SIX MONTHS IN THE HIJAZ

SIX MONTHS IN THE HIJAZ

JOURNEYS TO MAKKAH AND MADINAH

1877–1878

JOHN F. T. KEANE

With an Introduction by William Facey

barzan

Barzan Publishing

2006

Six Months in the Hijaz
Journeys to Makkah and Madinah 1877-1878

Barzan Publishing
Manchester & Beirut

Windrush Millennium Centre
Alexandra Road
Manchester M16 7WD
United Kingdom
www.barzanpress.com
info@barzanpress.com

Six Months in Meccah first published by Tinsley Brothers, London, 1881.
My Journey to Medinah first published by Tinsley Brothers, London, 1881.
Six Months in the Hejaz first published by Ward & Downey, London, 1887.
This facsimile edition of the two 1881 titles first published as
Six Months in the Hijaz, Barzan Publishing 2006.

ISBN: 0-9549701-1-X
ISBN: 1-905521-08-1 (quarter-bound edition)

CIP Data: A catalogue for this book is available from the British Library.

Printed and bound by SNP Leefung Printers Ltd
Designed by Dynamic Graphic, Lebanon
Index & glossary compiled by Lawrence Campbell

Endpapers: This engraving, of the Ka'bah and the Haram at Makkah during the pilgrimage, appeared in *The Graphic* magazine of 25 March 1882 with an article on Keane's visit to the holy city in 1877–78. Its caption states that the engraving is "from the first photograph ever taken". Keane or *The Graphic* must therefore have obtained one of the photographs taken by the Egyptian photographer Col. Muhammad Sadiq in 1880.

Contents

Introduction

Among European accounts of the Muslim pilgrimage, John Keane's stands out for its freshness and immediacy. During the course of what he referred to as a "life of the wildest adventure in every corner of the globe", this journey was perhaps his most audacious exploit of all. Though only a young man of twenty-two when he embarked on it, he was already mature in experience, having been at sea since the age of twelve and served on board sailing ships of many types and under the harshest of conditions, from the Arctic to the tropics. His account of his months in the Hijaz, from September 1877 to early 1878, is none the less a young man's story. What he lacks in scholarly and scientific background, the young Jack Keane makes up for in verve and vivid observation, expressed in a highly entertaining and occasionally irreverent style.

Very little has appeared in print on the life of this intriguing character, and much of what has been written centres on the mysterious affair of the "Lady Venus", who, he alleged, was an Englishwoman named Macintosh living in Makkah at the time of his visit. This arresting claim brought Keane a certain notoriety in the late 1870s and 1880s, and certainly helped to sell his books. But, as will soon be apparent, there was much more to the man and his work than that affair.

Keane's first book, *Six Months in Meccah*, was published in 1881 and attracted sufficient attention to be reviewed in the lofty pages of the *Athenaeum*, whose review opened:

> Those orthodox geographers who were startled by the American outsider's [Henry Morton Stanley] successful walk into Africa will receive a hardly less severe shock on learning that the pilgrimage to Mecca has been performed by a youngster of five-and-twenty [*sic*], apparently a sailor by profession, and with none of the special training enjoyed by his few predecessors.

This reviewer's sole comment on the Lady Venus was: "Mr Keane met at the house of a moulvi … the *soi-disant* English lady whose mysterious story was afterwards investigated in India with only partial success." Otherwise the review was distinctly favourable, finding *Six Months in Meccah* graphic and amusing and "a clever little *jeu d'esprit*", complaining only that Keane tells the reader almost nothing about himself or how he came to be in Jiddah.

Keane was simultaneously gratified by the favourable reception of his book, and exasperated by the scepticism of some readers. In the Preface to *Six Months in the Hejaz*, in 1887, he writes:

> The persistent incredulity of a large section of authorities deterred the publishers from increasing the venture to more editions [since the first edition sold out]; but as time has worn on, every new circumstance bearing on the subject has only tended to confirm my story, and now the truth of it (as was inevitable sooner or later) has been established by the test of time.

Six Months in Meccah was followed later in 1881 by *My Journey to Medinah*, and it is those two books that were sub- sequently republished in one volume, under the title *Six Months in the Hejaz*, in 1887. These volumes are extremely hard to find nowadays, and the first two are here reprinted for the first time, as far as can be ascertained, since the 1880s.

Early years, 1854–77

John Fryer Thomas Keane was born in the Yorkshire port of Whitby on 4 October 1854, the eldest of three sons and two daughters of the Rev. William Keane. His early years were spent at the parsonage, No. 5 Bagdale, in the strait-laced atmosphere of a pious, educated middle-class home. His father, born in 1818 in County Clare, Ireland, into a family of the Anglo-Irish ascendancy, had been educated at Charterhouse in London, where his fellow pupils included the Calcutta-born novelist William Thackeray, and at Emmanuel College, Cambridge. Feeling a vocation for missionary work, he had gone out East in 1846 as a Missionary Canon to St Paul's Cathedral, Calcutta. He seems to have had a gift for languages, for he was said to have preached to the Indians in their own tongue. While in India he also became chaplain to the Bishop of Madras, and perhaps it was there that he met his future wife Elizabeth, some nine years his junior, a daughter of the Hon. John Fryer Thomas, Member of Council of Madras, after whom they were to name their eldest son in 1854. Returning to England in 1852, William Keane took up the post of Association Secretary to the Church Missionary Society in London. In 1853 he was appointed Perpetual Curate of Whitby, and in the same year married Elizabeth Thomas in Brighton. He was to spend the remainder of his life in Whitby, becoming Rector in 1861, and dying in 1873 at the young age of fifty-five, having suffered from paralysis of his lower body for a number of years. Elizabeth Keane lived on until 1903, dying at the age of seventy-six.

John Keane refers to his mother not at all in his writings and to his father just twice. In *On Blue-water* he alludes to difficulties at home and to the disappointment he caused his "stern and hopeful" parent as a boy. The weight of family expectations on the lad can be deduced from other reports. The Rev. William Keane was renowned in Whitby for his indomitable spirit, even when confined to a bath chair, his boundless enthusiasm for causes of various kinds, and for his wit and a ready reply. He was "a most fecund pamphleteer" who "rushed into print whenever he possibly could in defence of or to promote any of his pet theories on India, the Church, Education, or Temperance questions". A newspaper cutting from 1926 recalls the Rev. Keane in Whitby before he was struck down by paralysis:

> There comes along Baxtergate [a main street in Whitby] a little active man, with the face of a mystic and heart of a saint. He strikes us at once as a man of authority, and as he moves rapidly along the street men take off their hats, and he has a kindly word for them all. He is the Rev. William Keane, the rector, or as he was then known, the Incumbent of Whitby. He was a true and ardent Churchman: a Protestant who had no use for the ritualism which began to make itself felt in Whitby during the later days of his service. But where there was sorrow or grief in the town, Mr Keane forgot everything in the fact that he was a Christian Minister first of all, and no man ever sought more earnestly to know his Divine Lord than he.

Many of his fine personal qualities, including his energy and eloquence in print, the Rev. Keane passed on to his son John, but not, alas, his interests, particularly not his devotion to his Maker – a common enough syndrome among parsons' sons, then as now. Given the young Jack's lukewarm religious outlook he most probably found a father who could pen a tract entitled "Let a Man Examine Himself, and so let Him Eat of that Bread, and Drink of that Cup", somewhat uncongenial, if not downright forbidding, as a parent. Later, in *Three Years of a Wanderer's Life*, Keane caustically remarked: "All my relatives belong to that better-off class of earnest Christians especially preyed upon and victimised by the ecclesiastical hawk and Gospel shark." A voracious reader, even as a boy at sea, Keane claimed to have read the Bible six times but only "when I had nothing else to read". In *On Blue-water*, in talking of books placed on board ship by the only charity, the Seamen's Library, for which he had any respect, he remarks: "I have often begrudged the space – one-third – taken up in the box [of books] by the drivelling twaddle put in as religious literature ... for palpable drivelling concoctions of babyish falsehood, commend me to some of the pious Tom Peppers that write religious tracts." It is only natural to wonder if he had his father in mind.

By his own account Jack was a difficult boy: "I have often wondered and wondered at that time if I really was a bad boy," he says in *On Blue-water*. On arrival around the age of eleven at "a large and well-known public school", he immediately gave evidence of a wandering streak and was expelled for repeatedly breaking school bounds to explore the countryside around. This school, which he does not name, was not Charterhouse, though his younger brother Robert did follow their father there. As a result of these escapades, he tells us, "the extremely doubtful reception I was given [at home] soon determined me to be off on my own account."

His wanderlust seems to have been aggravated by the experience of home and boarding school, developing into a compulsive need to escape whatever situation he might find himself in, whether bad or good – a condition that was to lead to a degree of self-sabotage in later life. By his late teens he had become an inveterate rolling stone who found it all too easy to quit a job on an impulse, most especially if a novel prospect presented itself. Naturally Keane could not resist romanticising this side of his nature, and thus makes much of the claim that he ran away to sea at the age of twelve. Whether he ran or was sent away is but one of several puzzling issues that his own story of his life presents us with.

Today Whitby has dispensed with the grim realities of its seafaring past but retains to an extraordinary degree the romance of its explorers and whalers. Standing on the low cliff up by the famous Abbey ruins, one looks down upon the old port clustered along both banks of the Esk, whose estuary ushered forth voyages of epic significance in the history of exploration: those of Capt. James Cook to the Pacific and Australia, and of the Scoresbys to the Arctic. There is a bracing whiff of North Sea salt in the air, and a sense of connectedness to the great blue yonder, that must have brought out the adventurer in many a physically active Whitby lad.

In young Jack Keane's case what seems to have happened is that his father sent him off on a long voyage in a small collier brig, the hardships of which temporarily tamed the boy. He was then sent to reside with a private tutor in a remote part of the East Riding of Yorkshire, thus somewhere south of the North York Moors. The tutor was a kind, elderly parson, but the boy soon turned out to be an incorrigible daredevil, being drawn to poachers and open-air pursuits. In *On Blue-water* Keane laments, perhaps a little disingenuously, the rebellious side of his nature:

> I often think how low my moral perceptions had fallen when I, a gentleman's son, thought it no sin to sit in a village tap-room,

> though a staunch teetotaller, listening to tales of adventure by flood and field from gamekeepers, poachers, and one old retired sea-captain, my greatest hero … Yes, I was a very wicked boy; but still I think my strong and peculiar bent, my strong zoological turn and passion for geographical discovery, might have been better directed. A boy whose love of climbing the most precipitous rocks and the tallest trees is so strong as to brand him among sober men as a youth of notorious suicidal tendencies, might still be preserved from such a hopeless though fascinating fate as the sea presents.

In any event, by 1883 Keane could claim that he had been at sea off and on for seventeen years, and by the age of fourteen was already inured to hardship, accidents and death at sea. But one can deduce from various other references that not all the time after the age of twelve was spent on board ship. For a time as a youngster he lived up-country in India, in the house of a gentleman, which perhaps implies he was living with one of his Fryer Thomas uncles, possibly in the Madras area. In *Three Years of a Wanderer's Life* he reveals that as a young lad of fourteen (i.e. in 1868) he was "living with a relative in Madras". On the next page that relative turns out to be "Lady A—", with a household that included a butler. Perhaps this was an aunt, a sister of Keane's mother Elizabeth Fryer Thomas. Elsewhere Keane recalls a scene of his boyhood: a cremation ground in Madras.

Nonetheless, the sea dominated his life and, if the stories of his early voyages in *On Blue-water* and *Three Years of a Wanderer's Life* are to be believed, an astonishingly colourful and adventurous life it was. Like his father, Keane was not a large man, but he turned out to be physically indestructible, very courageous and well able to look after himself if it came to a brawl. Anything was a challenge to him, and he became "fully determined to see if there really was any part of the world it would be 'impossible' for me to go". He started as a "premium apprentice" on board a small barque sailing between England and India and, at the age of eighteen, obtained a 2nd mate's certificate. This was the only paper qualification he seems to have gained, though he does once claim that he became a certificated officer in P&O at about the same time. He had been on a whaler in the South Seas and the Arctic. Between 1873 and the journey to Makkah in 1877 there followed voyages to the Black Sea, the Arctic, China (on a steamship), a spell in England in the Naval Reserve, Demerara (British Guyana) where he worked on a sugar plantation for six months, coastal trade in the North Sea, and several voyages between Bengal and England via the Cape of Good Hope aboard a "Britisher" sailing ship on which he served for about twenty months. That was an unusually long time for him though, to be fair, the difficulties he found in staying on a ship seem to have been due as much to the iniquities of a system that denied sailors their proper pay at the end of a voyage, as to compulsive bolting on his part.

In early 1877, he tells us, without giving reasons why, he took his discharge from the Britisher and paid his passage to Constantinople. There he claims to have joined the Ottoman army and served for two months in the Ottoman supply corps. In 1900 he told the *Whitby Gazette* that he had also served three months as a navigating officer in the Ottoman navy, that he had been a *bimbashi* in charge of a large ambulance train, and that he had been present at the fall of Plevna during the Russo-Turkish hostilities of that year.

However, while the siege of Plevna began in July 1877, its fall did not take place until December, when we know Keane to have already reached Makkah. This is another example of discrepancies in Keane's stories of his life that one has to be on the alert for: was his memory playing tricks on him as he grew older, or did he deliberately embroider those of his experiences he knew could not be independently verified, to impress an audience? If the latter is the case, it is a characteristic he shared with many travellers. Notable in an Arabian context is William Gifford Palgrave, who was adept at inserting a plausible fiction into an otherwise accurate record. His best-seller, *Narrative of a Year's Journey through Central and Eastern Arabia (1862–63)*, is full of valuable eye-witness material, but has to be read with a sharp eye for exaggeration and, in some instances, sheer invention. However, as will be apparent below, the overall verdict must be that Keane's account of his six months in the Hijaz is a truthful one.

Keane left Turkey to travel, as a passenger for once, by steamer to Alexandria, where he must have arrived by the late summer of 1877. "A few weeks after leaving Stamboul," he says, "I was granted an opportunity of performing the pilgrimage to Meccah and Medinah." He gives no hint of his reasons for this new adventure, stating only that he had been preparing himself for it for some time, that he was well qualified for it having served on board vessels with Muslim crews, and that this juncture, as he made his way down the Red Sea and found himself in Jiddah, seemed a good opportunity. After a few days in Jiddah, he had the good fortune to attach himself to the retinue of an Indian "Amér" who was making the pilgrimage. Exactly how Keane did this we are not told, his statement to the Foreign Office in 1879 merely hinting at some service he had managed to perform for this Hindi grandee. By continuing to make himself useful in the Amir's entourage, he was able to contrive the stay in Makkah and the journey to Madinah that he describes in the two volumes presented here.

Six months in the Hijaz, 1877–78

Keane's two books speak for themselves, but some background remarks are in order by way of introduction. He arrived in the Hijaz at a time when the impact of Western technology on Arabia was beginning to accelerate. European steamships had been calling at Jiddah for some time, and the opening of the Suez Canal in 1869 had made the Hijaz more accessible to the outside world – especially to the Ottoman Turks, who since the early 1870s had been tightening their military and administrative grip on the semi-autonomous province.

British attention too was becoming more focused on the Muslim holy land, as Britain's Indian empire produced the vast majority of pilgrims coming by sea to Jiddah every year. The British authorities were concerned for the welfare of British subjects in the Hijaz, and so tried to keep abreast of pilgrimage affairs. Throughout the latter part of the 19th century and the years up to the Arab Revolt in the First World War, the concern of the British Indian authorities for the security of the Red Sea route and the Muslim pilgrimage was to intensify greatly, conscious as they were that the majority of the world's Muslims at the time lived under British rule in what are today Pakistan, India and Bangladesh. Keane's account of his time in the Hijaz is as suffused with the populous subcontinent's links with Jiddah, Makkah and Madinah, as it is with his own personal familiarity with Indians and their ways.

Western attention and technology were penetrating in less formal ways as well. Photography had been invented in France and Britain in 1839–40, and had already become commonplace in those Arab countries bordering the Mediterranean. Though Keane himself did not bring a camera, his visit almost coincided with the earliest known photography of Makkah, by the Muslim Egyptian official Col. Muhammad Sadiq, in 1880. Indeed the engravings that accompanied an anonymous article in *The Graphic* magazine of 25 March 1882, recording Keane's journey to the Hijaz, included two engravings of Makkah and Madinah, each "from the first photograph ever taken". No longer would the reading public have to rely on the written accounts and drawings of the Muslim holy places by travellers such as Burckhardt and Burton.

Keane probably arrived in Jiddah during September 1877, as he reached Makkah itself during Ramadan, that is, some days before 8 October 1877, the last day of the holy month. There is no doubt that he made the journey he describes, as he gave his name and the addresses of friends to the acting British Consul in Jiddah, James Zohrab, informing him of his intentions, and called in again before he left Jiddah, probably in March 1878; thus officialdom was aware of his venture, and indeed the consul was later called upon by the Foreign Office to investigate the puzzling affair of the Lady Venus. Keane stayed in Makkah for the pilgrimage itself, and attended the standing at Jabal 'Arafat on Friday 14 December 1877. He estimated the pilgrims at 200,000, and *The Times* of 6 October 1878 reported the pilgrimage of that year as having been unusually large, attracting about 180,000 people, around twice the normal figure. In this new age of steamships, 42,718 of them had arrived by sea at Jiddah.

Keane, who could speak Hindustani, passed himself off amongst this variegated assemblage from all over the Muslim world as a pilgrim from Bombay or "a country called North". The vagueness of his provenance seems to have raised no eyebrows: Keane's successor in Makkah in 1908, A. J. B. Wavell, remarks on the profound ignorance of geography amongst Hijazis and pilgrims alike. Keane at first adopted the name "Abdur

Mohammed", "Servant of the Prophet", a distinctly odd appellation that seems to betray a certain ignorance of Islam and Arabic on his part, but he soon modified it to the more orthodox "Mohammed Amin". He quickly mastered the pious expressions and gestures of Muslim discourse, admitting when necessary to being a recent convert. Only once was he suspected of being a non-Muslim and then, having foolishly started a fight, managed to talk and act himself out of trouble by putting on a convincingly devout performance. His Arabic, rudimentary at first, doubtless improved considerably as time went by. He mixed freely with the common stream of humanity in the streets and in the Haram – the sanctuary around the Ka'bah – even at one point gaining admittance to the Ka'bah itself. He has the grace to confess to initial qualms of conscience about his "wild and unscrupulous" expedition, but came to act the lie so well that he soon believed in it himself. In six weeks he felt as much at home as if he had been a Muslim all his life. His companions found him an agreeable and harmless fellow, with a fund of good stories about his seafaring past. These, though probably for the most part true, they listened to with open-mouthed disbelief, while they tended to believe the many wonderful stories he "invented … to amuse them".

Unlike his predecessors such as Badia y Leblich/Ali Bey al-'Abbasi, Burckhardt and Burton, Keane travelled not as a grandee or learned doctor, but as a common man without pretensions to scholarship or scientific discovery. In this he was more like his immediate predecessor, the English Muslim Herman Bicknell, who made the pilgrimage in 1862. Keane was familiar with the classic accounts of their visits to Makkah and Madinah by Burckhardt and Burton, but spent longer in Makkah than either of those two explorers. As in his life at sea, he mingled with the lower orders and delights in reporting the daily life around him. Keane's sympathies were with the common man, and he had no time for snobbery, racism or bigotry. This attractive characteristic is explicitly revealed by passages in his other books. For example, in *On Blue-water* he comments: "I often thought, with shame, while on board her [an Austrian ship manned by Italians], how differently I was being treated from the way in which I had seen many a poor solitary foreigner treated in the forecastle of an English ship." His egalitarian outlook is often implied by the way in which he describes his relations with his fellow man, whether Indian, European, Chinese or black, Christian, Muslim or Hindu. "Along the career on which I have been urged I have seen many phases of life, most frequently from the point of view of those who endure them without a voice to speak for themselves", he reflects in *Three Years of a Wanderer's Life*. In the same book he describes defending a dying black man from an alcoholic American sailor, decries English aloofness from other races, and stands up for the rights of native peoples against imperial incursion. Throughout these two works on his life at sea, he shows himself to be a universal humanist:

> The happiest lesson taught a man in living with and mixing among men of all conditions is that if human nature is the same all over the world, the normal man is good, and wrongdoing is everywhere very rightly characterised as unmanly, unnatural, inhuman, and the like. A pessimist view of human nature may be held by the narrow-minded and self-satisfied; let them stagnate in their other worldliness.

A gifted writer with an engaging turn of phrase, Keane is highly skilled at conjuring up the life around him in the holy cities. At one extreme he can make us laugh out loud at the outlandish variety of dress in Makkah, and on the other move us with awe at the great spectacle of faith at the climax of the pilgrimage at 'Arafat. He is never short of an opinion, trenchantly expressed, as for example his discerning view of the institution of slavery in Islam. Most noteworthy are his descriptions of the Haram and the Ka'bah, the 'Id al-Fitr at the end of Ramadan, the prospect of Makkah from the summit of Jabal Qubais, and the varieties of pilgrim to be found.

Although dry statistics and quantification were not really Keane's style, he made a fairly thorough attempt to measure the Haram and the Ka'bah. To do this he used a bamboo cane exactly a yard long, which he would drop or casually lay down whenever a measurement was required. By means of this stick too he could get accurate heights of buildings, by measuring their shadows when the sun was at 45°; this he could be sure of by the cunning schoolboy method of choosing the moment when his stick's shadow measured exactly its own length. The dimensions of the Ka'bah itself he obtained by the somewhat bizarre and undignified method of crawling round it at night, laying his cane as he went, "by way of a prayer mumbling the number of times he moved his stick". His description of the Haram as a whole appears to be entirely his own. Unlike Burton, Keane does not spare himself the inconvenience of describing it anew on the grounds that, as Burton had it, "the House of Allah has been so fully described by my predecessors [Ali Bey and Burckhardt], that there is little inducement to attempt a new portrait". Keane appears not to crib from Burckhardt's detailed description, nor, where they measure the same structures, notably the Ka'bah itself, do they seem to conflict. Their two independent descriptions, therefore, usefully complement one another.

At Muna Keane witnessed the procession of the Sharif of Makkah and the Ottoman governor, and gives an eye-witness description of them. This Sharif was the mild and just Husayn b. Muhammad b. 'Abd al-Mu'in of the Dhawi 'Awn clan, who had assumed the rule in 1877 – the same Sharif who was to receive Doughty with great courtesy at Taif in August 1878, and who was to fall to an assassin's knife in 1880. Keane notes the limits of Ottoman provincial rule: the Turks held the cities only, and wielded no control over the bedouin tribes.

Perhaps most vivid of all is his description of the storm at Makkah, about eight days after the 'Id al-Adha, or Feast of Sacrifice, which flooded the Haram to a depth of six feet round the Ka'bah, leaving the city awash with putrefying waste and causing an epidemic of cholera and typhus. This storm must have broken on about the 18th day of Dhu al-Hijja, the last month of the Muslim year, and twelve or so days before the beginning of the new Muslim year 1295 on 5 January 1878.

The outbreak of disease prompted Keane's Indian Amir to embark with some of his entourage on the overland journey to Madinah. At first Keane tried to wriggle out of this expedition, but then, typically for him, entrusted the decision to the toss of a coin. Madinah it was; and it is his visit to the City of the Prophet that he describes in his second book, *My Journey to Medinah*. We are not told when they set out, but perhaps it was towards the end of January 1878. Keane's sense of the passage of time was somewhat challenged during this journey, as he was stabbed in the leg by a *badawi* shortly after leaving Rabigh. The wound almost killed him, and he passed some of the time en route in a coma.

The hardships of the pilgrims on the long march to Madinah are inconceivable to us today. Many pilgrims died by the road, unable to struggle onwards; others were picked off, robbed and murdered by bedouin. In contrast to Burton's which went by the most easterly of the inland routes, Keane's caravan like

Burckhardt's went to Madinah via Rabigh on the coast, and his account is interesting on that score alone, though he exaggerates the distance somewhat. There is a most graphic description of a dust-storm on the way back to Rabigh which will be painfully familiar to all those who have experienced such meteorological events in Arabia. The round trip, including the ten days they spent in Madinah, took about five weeks. Apart from that, Keane is vague on dates, and it is not clear precisely when in 1878 they returned to Makkah; most probably it was in March. The party spent four days in Makkah, and then returned to Jiddah and boarded a steamship with the Amir for Bombay.

The Lady Venus affair

Allowing for slight exaggeration here and there, perhaps inevitable after he had spent several months in an environment where he found "truth less credited than fiction", Keane's account has the ring of authenticity about it. He is in a real sense the first recognisably modern traveller to Islam's holy places: less interested in Islam *per se* than in universal human nature, he travels as an ordinary man and records his personal experiences as he moves freely among his fellows, casting his net to catch whatever is available, just as he recorded his maritime adventures and companions. He is not an explorer; in a way he is travelling to write – a very modern pursuit – and his own personality is part of his tale.

However, his first book, *Six Months in Meccah*, faced a challenge from sceptics when it appeared in 1881. This scepticism centred on his account of his meetings with the "Lady Venus", a name which Keane represents as a literal translation of "Begum Zarah", though he is not quite correct in doing so. This lady Keane presents as an Englishwoman who had been living in Makkah for almost twenty years, having been abducted in Lucknow during the Indian Mutiny of 1857–58 and converted to Islam. Subsequent writers on Arabian travel, such as Bidwell and Trench, have tended to accept the truth of his story in its entirety, and "Miss Macintosh" has been duly elevated into her peculiar niche in the annals of European travellers in Arabia. That *Six Months in Meccah* brought Keane a certain celebrity at the time was due to British sensitivity over the Indian Mutiny. Any suggestion that an Englishwoman might be living under the duress of an ex-Mutineer was liable to arouse almost hysterical indignation even at the highest levels of government.

In the winter of 1878 Keane took his story of the Lady Venus to "a number of gentlemen who had been either long residents in India or who were well-known travellers in the East". These included one of his maternal uncles, E. B. Thomas, a retired official of the Madras Civil Service, who took up the case with vigour, consulting the explorer and Arabian traveller Richard Burton and submitting it to the Foreign Office, where Lord Salisbury himself showed interest. The papers relating to the affair are preserved in the British National Archives (formerly the Public Record Office) at Kew, London, in file F. O. 370/461. The Foreign Office, always on the lookout for ex-Mutineers who had taken refuge in the Hijaz, instigated investigations through the consul in Jiddah, James Zohrab. Zohrab sent an agent to Makkah and established the existence of a Muslim lady living there who was generally believed to be an Englishwoman; unfortunately her protector in Makkah, an alleged ex-Mutineer named Faiz Ahmad Khan of Datauli, Aligarh, had recently died, and she had just, on 3 March 1879, departed from the Hijaz to return to India in the train of his son, Muhammad Ismail Khan of Datauli.

So the case was passed to the India Office. E. B. Thomas, in a letter of 24 April 1879 to the India Office that conveys the scandal-ised tone in which the affair was being pursued, fulminated:

> If she has ever been, as is conjectured, a lady, or even any respectable European female, it is impossible to suppose that she can desire to remain in her present degraded and painful position or be really, (as may be pretended), a willing captive, and convert to the Mahomedan faith.

After much investigation the lady in question was eventually tracked down in India by the magistrate at Aligarh, W. T. Martin. Towards the end of June 1879 Martin managed to arrange for his wife to interview her, and also to obtain a written statement from her about her origins. It emerged that she was indeed named "Zuhra Begam [*sic*]". *Zahrah*, meaning "flower" or "beauty", and the related *Zuhrah* meaning "beauty" or "light", are not uncommon Arabic girl's names in the Muslim world, while *zuharah*, from the same root, is the name of the planet Venus, the Evening Star. Thus Zuhra Begum does not quite translate as "Lady Venus", as Keane has it: he had stretched a point, no doubt to titillate his readers. But Martin had no doubt that he had found the right woman. Except for her alleged origin in England and abduction and conversion to Islam, "all the other details of Mr Keane's description are found in her" (Keane had submitted a lengthy statement to the Foreign Office about the lady in early 1879). She herself claimed to have been born in Lucknow, of a Kashmiri mother, and to have had no knowledge of her father. Martin's report confirms the excellence of her English, observing that "she appears to be an intelligent and educated Englishwoman". He goes on:

> In the face of her repeated and unreserved statement, it is difficult, if not impossible, to believe that she is an Englishwoman, although fair enough to pass for one; and yet her English accent is hardly at all East Indian, while her speech is so fluent and natural, that it is not easy to suppose that she could ever have acquired English, which she seems to have learnt as her mother-tongue.

The lady insisted that she was under no coercion whatsoever and was very content where she was. There was thus no question of her wishing to be freed from a non-existent captivity. Martin concludes that the father may have been an Englishman; so Zuhra Begum would have been an "Angrezin", or Eurasian, who had been brought up from infancy to speak English. She was about forty-five years old (Keane had estimated forty), of middle height and of a light olive complexion with eyes of a light colour, and had the general appearance of a reduced gentlewoman. She confirmed the story of her long residence in Makkah and its circumstances. She admitted that she had met four Europeans there, though was evasive about meeting one as recently as Keane's visit, and denied ever having done so in the Haram as Keane describes. Finally, she denied having been abducted during the Mutiny or ever having expressed a wish to escape.

What emerges most clearly from Martin's report is the difficulty he found in believing that Zuhra Begum was not an Englishwoman, though he felt compelled to accept her word for it. His niggling doubt was compounded shortly afterwards as a result of exchanging letters with her. Martin expressed the view that "it is all but impossible to believe that she would have been brought up otherwise than as an English-speaking person, and therefore the mystery about her is only enhanced". As a result his reports were regarded as not absolutely conclusive, although in the light of Zuhra Begum's insistence that she was perfectly content where she was, it was decided not to pursue the matter further.

The overall effect of Martin's investigation must be to confirm much of Keane's story: if Martin found it hard to believe that Zuhra Begum was not English, Keane can be forgiven for doing likewise. So far from inventing her, he had unearthed a well-known character in Makkah and went along with the local and very plausible belief that she was an Englishwoman. In the light of all the corroborating details as to her appearance and personality, it is going too far to suggest, as M. D. Allen does in "The Curious Affair of the Lady Venus", that Keane never actually met her in Makkah, but only heard about her, and invented his meetings with her in order to sell his book. The most one can lay at his door is the fiction that she was really a Miss Macintosh, a doctor's daughter from Devon kidnapped and converted in Lucknow, who wished to be liberated from her Muslim confinement. He may also have embroidered the substance and locations of their conversations. But he almost certainly genuinely believed she was English, as everyone else who met her was inclined to do, and, like his uncle, found it impossible to accept that, being English, she would not wish to reclaim her origins. He thus convinced himself that she was an unwilling convert too fearful to speak out, and it was a short step from there to campaigning for her rescue.

It is clear from the Appendices to the two books reprinted here that Keane found it impossible to let go of the idea of Zuhra Begum's Englishness. The personal letter he claims, in the Appendix to *My Journey to Medinah*, to have received from her "which proves most conclusively that the statements made in *Six Months in Meccah* – so far at least as she is concerned – are correct", perhaps did not exist, as he nowhere divulges its contents. If that too was an invention, it would at least be symptomatic of his inability to relinquish his belief in Zuhra Begum's English origin.

In 1886, Keane's description of Zuhra Begum received accidental confirmation from another source, of which Keane himself was most probably unaware. The Scottish missionary Ion Keith-Falconer was making his way down the Red Sea by steamer to Aden, and stopped off at Jiddah around the end of November 1886. He takes up the story (in *Memorials of the Hon. Ion Keith-Falconer*, by Robert Sinker):

> … we stopped at Jidda, but to my great disappointment, quarantine prevented me from going ashore. I gazed long at the hills which hid Mecca from us. At Jidda, the only other 1st class passenger got off, an Indian Musalman going to Mecca. His card runs thus: H. M. Ismail Khan, of Datauli, Aligarh … As he was going to relations at Mecca, I asked him whether it was true – as Keane states in his *Six Months at Mecca* [*sic*] – that an Englishwoman had lived there as a Muslima for many years. He said, "Yes, she now lives in my house at Aligarh." I then asked him some questions, and his answers tallied exactly with Keane's account. She is known as Zuhra Begum, which might very well be rendered Lady Venus, as Keane does. Was that not a curious coincidence?

A coincidence indeed, and Keith-Falconer's account serves, like Martin's, only to deepen the mystery surrounding Zuhra Begum's origin. In conclusion, one must certainly acknowledge that the reports of Zohrab, Martin and Keith-Falconer, if they do nothing else, so far from undermining Keane's account of his visit to Makkah, actually provide independent confirmation of it. In so doing, they lend authenticity to the rest of Keane's highly entertaining story of his six months in the Hijaz.

Keane's later life, 1878–1937

After his Hijaz adventure Keane returned to England to write up his journey and, just as pressing, to find a career. Despite – or, as he would no doubt say, because of – his lack of a conventional education he was an inventive and clever person of wide reading and independent mind. He enjoyed a reputation among his fellow crewmen as "book-larned", and was able to deploy in his writings references to Darwin, Shakespeare, Marlowe, Lewis Carroll and Hakluyt's *Voyages*, as well as Burckhardt and Burton. It seems that during his sojourn in England, as the affair of the Lady Venus was being investigated and while he was penning his two books, he decided to take up medicine. At the age of twenty-three, by his own account, he

> became possessed of means sufficient to allow me to choose other and more inviting lines. I matriculated in the Edinburgh University, and took up medicine, which I studied for three years. My source of supply was, unfortunately, an Irish one, which failed with the rent, and I was thrown entirely on my own resources; hardly with the millstone poverty about my neck, though assuredly with the tin-kettle necessity at my tail – an incitement which has kept me running ever since, even though without a goal.

Despite having to curtail his medical studies, he claimed to have won some sort of medical diploma and "held for a year two unqualified assistantships in crowded parts of London", finally having to relinquish the attempt and return to the old wandering life of adventure.

Six Months in Meccah and *My Journey to Medinah* were published successively in 1881 by Tinsley Brothers of London. William

Tinsley (1831–1902) was a well-known figure on the London publishing scene between 1854 and 1888. He was always on the look-out for new talent, and his name often crops up in the biographies of celebrated authors whose work he published – among them George Meredith and Thomas Hardy. He was doubtless attracted by the young Keane's lively style and the colourful story he had to tell.

The authorship of *Meccah* was puzzlingly attributed on the title page to "T. F. Keane", while *Medinah* was ascribed to a more recognisable "John F. Keane". That "T. F. Keane" was not a mere typographical accident can be presumed from his article "Mecca and its Pilgrims" in *Frank Leslie's Popular Monthly* of December 1882, published under exactly the same byline, which repeats large sections of *Six Months in Meccah* verbatim. John Fryer Thomas Keane does not seem to have settled to his full set of initials until late in life. Whether "T. F. Keane" is symptomatic of a youthful wish to disown himself, or just a feeble attempt to disguise his identity, we shall probably never know. Perhaps a man who cannot be trusted to get his own initials right cannot wholly be trusted in larger matters relating to his life. Yet, as we have seen, his tales of travel must be regarded, by and large, as veracious.

While his writing, medical pursuits and the investigation of the Lady Venus were going on, Keane also tried his hand at freelance journalism. For this he certainly had a rich talent, as his books testify. He would have made a good campaigning journalist, and one feels that he missed his real *métier* in life. The success of his two Hijaz books led to *On Blue-water* (1883) and *Three Years of a Wanderer's Life* (1887), both of them autobiographical exposés of the life of British merchant seamen in the 1860s, 1870s and 1880s. They are stinging and eloquent indictments of the brutality of mates and captains, the grisly diet, the cavalier attitude to life and limb on board ship, the exploitation of seamen and lack of prospects which forced them to keep changing ship. One should disregard his disparagement of his own talent as a writer: "It did not take me long to learn that I need never hope to make my pen my legs, though it might do for a crutch," he sighs, after describing his efforts at freelance journalism in 1883/4.

In this respect Keane is certainly too hard on himself. He is worthy to be classed as a Victorian Alan Villiers or Eric Newby, except that he is less interested in recording epic voyages than everyday life at sea. Like both those men he had sailed on a grain ship round Cape Horn, but it merits no more than a mention. His is the record of his fellow man: he is the George Orwell of the Jack Tar under-class, no less down-and-out around the globe than at home. Reduced on one occasion in 1886 to walking from Liverpool to London and begging en route, he could sympathise with his fellow tramps, who like him were unable to hold down a job. Unlike them he was able to write about his experiences, not just with biting wit but with a light-hearted empathy: "Just before I reached Congleton, a dog flew out of a gate and bit me on the right calf; luckily he only nipped up a little bit of skin with his incisors – a very sincere form of flattery, after which there could be no doubt but that I was doing justice to the *rôle* of tramp."

Working when he did, Keane had a wide experience of both sail and steam. His books are a rich repository of the nautical jargon of the time, and while one occasionally has to persevere through such sentences as "I was sent up on the jaws of the gaff, to bend the head of the spanker", his evocations of life at sea can be masterly. Some of his depictions of the routine terrors of a sailor's life, such as hurricanes, near shipwrecks, or the truly petrifying task of taking in sail up aloft in high winds and heavy seas, are not for the faint-hearted.

Keane's interests were extensive. He had a bent as a naturalist, and makes entertaining observations on wildlife that demonstrate his respect for his fellow creatures. Just as he treated all mankind as equals, so he abhorred the infliction of gratuitous suffering on animals, even on sharks, which he specialised in catching. His observations on meteorology and fish, reptile and bird behaviour are expert and sometimes intriguing. If you want to know how to catch an albatross or make a weather vane from a seabird's head, Jack Keane is your man. On one Indian Ocean voyage he collected specimens, pickled them and subsequently took them to the British Museum for identification.

But his grand ambition was to be an explorer. New Guinea's allure as virgin territory for exploration led him to hatch a long prospectus for his own freelance investigation, of a humane and enlightened nature, of that mysterious island. He even goes so far as to say in one place that he undertook his Hijaz journey with the sole purpose of publicising himself as a potential explorer of New Guinea, but it is hard to take that too seriously. His hopes for New Guinea had to be abandoned in 1883 in the face of other expeditions being planned with official support, but he did eventually end up in Australia, a country that from early voyages he had come to regard as "the land of every wise man's adoption".

Three Years of a Wanderer's Life is Keane's autobiography during the years 1883–6. 1883–4 found him suffering from dengue fever in Calcutta; serving as 2nd mate on board a steamship that was wrecked on Perim Island at the mouth of the Red Sea; in Aden; sailing up the Red Sea in genteel company; in the Suez Canal; on a Cook's tour to the Pyramids; in London; on an ice trader in Norway; in London again; sailing the Atlantic to New York; shanghaied onto an American sailing ship; kidnapped in Brazil; and serving on a British ship delivering rice from Burma to Rotterdam.

In the summer of 1884 he announced his return to London to anxious friends and relatives, and found that his book *On Blue-water* had been a success. So he settled down in Dublin to write another, *Mere Shakings*, which, as he tells us, was a series of seafaring stories and pieces on his life at sea that was published initially in *Tinsley's Magazine*. When it came to the question of their publication in book form, a falling-out seems to have occurred between Keane and Tinsley. Certain it is that no book entitled *Mere Shakings* seems to exist, and that Keane's subsequent publications, *Three Years of a Wanderer's Life* and *Six Months in the Hijaz*, were published not by Tinsley Brothers but by Ward and Downey, whose Arabian track record included *The Memoirs of an Arabian Princess*. Both publishers specialised in feeding the Victorian reading public's voracious appetite for popular, readable fiction and non-fiction.

The difficulty over *Mere Shakings* decided Keane on a whim to work his passage to China to take a look at the Franco-Chinese hostilities then brewing. After a time characteristically down-and-out in Hong Kong, he managed to put his journalistic talents to use, first on the *Hong-Kong Telegraph* and then on the *Shanghai Courier*. In March–April 1885 he inveigled his way into Ningpo as the sole war correspondent, reporting on the French blockade for the *Shanghai Courier* and other papers.

He then worked his passage to Calcutta and paid a visit to a cousin, Mr Bruce, on his tea plantation, whom he had not seen for ten years. On his return to Calcutta, he settled to a steady job on the railways, with occasional journalism, but was temperamentally unable to hold it down. He left for Burma and took ship for Liverpool where he arrived, destitute once more, in August 1886. His account of his tramp from Liverpool to London is worthy of George Borrow's *Wild Wales*.

On 1 September 1886, Keane sat down to write *Three Years of a Wanderer's Life*, and finished it on 20 November, which gives some idea of his facility with a pen. In 1887 the book was published in two volumes. In the same year *Six Months in Meccah* and *My Journey to Medinah* were republished in a single volume entitled *Six Months in the Hejaz*, with an amalgamated Appendix on the Lady Venus affair.

Reading *Three Years of a Wanderer's Life*, one constantly wonders why so talented, resourceful and versatile an individual was so often compelled to take ship under such vile conditions. He gives us no clear answer, except the recurring shortage of funds which he implies from time to time. Here he is guilty of exaggerating his plight a little: in one or two tight spots he was able to write off to relatives for emergency funds, and it emerges that an uncle had guaranteed his bills at the Sailors' Home over a period of nine years in his early seafaring life. Such safety nets are of course denied to true down-and-outs. As far as his career as a sailor goes, he does make the case that the seafaring life held out no prospects for him because his service in foreign vessels and his many broken voyages disqualified him for examination at the higher grades. These explanations are not however sufficient. Though he was unable to maintain a relationship with a job, he did not lose touch with his wider family, despite never mentioning his mother or the death of his father in 1873. But other family members, particularly his brother Robert, his maternal uncle E. B. Thomas, and his brother-in-law the Rev. G. C. Carter, an under-master at Charterhouse, surface in his life from time to time and were clearly disposed to lend him support. We must invoke a deeper psychological reason for Keane's recurrent destitution: his compulsive urge to throw himself upon fortune whenever an opportunity presented itself. A revealing instance was his making the decision whether or not to go to Madinah dependent upon the toss of a coin. It is the only explanation for his constant inability to stay in a ship or stick with a career.

Henceforth details of Keane's life become sparser and, as hitherto, he is our only source for them. During 1887–90, as he claims, he was "on the press and twice visited America," and "wrote a great deal for the London daily papers, principally the *Pall Mall Gazette*".

Then began his Australian period, which was to last until the end of his life. In 1890 he "went to Australia and spent seven years prospecting and exploring in the far north of south Australia, and the far interior of the northern territory, always in little known, often in altogether unknown country". 1899 found him editing the *Port Augusta Despatch.* In 1899–1901 he was back in England, "employed by Central Australian Exploration Syndicate, London, Davidson Expedition". In 1900, he visited Whitby and announced to the *Whitby Gazette* that he had

> now returned to England to write a book, or books, on my discoveries and adventures in Australia. But first, by way of keeping the pot boiling, I delivered a few lectures in London, in pilgrim garb, to very critical audiences, on Mecca and Medina, which were received much better than I had dared to hope. So much so that I have been encouraged to come down to Whitby, where I should be personally remembered by many people, to try to raise a larger audience than any I have hitherto addressed.

This talk was to be delivered before the Whitby Literary and Philosophical Society, but was mysteriously postponed at the last moment "with Mr Keane's entire concurrence". One can only speculate as to the reasons.

The remaining glimpses of Keane's life are given by his entry in *Who Was Who* of 1941. In 1903 he "worked for 95 days of 12 hours each as a cane-cutter in the northern cane-brakes of Queensland, to prove that the work could be done by white men". He claimed to have invented a method of wire fencing that was adopted by the Queensland government, and in 1908 "purchased 655 acres of agricultural land" from the same government. 1905 allegedly saw the publication of *Matthew Walker* which, like *Mere Shakings*, eludes capture these days. But unlike *Mere Shakings*, we have not an inkling what *Matthew Walker* was about. If indeed it was published at all, it was Keane's last literary venture. 1909–13 saw him "residing on land and effecting improvements necessary to establish ownership of 354 acres". He would now have been almost sixty years old and, from 1913, his time was "almost entirely devoted to agricultural experiment and independent criminal investigation, with very surprising results." This last remark, left unexplained, demonstrates that his penchant for tantalising the reader had not deserted him. His recreations, listed as rod fishing and horse training, show that he never lost his taste for the outdoor life. Finally, on 1 September 1937, at the age of eighty-two, John Keane died at the Eventide Home, Charters Towers, the former gold rush town in North Queensland. His burial record, under the heading "Remarks", reads "Senile Decay".

That Keane merited an obituary in *The Times* is testimony to the short-lived fame that *Six Months in Meccah* and *My Journey to Medinah* had brought him in the 1880s. The obituary, which is otherwise basically the same as Keane's entry in *Who Was Who*, concludes:

> Keane was probably unknown to the present generation, but there will be many old travellers and students of Mahomedan life

> who will be sorry to hear of his death. He had all the qualities which enabled him to lead the kind of life that suited him. He was adventurous to the point of recklessness, and being indifferent to his own interests he never sought any recognition.

One might quibble with the final phrase, but it is otherwise a just epitaph. Time now to let Jack Keane speak for himself.

Acknowledgements

My account of John Keane's life and that of his father, the Rev. William Keane, could not have been written without the ready help of Mr Parry Thornton, of the Whitby Literary and Philosophical Society, to whom my warmest thanks are due, not least for drawing to my attention the important article by M. D. Allen on "The Curious Affair of the Lady Venus". I also acknowledge with gratitude valuable assistance of various kinds from the late St John Armitage; Dr Peter Clark; Peter Harrigan; Carl Phillips; John Shipman; Frances Topp; Ann Wheeler and Margaret Mardall of the Charterhouse Archives, Godalming; and the Whitby Archives Heritage Centre.

William Facey
London, January 2006

Note on Transliteration

Throughout his narrative Keane adopts the spellings, common at the time, of Meccah and Medinah, Jeddah and the Hejaz. These are preserved in the facsimile text and used in associated index and glossary entries provided in this Barzan edition.

However, to conform to current accepted usage, the Introduction and other newly set pages adopt the spellings, more academically current today, of Makkah and Madinah, Jiddah and the Hijaz.

The full transliterated names of the Holy Cities are Makkah al-Mukarramah and Al-Madinah al-Munarawwah, literally Makkah the Blessed and Madinah the Radiant (rather than "Medinah the Honoured" as Keane translates it on pp. 89 and 91 of Volume 2).

The Hijaz: Keane's route from Makkah to Madinah and back.

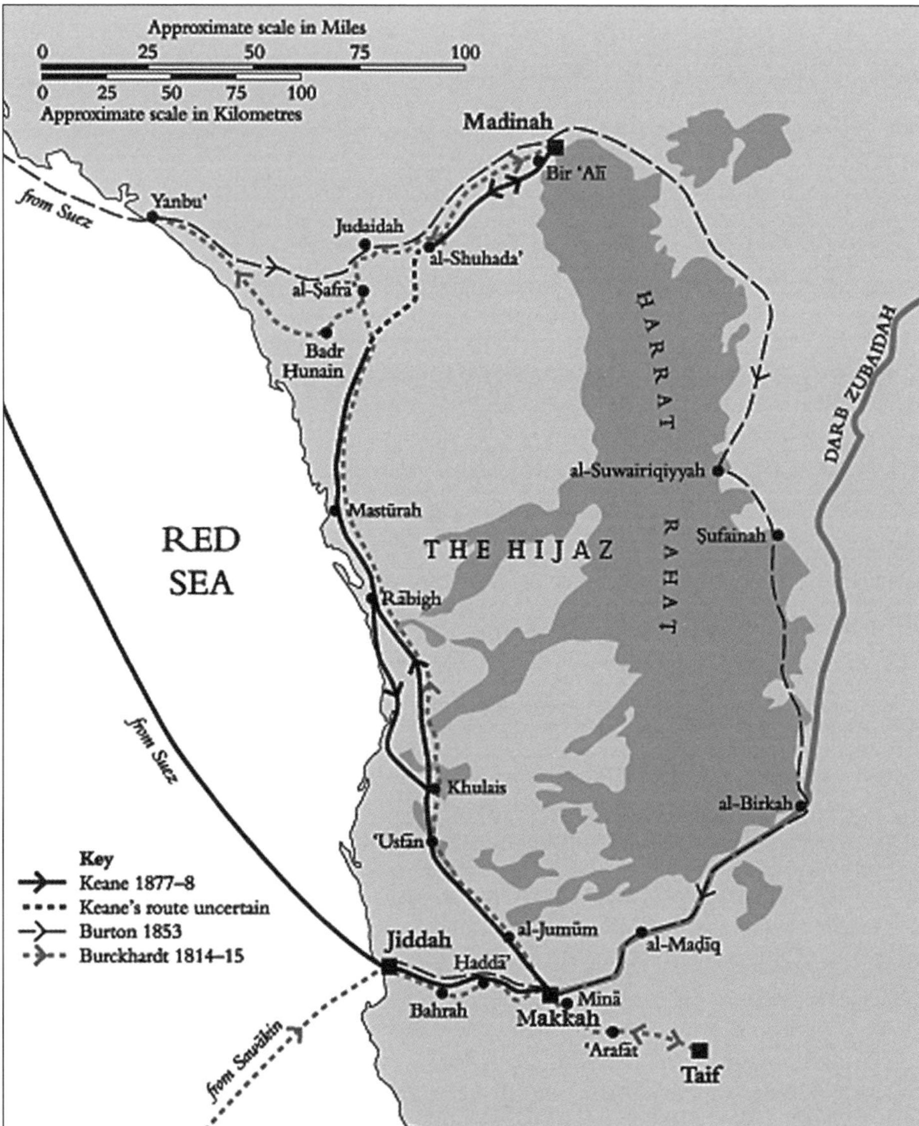

Bibliography

Allen, M. D. (1998), "The Curious Affair of the Lady Venus" in *Shaw and Other Matters: A Festschrift for Stanley Weintraub on the Occasion of His Forty-Second Anniversary at The Pennsylvania State University*, ed. Susan Rusinko, Selinsgrove: Susquehanna University Press/ London: Associated University Press.

Badia y Leblich (1816), *Travels of Ali Bey in Morocco, Tripoli, Cyprus, Egypt, Arabia, Syria and Turkey, between the Years 1803 and 1807*, London: 1816. Reprinted 1993, Reading, UK: Garnet Publishing.

Bicknell, Herman [El-Haj Abd el-Wahid] (1278 AH/AD 1862), letter to *The Times*, reprinted as Appendix VIII in Burton 1893.

Bidwell, Robin, (1994) *Travellers in Arabia*, Reading, UK: Garnet Publishing.

Burckhardt, John Lewis (1829), *Travels in Arabia, Comprehending an Account of those Territories in Hedjaz which the Mohammedans Regard as Sacred*, London: Henry Colburn. Reprinted 1993, London: Darf Publishers Ltd.

Burckhardt, John Lewis (1830), *Notes on the Bedouins and Wahábys*, 2 vols., London: Henry Colburn. Reprinted 1992, Reading: Garnet Publishing Ltd.

Burton, Richard F. (1893), *Personal Narrative of a Pilgrimage to al-Madinah and Meccah*, Memorial Edition, 2 vols., London: Tylston & Edwards. Reprinted 1964, New York: Dover Publications, Inc.

De Gaury, Gerald (1951), *Rulers of Mecca*, London: George G. Harrap.

Doughty, Charles M. (1936), *Travels in Arabia Deserta*, 2 vols., London: Jonathan Cape Ltd. Reprinted 1979, New York: Dover Publications, Inc.

Facey, William (1992), *Riyadh: The Old City*, London: IMMEL Publishing.

Facey, William, and Grant, Gillian (1996), *Saudi Arabia by the First Photographers*, London: Stacey International.

The Graphic magazine (1882), anonymous article "The Pilgrimage to Mecca", edition of 25 March 1882, pp. 287, 292–3, 296.

Hogarth, David G. (1904), *The Penetration of Arabia*, New York: Frederick A. Stokes Company.

Hogarth, David G. (1978), *The Hejaz before World War I: A Handbook*, Cambridge: Falcon–Oleander reprint of Cairo: Arab Bureau 1917.

Keane, T. F. [*sic*] (1881), *Six Months in Meccah: An Account of the Mohammedan Pilgrimage to Meccah*, London: Tinsley Brothers.

Keane, John F. (1881), *My Journey to Medinah: Describing a Pilgrimage to Medinah Performed by the Author Disguised as a Mohammedan*, London: Tinsley Brothers.

Keane, T. F. [*sic*] (1882), "Mecca and its Pilgrims", in *Frank Leslie's Popular Monthly*, Vol. 14, December 1882.

Keane, John F. (1883), *On Blue-water: Some Narrative of Sport and Adventure in the Modern Merchant Service*, London: Tinsley Brothers. Reprinted 1888.

Keane, John F. (*ca.* 1884 and later), *Mere Shakings*, a series of articles in *Tinsley's Magazine*. [Perhaps never published in book form.]

Keane, John F. (1887), *Six Months in the Hejaz: An Account of the Mohammedan Pilgrimages to Meccah and Medinah*, London: Ward & Downey.

Keane, John F. (1887), *Three Years of a Wanderer's Life*, 2 vols., London: Ward & Downey.

Keane, John F. (1905 according to Keane), *Matthew Walker*, place and publisher unknown.

Keighley, Marion (1957), *Whitby Writers: Writers of Whitby and District 1867–1949*, Whitby: Horne & Son.

Kiernan, R. H. (1937), *The Unveiling of Arabia*, London: George G. Harrap & Co.

National Archives, Kew, London (formerly the Public Record Office): Foreign Office file F.O. 376/461. [Unpublished]

Newbolt, Peter (2001), *William Tinsley (1831–1902), "Speculative" Publisher: A Commentary, with a Check-list of Books Published by Tinsley Brothers, 1854–1888*, Aldershot, UK: Ashgate.

Palgrave, William Gifford (1865), *Narrative of a Year's Journey through Central and Eastern Arabia (1862–3)*, 2 vols., London: Macmillan.

Peters, F. E. (1994), *Mecca: A Literary History of the Muslim Holy Land*, Princeton University Press.

Peters, F. E. (1994), *The Hajj: The Muslim Pilgrimage to Mecca and the Holy Places*, Princeton University Press.

Pirenne, Jacqueline (1958), *À la découverte de l'Arabie*, Paris: Le Livre Contemporain.

Ralli, Augustus (1909), *Christians at Mecca*, London: William Heinemann.

Sinker, Robert (1903), *Memorials of the Hon. Ion Keith-Falconer*, new edition, Cambridge: Deighton, Bell & Co., and London: George Bell & Sons.

Smales, Rev. Gideon (1867), *Whitby Authors and Their Publications*, Whitby: Horne & Son. [A short life of the Rev. William Keane, plus a list of 18 of his published pamphlets.]

The Times newspaper, 23 November 1937. [Obituary and announcement of Keane's death.]

Tinsley, William (1900), *Random Recollections of an Old Publisher*, 2 vols., London: Simpkin, Marshall & Co. Ltd.

Trench, Richard (1986), *Arabian Travellers*, London: Macmillan.

Wavell, A. J. B. (1912), *A Modern Pilgrim in Mecca and a Siege in Sanaa*, London: Constable & Co.

Whitby Gazette, 31 May 1873, "In Memoriam: Rev. William Keane, M. A., Born 1818: Died May 26th, 1873".

— 11 June 1881, "A Book by a Native of Whitby: *Six Months in Mecca* by T. F. Keane [*sic*], (Hajj Mohammed Amin)", review reprinted from *The Athenaeum*.

— 15 November 1889, "Literary: Mr J. F. Keane", announcing series of articles by Keane in the *Engineers' Gazette*, on "Life on an Ocean Tramp".

— 23 May 1894, "To Such Base Uses May We Come at Last".

— 20 July 1900, "Our notable fellow-townsman, Mr Keane …".

— 20 July 1900, "An Interview with Mr. John Keane (All Hajj Mohammud Amin [*sic*]): A Famous Traveller and Author".

Who Was Who 1929–1940 (1941), London: A. & C. Black.

Wolfe, Michael (1997), *One Thousand Roads to Mecca: Ten Centuries of Writing about the Muslim Pilgrimage*, New York: Grove Press.

SIX MONTHS IN MECCAH.

SIX MONTHS IN MECCAH:

AN ACCOUNT OF THE MOHAMMEDAN PILGRIMAGE TO MECCAH.

RECENTLY ACCOMPLISHED BY AN ENGLISHMAN PROFESSING MOHAMMEDANISM.

BY

T. F. KEANE.

(*Hajj Mohammed Amin.*)

"The first of the Pilgrims to Meccah and El-Medinah who has left an authentic account of the Holy Cities is Lewes Wertomannus (Ludovicus Bartema), gentelman, of the citie of Rome. 'If any man,' says this author, 'shall demand of me the cause of this my voyage, certeynely I can shewe no better reason than is the ardent desire of knowledge, which hath moved many other to see the world and the miracles of God therein.'"—*Burton's Pilgrimage*, Appendix II. First Edition. Longman. "The Navigation and Voyages of Ludovicus Vertomannus, gentelman, of Rome. A.D. 1503."

LONDON:

TINSLEY BROTHERS, 8, CATHERINE STREET, STRAND.

1881.

CHARLES DICKENS AND EVANS,
CRYSTAL PALACE PRESS.

CONTENTS.

A *

CHAPTER VI.

CHAPTER VII.

CONCLUSION.

SIX MONTHS IN MECCAH.

PREFACE.

My object in the following pages is to give an account, in as short and inviting a manner as I can, of everything of interest that came under my notice while in Meccah, during the pilgrim season 1877–78; and chiefly for the benefit of those who may not have had the leisure, or perhaps inclination, to read the complete and exhaustive descriptions of the same scenes in the volumes of the well-known Swiss traveller, Johan Ludwig Burckhardt (Shaykh Hajj Ibrahim) and of the better-known learned traveller and author, Captain R. F. Burton (Shaykh Hajj Abdallah).

So, promising to make up for my lack of further prelude by what I only hope may not be deemed my too frequent interludes, I will with your permission proceed at once to "spin my yarn" in my own way.

J. F. KEANE (Hajj Mohammed Amin).

EXTRACT FROM *THE TIMES*, THURSDAY, OCTOBER 23, 1879.

"I SHOULD strongly recommend to such of our countrymen as take a morbid delight in depreciating the power and influence of England to take a cruise in the Persian Gulf. If, as we are so constantly told, our word in the Councils of Europe counts for nothing, it is gratifying to see that at all events it stands for something in Asia; and that the Persian Gulf, for instance, in which we do not possess one yard of territory, is for all practical purposes an English lake. Such, indeed, is the case. The shores of the Gulf may actually be situated either in Turkey, Persia, or Arabia; but the one controlling power which keeps everything in order and in its proper place, which has put a stop to piracy, and enjoys the usufruct of peaceful trade, is this same effete, worn-out England: and all this good is effected without the smallest fuss and bluster, simply by the quiet action and influence of a few Englishmen, official and commercial, whose very names are unknown beyond the immediate sphere of their influence, and who are backed by no greater physical force than two or three of Her Majesty's smallest gun-vessels and a single company of Sepoy Infantry."

SIX MONTHS IN MECCAH.

CHAPTER I.

MECCAH'S PILGRIMS.

Meccah's pilgrims, confident of Fate,
And resolute in heart!—LONGFELLOW.

THOUGH Mohammedans are divided into almost as many sects and schisms as Christians, they are all* agreed on one point, namely, that it is imperative on every Mohammedan who can afford it to make a pilgrimage to Meccah at some time in his life. And it is even considered obligatory on those who may have undertaken the pilgrimage during childhood to remake it when they become adult. This pilgrimage must be performed after prescribed rules and forms, and certain ceremonies must be gone through on the proper days of the year; consequently many thousands of Moham-

* Excepting a few barbarians, who can no more be called Mohammedan than some of the tribes of missionaries' pets in South Africa can be called Christian.

medans assemble at Meccah from all parts of the East during the pilgrim season, some of whom come in caravans across the Arabian deserts, while by far the greater number come by sea, giving employment to a number of English ships, and during the season of which I am writing 42,718 disembarked at Jeddah.* It was at this place that I was enabled to attach myself to the train of a youthful Hindi † Amér,‡ whom I accompanied on pilgrimages to Meccah and other places in the Holy Land of Islam,§ and of my expedition to Meccah I shall now attempt to give some account.

On the first landing of these pilgrims at Jeddah, what struck me most was their helplessness and gullibility, for no party of English tourists in Egypt could have been more victimised than were the pilgrims by their brother Mohammedan touts and crimps

* "The British Consul at Jeddah states that in the season of 1877–78 there were 42,718 pilgrims landed at that port, an increase of nearly 4000 over the preceding year; but this was more than counterbalanced by the falling off in the numbers at Zembo and Leet. . . . The concourse at Meccah on the Great Feast-day was estimated to have exceeded 180,000 souls."—*The Times*, October 26th, 1878.

† Mohammedan native of India as distinguished from a Hindoo.

‡ Properly, and in this case really, a lord of the land under a ruler, and subject to feudal conditions.

§ The Hejaz.

of Jeddah. Before they landed a Turkish Custom-house official demanded one rupee a head on no apparent grounds whatever, and then, on landing, charged them a rather high duty on all their baggage, by weight, so that as most of the wealthier pilgrims bring almost sufficient food to last them during their stay in the country they get a pretty good foretaste of what is coming ere they are handed over to the native cicerones to undergo further extortion. Many of the wealthy pilgrims bring introductions to friends or countrymen resident in the Hejaz ; with these introductions my patron was well provided, and thus we secured a tolerably peaceful reception. I cannot describe polyglot Jeddah, as I was not there long enough to find out anything new or interesting about it. To the gentleman acting as British Consul I gave my name and the addresses of friends in England, informing him of my intentions. He said much to dissuade me, telling me the roads were in an unsafe state and the country rather disturbed on account of the withdrawal of Turkish troops to the war in Europe; but I had already made up my mind on the subject, and accordingly sold such of my clothes as would be unsuitable and provided myself with a native wardrobe ; then, after a three-days' rest in

Jeddah, I entered into the preparations of our party en route for Meccah. About noon on the third day, camels were hired from the Bedawins (the real sons of the Desert, as distinguished from their spurious brethren in Egypt, Palestine, and other countries generally visited by Europeans), whom I now met for the first time, and of whom, notwithstanding their wretched appearance at first sight, their haggling, and their shrill voices, I formed a favourable opinion, and still believe to have their good points. One conclusion I quickly arrived at: the "wily Hindi" would be no match for the "swarthy Paynim" in a "rough-and-tumble." After a great deal of hard swearing in a Babel of tongues, the camels were laden and got under way, and I, following the example of my companions, performed the greater ablution (i.e. the bathing of the entire person), and put on the pilgrim's garb, which consists of two pieces of white or light-coloured cotton fabric, one piece round the body over the left shoulder, leaving the right arm bare, the other round the loins, enveloping the body from the waist to below the knee (the head is left uncovered and the upper part of the foot bare), and then said a two-prostration prayer, which is a supplementary act of devotion for special occasions. We afterwards joined our camels, which had become part of a larger caravan outside the walls of Jeddah. I had no difficulty in getting through the gate in the crowd, nor did I hear of any pass being required from the pilgrims, either here or at Meccah, though one may have been got for me by the Amér as Abdur Mohammed, the name I had adopted.

As we went through the gate two fine soldierly-looking Turkish sentries stood leaning on their rifles, smoking cigarettes, and seemed scarcely to notice even the camels passing them. Our party was composed of about fifty in all, men and women; and, as only fifteen camels had been hired, ten with shugdufs, or litters, and five pack-camels (four of these latter with shibriyahs), and as each of these (the shugduf and the shibriyah) carries only two persons, about twenty of our party had to walk by the camels, in company with a number of fakirs, or beggar-pilgrims, who had attached themselves to us and who were accepted as a matter of course, receiving a great deal of charity in the shape of broken victuals and water, which latter has a money value in this country. I found I had to share a shugduf with one, of whom I shall often have to speak, since he was my camel-mate during the whole pilgrimage, and, as I intend, for reasons that will readily suggest themselves to the reader, to suppress or translate all my companions' names, I shall call him (as I always thought of him), the "third warrior," the junior of the three armed retainers who formed the Amér's body-guard.

The kind of panniers or litters, in which we sat or lay at full length when riding, are known by the names of shugduf or shibriyah. Inside the shugduf is a pocket for food, tobacco, and other little necessaries; outside, at the tail end and within easy reach, a wicker-basket containing a bottle of water. Having mounted, that is to say, having, by the help of a ladder, ascended into this construction of bent boughs and old bags, resembling a rickety wigwam poised airily on the hump of a camel, the impression I laboured under was that we were instantly to plunge off in mad bounds across an exceedingly rough country, feeling at the same time pity for the poor beast under what I supposed could only have been an immense burden, spiced with momentary expectation of a spill. But on looking out I found the road a perfectly level sandy plain, the camel crawling along at a slow walk, jolting more than the fastest pace of the hardest trotting horse; moreover the platform on which you lay is on a level with the top of the animal's hump, and the whole structure of the shugduf so top-heavy that it requires the nicest adjustment of weight on either side to prevent the saddle, to which the shugduf is securely lashed (but which has no attachment whatever to the animal, merely adhering to its back in some mysterious way), turning a complete somersault—a thing which not unfrequently happens, for the art of balancing a shugduf is only acquired after long practice. Our camel-driver threatened and abused us wildly for our awkwardness, my companion being as much a novice and as unaccustomed to this mode of travel as myself; however, we purchased peace at the price of a few dates and a little bread. I, for my part, spent one of the most wretched and apparently perilous nights I have ever had the misfortune to undergo, for the pitching and rolling of that desert-ship could not find its equal afloat; so that I, old sailor as I was, became exceedingly sick, a thing which had not happened to me for many years while at sea. The country over which we passed was a sandy plain, if anything, a slight ascent; our course, by the stars, nearly east; and the distance, I was informed, twenty-eight miles to Haddah, where we halted at daylight. Haddah is the stage, or half-way halting-place, between Jeddah and Meccah. Here there are about four or five square miles of cultivated ground, dotted over with groups of Bedawi huts. A stream of brackish water rises in the north-east, and flows a mile or two over stone-built watercourses before losing itself in the desert. Around are what would be called the foot-hills of the approach to a range of mountains, the first out-cropping of stone from the sandy plain, gradually increasing into rocky ridges and higher hills to the eastward. In the shade of a large shedlike caravanserai we spent the day, praying, eating, and resting; but sleep could not be got, for some of the more devout pilgrims kept up the "Talbiyat," or Pilgrim's Prayer:

> Labbayk' Allahumma, Labbayk!
> La Sarika laka, Labbayk!
> Inna'l Handa wa'n Niamata laka w'al Mulk
> La Sharika laka, Labbayk!*

Imagine for yourself an unmusical old man of ninety, with his nose in a rat-gin, trying to sing at the top of his voice those words to the tune of "Silent, oh Moyle," or "The Sailor's Grave," for the first time in his life, and you will be able to faintly

---

* "Here I am! O Allah! here am I:
No Partner hast Thou, here am I.
Verily the Praise and the Beneficence are Thine, and the Kingdom:
No Partner hast Thou, here am I."

Translation from "Burton's Pilgrimage." Third Edition. W. Mullan and Son. London, 1879.

realise the excruciating discord and ghastly contortions these pilgrims keep up for hour after hour while on their way to Meccah, to say nothing of many other almost equally disturbing devotional cries. I now found I could perform my ablution and prayer without attracting notice by any awkwardness on my part, audacious imitation giving me considerable help.

About an hour before sunset we got under way for Meccah; after this the road became a more decided ascent, the hills around being higher and more rugged as we passed through rocky defiles in which the moaning of the camels and the labbayks of the pilgrims were echoed and re-echoed with a truly weird effect. At daylight, when we seemed to have reached the summit of a rocky platform, the increased intensity of the labbayks and the dismounting of those ahead told that "the Meccah" was in sight. The distance we had come from Haddah was about twenty miles, and the course still easterly. The approach to Meccah by this road does not give a good view of the town. You arrive among collections of high stone buildings scattered over rocky slopes, then dismounting—for it is the proper thing to enter Meccah on foot if possible, women and invalids only being excepted—you find yourself passing along rather wide streets, and between houses of some height; and as you continue on a downhill course the streets become more narrow and dirty towards the centre of the city, where a house had been prepared for us in the walks of the Haram or square enclosed for public worship, where is situated the Moslem Holy of Holies, the Kaabah.

Now here was I, a veritable "Britisher," looking through a plain iron-barred window, estimating the dimensions of that Mohammedan pivotal point of the world—"Hub of the Universe," the Kaabah, a shrine for which to die at hundreds of thousands stint and pauper themselves in their old age, and towards which millions of eyes from all points of the compass turn with reverence five times daily. But my calculating mood was soon cut short, for having established ourselves on the premises, there was no escaping the forms and ceremonies appropriate to the occasion, which, tired and weary as I felt, kept me going the whole day. Besides the usual everyday five prayers and ablutions, we had to perform a two-prostration prayer in one part of the Haram and another in another part; to do the tawaf—i.e. walk, or rather trot, round the Kaabah seven times, kissing the Black Stone let into a corner of the building, and touching another stone in it, at every circuit; to run seven times about one-third of a mile through the streets repeating (after a guide hired for the purpose) proper prayers—this latter ceremony is called El-Sai, and is done in commemoration of Hagar's running up and down searching for water on the same spot. The street is in the middle of the city, skirting the Haram on the east, and crossing the valley of Meccah indirectly from side to side. Lastly, the head must be shaved. And now I was at liberty to take off the pilgrim's garb. My companions only shaved as much of the top of their heads as could be covered by a skull-cap, but I preferred, for reasons of cleanliness, to do all the shearing, moustache-clipping, and nail-paring of the most close-shaving Mohammedan, leaving my beard, the ends of my moustache, and two small locks under my temples, the only hair about me. The costume I assumed was a sort of mixture of Hindi and Turk, with perhaps as much of the Arab as of either in it. My headdress was a Turkish tarbóuche, with a long silk handkerchief tied round it; on my feet the Hindi sandals, a strip of leather protecting the entire sole of the foot, and kept on by a band over the instep and down between the big and second toes; by way of breeches, a pair of Hindi cotton pyjamas, four feet round the waist and tight at the ankles; a tunic of the same material, girded about the loins with several folds of a cotton scarf;

and over all, when in the open air, an Arab-brown cloth mantle, having wide sleeves and reaching down to the ankles.

Right glad was I on this my first night in Meccah when we had said our last prayer and had laid down for the night to sleep, although the Amér and some thirty other "True Believers," packed head and tail in the same room, were snoring like pigs around me —yes, such was the thought, even the name of the unmentionable animal—literally unmentionable to all strict Mohammedans. Notwithstanding this impious thought my conscience did not prevent my sleeping soundly. Nor did I wake at the 2 A.M. meal—for this was the month Ramazan, when all food must be eaten between sunset and sunrise—but my well-meaning friends took sufficient interest in my spiritual welfare to turn me out for the morning prayer, for which service I appeared properly grateful, exhibiting a great deal of cheerful alacrity in the shape of a cold-water wash before sunrise on a chilly morning, and a quarter of an hour's gymnastic praying. One convenience was that the room in which we lived had three large recess windows looking straight into the Haram, so that we could see the Kaabah to which we prayed, and which is known as the "Ear of God" and by a dozen other flowery Eastern appellations, without going out. Neither the Amér nor any of his superior retainers went into the arcades surrounding the Kaabah to pray except at noon on the Mohammedan Sunday, which falls on our Friday, and on a few other festive occasions. At first I always secured a place at these windows, not caring to show myself more in public than was necessary.

As this narrative is written chiefly for those who know little of Mohammedanism or Meccah, before going farther I will explain what this pilgrimage is, and endeavour to demonstrate my position in Meccah. I had often heard it said and myself believed that this great concourse of people which every year assembles at Meccah, ostensibly on a pilgrimage, really meets for a great mart or fair held there; but now having made the journey I know that this is not the case. It is a true pilgrimage, the outcome of a belief in the tenets of a religion, the commands of the Prophet. I think I might truly say that a very small minority go for temporal gain, though the majority do not go from disinterested motives (the devotion of love talked of by Christians playing a small part in Mohammedanism, so far as I have seen). The journey and hardship are undertaken professedly with an eye to the future, as believed to be necessary for the salvation of the soul from the punishments and in the hope of the rewards promised in the Koran, and are, as I said before, the outcome of a wonderful and widespread belief, difficult to understand, and which could only exist among such races as imaginative miracle-mongering dwellers of the East. From this it will be understood that the community of Meccah is composed of the most bigoted Mohammedans, the fanatical scum of the whole Mohammedan world. Now, the precarious position of an unbeliever in any wholly Mohammedan town is well known; but let a Jew, Christian, or idolater approach to defile ground so holy and held in such veneration as is Meccah in the eyes of Mohammedans—ground of which many declare that should any but a True Believer stand on, it would open and swallow him—to say that he would be stoned to death, torn in pieces, burnt and his ashes sent out of the country, would only be repeating what I have heard Mohammedans declare. I am confident the life of a solitary white man refusing to make "profession of that faith" would not be worth an hour's purchase—two hours outside the walls of Jeddah—even at this day: so that should any but a Mohammedan, from motives of curiosity, gain, or for adventure wish to enter the Hejaz, he must conform to the customs and habits of a Mohammedan, and adopt great caution; for, notwithstanding the security in which the majority affect to live, there are many jealous and inquisitive watchers, self-constituted spies, who would soon seal the fate of anyone suspected of insincerity. But let him be master of the thousand little signs and allusive phrases of Mohammedan Freemasonry, and let him affect minutely all observances and points of etiquette among Mohammedans, and sustain throughout a character for devotion, and he need fear no inconvenience on the score of his nationality in a place like Meccah. He may declare himself a Peckham Ryot, a native of Belgravia, or a country called North, as I have done, and he will meet with courteous, polite credence; for there is so much dissembling and cunning in the Eastern character and respect for deceit that a Mohammedan will outwardly appear to believe a lie, in inverse proportion to its obvious untruth. I have told an Arab that I was by profession mate of a steamer, which must have seemed an imposition in such a poor wretch as I looked at the time, and he has immediately after, in my hearing, declared as a matter of fact that I was captain of a steamer, giving me my promotion out of compliment to what must have appeared to him the immensity of my first crammer. All through I made assurance my strong suit and my acquaintance with India and hailing from Bombay my trump card; but if ever really cornered, as on one or two occasions, a little hand-play, implying that I was a recent convert, would in every case call forth nothing but approval and commendation. To undertake an expedition of this kind was certainly a wild and unscrupulous thing, and I suffered many qualms of conscience and felt the veriest hypocrite; but having once entered into it there was no drawing back and the ordeal had to be gone through, though I often at first longed to declare myself a humbug. I remember once hearing a sailor say to another: "You have told that lie so often, Jack, you believe it yourself." I now found this to be no impossibility. It became my case to a nicety, and in less than a month I was to all intents and purposes as honestly Mohammedan as any born Arab among them. I, in fact, acted that lie so well I believed it myself! The name I had adopted, the "Servant of the Prophet," though common in several forms in India, was objected to by the most correct of our party as not strictly orthodox, for, said they, was not Mohammed himself the servant of God? I thought this would be very inconvenient, as a cause of discussion bringing me into uncoveted notice, and added " Amin " to the name I had already adopted, then dropping " the servant," by an easy transition I became known as " Mohammed Amin," a name which I supposed could not be objected to by any Mohammedans, no matter of what peculiar persuasion. Though I do not pretend but that I should be very much out of my depth were I to enter into any description of the discrepancies of belief existing among the various sects of the Mohammedans, still I do know more of Wahhabis than of the Wesleyans, and the Shafei is not altogether such a mystery to me as the Shaker; but I will spare the reader the infliction and myself the risk of exposure, having received probably much misinformation from so fertile a source as a Hindi one-sided education, and so I shall continue my narrative as the pilgrim Mohammed Amin, a Suni Mohammedan of the " reasonable class."

CHAPTER II.

IN MECCAH.

I WAS now settled in Meccah, living the ordinary everyday life of a pilgrim waiting for the "Great Pilgrimage." My ablutions were performed with the water of the well Zem Zem—Hagar's well in the wilderness, as tradition has it—and for appearance' sake I drank not a little of it, disagreeable as it was, being a mineral spring tasting like a weak solution of Epsom salts, and having a similar medicinal action. For each prayer said in Meccah, I was supposed to get credit for a thousand said elsewhere; still it is not desirable for any but the very devout to reside wholly in Meccah, as one's sins are multiplied in like proportion. I was not supposed to have any intercourse with my harem, if I had had one, nor to indulge in any feasting, sports, or amusements other than those allowable on religious grounds. Fighting and the shedding of blood were especially to be abstained from, and killing of vermin, flies, worms, etc. were almost equally reprehensible, on account of the probability of offending a "djin"—a class of spirit which is believed to take this form and to be especially abundant in Meccah—and on account of the sanctity of all living things Meccan, whether "djins," men, or insects. I have heard a hot discussion as to the advisability of killing a human parasite, the slaughterer defending himself on the plea that the insect was undoubtedly of foreign extraction and but recently imported. My food consisted of the native diet of India, two meals of curry and rice a day, morning and evening, supplemented by such sweets, fruit, or tea as might be going in the household; for the rice I ate, no matter how much, never satisfied my cravings, it having, as far as my experience goes, much the same effect on a hungry man as salt water on a thirsty one. I sometimes went out into the streets and purchased bread from the Turkish soldiers, who sell their rations, and judging from the quality of their bread and the quantity they have to dispose of, they must be in clover here. After a week or ten days I found I could walk about the crowded bazaars without attracting notice, my fair complexion exciting no curiosity among the chequered masses, nor my ignorance of Arabic giving me any inconvenience where so many nationalities were gathered, speaking more languages than I will stay to enumerate here, only mentioning that you may jostle against a Tartar, Malay, Negro, and Turk round any Hindi tea-stall. Nor does the style of your get-up make any difference, except that it is advisable not to be too "swell" in order to avoid attracting beggars, but otherwise the Archbishop of Canterbury doing the tawaf in his mitre and robes would not occasion a passing remark, and would be placed nowhere by twenty much more wondrously-attired figures. There was always something about that procession round the Kaabah that made me think of it as Madame Tussaud's male waxworks out for a walk—the many varieties of costume, the stolid expressionless faces and the peculiar Tussaud complexion, were all there.

I suffered at this time from small boils on the hands, feet, or face, accompanied by feverishness, a complaint (apparently peculiar to Meccah) which foreigners are seldom known to escape during the first month of their residence there. For a few days I was laid up with a very sharp touch of fever, lost count of time, nor did I attempt to recover any dates until my return to Jeddah. About this time the end of the Fast Ramazan came, and the Great Feast lasting for three days brought out the whole population, decked in their gaudiest apparel, while the guns from each of the three Turkish forts fired a salute of twenty-one at the times of the sunrise, noon, and sunset calls to prayers on each of the three days. The worship round the Kaabah in the great square was attended by larger numbers than I saw at any other time, notwithstanding that but few of the pilgrims had as yet arrived. I estimated that there could not have been less than thirty thousand assembled at the sunset prayer on the second day. It was an imposing spectacle to see those thousands of bearded, turbaned, hard, worldly men standing, circle widening upon circle, round their sacred Kaabah, silently following the imam as he praised God and blessed Mohammed. Then as from one voice rises the great cry, "God is great!" stirring emotions that must be felt to be appreciated, and simultaneously all bow and prostrate themselves with their faces to the earth. I have often stood in my window-recess going through these motions, unconsciously wrapt in the scene before me; every bright-coloured dress or brilliant turban a contribution to an extent of blended colour which the eye could not take in, each wave of prostration as it swept over this rainbow-tinted space making aurora-like transformations. In the twilight it was beautiful and impressive beyond most human displays. At this time the Kaabah was opened, but I did not now venture to seek admission, though I did so on a future occasion. At the end of three weeks I began to know the ropes and find my way about pretty well. I had taken the bearings of most remarkable objects by the stars and sun, inquiring their names and the histories connected with them.* One day I took a rather wider cruise to the top of a hill (Jebel Kubays), about a quarter of a mile south of the centre of the city and five or six hundred feet high, and rather steep on the north side, from which I hoped to get a good view. On this hill Mohammed is said to have wrestled with a great infidel, one Nimrud, and defeated him by a miracle, Nimrud being much the stronger man. It was on this hill also that Mohammed commanded the moon to rise half in the east and half in the west, then disappear down the sleeve of his mantle. On the highest point will the Haram be perched on the Day

* I must here caution the reader that most of my observations and statements depend on correctness of judgment, and may be, in some cases, but the widest approximations. I had not the simplest instruments—as a watch or a compass, to make no more scientific pretensions—and my notes were necessarily very scanty. I had, moreover, to look for nearly all information to the most ignorant and superstitious of Easterns, the Hindis.

of Judgment, previous to ascending into heaven, carrying with it all saved Mohammedans. Here there is a small mosque, from which, as I expected, a bird's-eye view of the whole city can be obtained. The town lies in a basin among steep hills of from five hundred to seven hundred feet in height, and probably not more than one thousand two hundred to one thousand five hundred above the sea. The whole of this valley, about one mile and a half long by one-third of a mile across, is packed and crammed with buildings of all shapes and sizes, placed in no kind of order, climbing far up the steep side of the surrounding hills, with here and there an outlying house on the summit of some rock, looking as though crowded out and waiting for a chance to squeeze into the confusion below; a curious gray mass, flat-topped, to an European eye roofless, half-plastered, for plaster in this climate is always either being put on, or well advanced in coming off, but never to be seen in its entirety. The walls of the houses are composed of uncut stone and rubble from three to six feet thick, in very high buildings even thicker, but stone is used only for the sills of windows or jambs and arches of doorways, and very little brick is employed anywhere. Notwithstanding the substantial thickness of the walls, tottering ruins may be found by the sides of the most thronged thoroughfares in every part of the city. Many of the houses are of great height, large and factorylike, full of little windows ; seldom two adjacent houses face the same way or are the same height ; nothing resembling a row or street could by any stretch of imagination be extricated from such a chaos of masonry. It was impossible, even from my elevated point of view, to trace a hundred yards of open space between houses in any direction (many of the passages are boarded over, which to a certain extent conceals them), except on the outskirts of the town, where two or three suburbs straggle off up the less inclined outlets from the valley, and where the ground is not so thickly built over, though with the same systematic irregularity. The rule seems to be that no two things must be alike, an Eastern characteristic developed into a fixed law of non-uniformity in everything about Meccah, a town which —built as it is of fragments of the crumbling rock about, made to adhere with thirty per cent. of coarse lime, together with the dusky crowds creeping in swarms about its dark lanes and streets, if such mere tortuous intricacies can be called so—suggests the simile of the giant ant-hill most strikingly, and indeed it applies better than any other description. There is a great sameness about all this detailed dissimilarity, from the midst of which the Haram stands out most prominently, at once fixing the attention, and indeed it is the main feature of Meccah. It is a large quadrangular open space, its longest direction north-east by east and south-west by west, enclosed within four arched colonnades or arcades, one hundred and ninety yards on the longest sides by one hundred and twenty-seven yards on the shortest, close up to which, on the exterior, houses are built, except on the east side, where it is bounded by a street skirting the wall of the Haram.

The arcades, which are twenty-five feet high, have a row of little domes, thirty-six on the long and twenty-four on the short sides, running along the centre of the top, which is fifty feet wide; but at the two principal entrances, in the middle of the north and west sides, there begins a widening of the roof, which has two more rows of domes. These I did not count, and under the arcades the projection of the roof is not apparent, the space being occupied by offices of the Haram built under them. There are six tall minarets, placed at intervals round the outside of the enclosure, one or two of which must be considerably over one hundred and fifty feet in height. From the inside of the arcades a number of stone pathways lead across the gravelled square to a central-paved oval space round the Kaabah, a plain unornamented oblong, of closely-pointed, massive, cyclopean masonry, thirty-eight feet by thirty square, and forty feet high, as I afterwards ascertained when some portion of the cover was removed. It is covered with a heavy black cloth, which has a good deal of silk in its composition, and all round it, ten feet from the top, a band about two-and-a-half feet deep, very richly worked in bullion, with the Caluma, the Mohammedan profession of faith, the whole of the black cloth being damasked with the same characters. The marble pavement glistens in the sun from the high state of polish in which it is kept by the feet of the pilgrims, who may be seen at all hours, both night and day, performing the tawaf. There are a few little buildings in the square, such as an erection over the well (Zem Zem) and the stations of the imams of the different sects. Add to these flocks of blue rock pigeons settled in the square, flying over and about it, perched on every available ledge not covered with little wire spikes, and I can show you no more of the Haram from my present standpoint. There are three Turkish forts or castles on the highest points of the hills around commanding the town, and covering its three principal approaches; they form a triangle with one another—north-east, west, and south. Jebel Kubays, like every other resort of pilgrims, is frequented by sturdy beggars, the sturdiest occupying the best positions, having handkerchiefs spread out before them with a few suggestive copper coins laid out on them. Before I left I was mulcted of, for an Eastern, a fabulous amount of coin by these beggars. A young Arab damsel with lovely eyes, by no means coy, followed me down from the top and beguiled me of my last half-piastre when she uncovered the lower part of her face in a dark passage near the bottom of the hill.

The measurements and numbers given were obtained at different times by a regular system, which I followed on every opportunity. I carried with me wherever I went a bamboo stick exactly a yard long, which I dropped or laid down carelessly as I moved about. No one would have suspected the zealous devotee crawling on his hands and knees at night round the holy Kaabah was by way of a prayer mumbling the number of times he moved his stick. The height of buildings I got by measuring their shadows, which bore the same proportion to the object as my stick's shadow bore to three feet, provided I had a plain surface, as in the Haram. All the measurements given in feet may be relied on as tolerably accurate, and were noted down at the time.

On the afternoon of this day I ventured into the Haram alone for the first time. On the day of my arrival in Meccah the occasion had been one on which I had not been in a condition to observe much, seeing the desperately tiring journey that had just transported me into such a whirl of strange surroundings. But I had now got the run of things, and felt sufficiently at home to go almost anywhere in Meccah. Each of the gates of the Haram is kept by a man—generally Hindi—who takes charge of the shoes of the worshippers as they pass in, and deposits each pair separately in a large wicker framework divided into pigeon-holes. Should you be in the habit of always using the same gate, you may give this man an occasional present on any special feast or fast day, but, if entering for the first time, or by a gate you are not accustomed to use, he looks for some trifling copper coin; though, as a rule, these men do not openly beg, from which fact I infer they must be paid from the funds of the Haram.

What is very noticeable on first entering the sacred precincts is the general solemn expression of the faces round you; everybody has on his Sunday-go-to-meeting countenance, and converses in a sober subdued tone, while those sitting have their feet carefully tucked under them—this is a point of etiquette everywhere, but especially to be observed in the Haram—and those lying down have their feet turned away from the Kaabah. Should you carry your shoes in your hand, as some do who may be going out by a different gate from the one by which they entered, you must hold them sole to sole, and no one would think of spitting while in the Haram, except on the soles of his shoes. Only privileged beggars are to be met with in the Haram, such as maimed or very old, and these do not force tribute from you after the manner of "bakhshish," merely getting in your way, and making themselves and their infirmities conspicuous. One old blind fellow puzzled me for a long time, by the rapidity of his movements from place to place among the thickly-set pillars supporting the arcades without a stick or any other apparent means of guiding himself, until I found by watching him that he was guided by the joints of the pavement over which he walked, feeling their direction and length with his big toes. A number of water-carriers go about among the crowd standing liquors-up indiscriminately, or getting paid by anyone liberal enough; sometimes, if you don't give them a trifle after imbibing, their generosity exceeds all bounds, and they douche you from head to foot with a second cupful. As the water is Zem Zem, you, of course, deem it too great an honour, and bestow a blessing with a benign grin in return for your drenching;

beaming outwardly, while the chilly liquid trickles down the small of your back.

Here and there may be seen, at any time night or day, parties of devotees sitting in circles droning out short prayers, over and over, hour after hour, with a uniformity of sound and expression—ecstatic grunts and swaying of the body—which to call monotonous would be to speak of the hundred-ton gun as a trifle large, or the *Great Eastern* as a tidy craft indeed. This sort of thing is kept up with a persistent monotony that becomes simply bewildering. Enthusiasts after some hours go into a religious frenzy, and what between sheer exhaustion and their mental condition, work themselves up to foaming inarticulate idiotcy. I have seen these fits present the symptoms of epilepsy. To be able to do this well is considered not exactly an accomplishment but rather a gift, and the possessor is looked upon with great reverence.

Men's convictions should be respected whatever they may be; but the contemplation of this fanaticism gave rise in me to an unhappy train of thought. To think that the noble faith founded by that redeemer Mohammed, at whose coming "the whole world was lost in the darkness of sin," if it ever was, and to the stimulating influence of whose hostility

Christianity may be said to owe its present state, if I read my history aright. To think that the faith preached by such as the earnest Omer, the faith held by the illustrious Moors and many a chivalrous Saladin, should have fallen off in the hands of these Eastern weaklings to a mere belief in prayer doing. How much cant do we hear iterated and reiterated about the "essential unprogressiveness of Mohammedanism?" I fear, as that stirring faith has failed to make anything of the Eastern, there is but a poor look-out for Christianity. If every tinted skin from light straw to ebony were Evangelical Low Church to-morrow, there would be as much opium and tobacco consumed as before: the only benefit to humanity would be found in the workings of the Protestant alcohol and six-shooter, those sturdy irregular followers of the Christian Church militant, whose cutting-up of the retreat none but the very fittest of the fit survive. "Keep off the grass." I do not charge my readers with habitually infringing Park bye-laws, when I suppose that at some time they may have found it convenient to cut across the tender turf in spite of the above admonition. Well, while promenading the arcades of the Haram for the first time, I felt a precisely similar sensation of uncomfortableness as I have felt while committing the above offence, no more! And yet I remember only a very few years ago being oppressed for days by the horrible guilt of having attended divine service in a Dissenting chapel.

How a few years of roughing it does knock "hereditary prejudice" out of a man, to be sure! It is now enough for me that I have met many good men, "aye, good men and true," of most religions—Catholic, Moslem, Protestant, or Buddhist—more good than bad: so the world may still be lived in, thank goodness! How I could ramble on! But I must not do so here, though I may remind the reader that I have only promised to "spin my yarn in my own way," and ask him to bear with my occasional wanderings; so just another word before "standing off on the long tack," and if you are the reader I suppose myself writing for, I shall not offend by offering the following little bit of instruction.

The name Mohammedanism is applied by Christians to a faith, the followers of which do not know it by any such name. They call themselves "worshippers of the one God," and have, in my humble opinion, a rather fine conception of that deity. They are "true believers" in all the patriarchs and prophets from Adam down, through Abraham, Moses, Jesus Christ to Mohammed, whose coming they believe to have been prophesied by the "Man of Peace," whose reappearance on earth is prophesied by Mohammed. And it is generally held by so-called Mohammedan theologians that the time of his reappearance is very near at hand; so much so that the mere repetition of such a statement was a standing byword among the pilgrims of every nation while I was in Meccah. Also the old idea of the near approach of the end of the world is very prevalent in the East just now, which, all in all, is about as ripe for the reception of some Darwaysh "Peter the Hermit" as it well could be, and were he to come upon the scene in some such a centre as Hyderabad in the Deccan, Mohammedanism might be giving some very troublesome death throes in a year or two. However, we need not be very much alarmed, as they have not sufficient unity left among them to organise anything like a formidable "jihad"—crescentade—anywhere.

To return to Meccah. Observing and inquiring were now the only things which recalled me to my identity. I had become so accustomed to my surroundings, and accommodated myself to circumstances so rapidly, that in six weeks I was as much at home as if I had been a Mohammedan all my life. I formed friends, had little tiffs and jealousies with my companions in the household—we all having the same interests, and even eating out of the same plates, without offering to bite, though the disposition to do so is so strong as to be barely under control. Darwinites may safely take my word for this fact, and are at liberty to make use of it as a startling analogy. My trencher-mates were a blind Moulvi,* and a gentleman with only two fingers on his right hand, the only one with which a Mohammedan may take food. I had, with infinite pains, worked this myself, thinking I would stand a better chance; but the first time I sat down I found I had immensely underrated my friends' abilities, for I never saw two men with such an alarming capacity for curry and rice, or who showed such extraordinary skill at putting it away. At first I was a little fastidious, and had rather a prejudice in favour of not seeing a greasy black hand scratching merrily among my food. I did not seem to enjoy it as much as I ought; however, it was only a prejudice which I had to overcome. I began by imagining lines drawn over the dish, separating a corner of it to myself and operating inside these bounds. This sort of thing did not last long, the two-fingered gentleman's two long fingers would come ambling along through

* Doctor of Divinity.

my little rice wall before I had got my third fistful swallowed; or the Moulvi's skinny hand would wave like a mesmeric pass over the dish, scatter grains that had stuck to his fingers from the last mouthful over it, and then alight on my most meaty morsel, a piece I had perhaps had my eye on from the first; but it would have shown greedy haste on my part to have taken it so early in the play. No, I hadn't a chance with these two thieves, for they got away five-sixths of the mess every meal, and with such grace too. "Bless you," they would say, "how little you eat, Mohammed Amin!" as they shared the last mouthful between them.

There was a time when I thought, to pretend to know anything about India, you must at least own to a passion for curry and rice. Ah yes, that was before I set myself up for an authority on the matter, when I could not have given you the following recipe for a real native curry:—Set a pot on the fire, put anything and some water into it, add saffron and powdered chillies till you are perfectly satisfied that the keenest palate could detect nothing else and it is so hot that you would rather be skinned alive than eat a spoonful of it, call it by the name of the next chief ingredient; cook it in any way, as long as you like, and in the meantime cast about for something else to put in it, it does not in the least matter what—a handful of shot or a piece of brown paper—just throw anything at it, you're perfectly safe. Serve it at any meal—breakfast, lunch, or dinner, all are equally suitable; and, if a victim hints that it is rather hot, and you want to be thoroughly native, swear "by Allah, it has not heard the name of chilly."

After the evening meal, we all used to sit round a lamp in the middle of the room, eating sweets, smoking hookahs, and telling stories. I got to be very fond of the hookah; the smoke passes through a chamber full of water which takes up the more solid particles and condenses the steam from the tobacco and cools the smoke, which is always inhaled right into the lungs and has a very soothing effect, though somewhat painful to a beginner.

Sometimes I would tell a story, something in this style:—The Amér begins by asking me, "You have been in many countries, Mohammed Amin?"

"Why not, your honour? Is not my work sailing?"

"I have heard there is a big fish in the sea, bigger than a ship?"

"I have seen many and hunted them in the sea to the south of India!" and so go on to give a long account of whaling to which all would listen most attentively, the Amér occasionally asking shrewd questions; or I would tell of a country where the sun does not set for six months, where there is hardly any land to be seen, all ice, ice, ice.

The Amér has said, "Good! Is there such a place in the world?"

"Yes."

"Good! If there is nothing but ice, for what do ships go?"

This is expected to be a poser, and the whole circle say "Yes, yes," and look inquiringly at me.

"Oh, there is a big animal called walrus, as big as two camels, having the body of an ox, the feet of a crocodile, the head of a tiger, tusks like an elephant, and tail of a fish; it is very fat, and we went to hunt them."

I can see incredulity on every countenance, and the Amér puts a final clencher with "Good! and what can it get to eat to make it so fat?"

"The fish in the sea!"

Here follow general laughter and exclamations of "God! what a father of lies!"

I invented many wonderful stories to amuse them and found, here as everywhere, truth less credited than fiction. I have been simply disbelieved when I said I had seen the late Sultan

Abdool Azis and Her Majesty; even an attempt to describe their appearance would not carry conviction.

Altogether I was not at all unhappy, and remember many pleasant evenings with my Mohammedan friends, with whom I was, I believe, a bit of a favourite all round, and looked upon as an agreeable harmless fellow, my punctilious observance of all religious duties making me much approved by the most devout. I often astonished even the blind Moulvi by my knowledge of divinity and the soundness of my principle—though I could neither read nor write much, and had spent my whole life among men who were only Mohammedan by name. I made also a number of acquaintances outside; a chatty old barber to whom I went twice a week to get my head shaved, and who had been a "Company's sepoy," I found very entertaining. He knew Bombay well, and liked comparing notes with me, talking about those "Shaitan" English, whom I could not help thinking he remembered kindly, though he of course joined me in my Mohammedan disapproval of them, expressing a little proper patriotic antipathy.

One day, when work and talk were rather "slack," the old fellow casually remarked, *à propos* of the previous conversation, "There is an Englishwoman in Meccah, 'The Lady Venus' by name.'

This was an eye-opener, though I took care not to show it, merely replying in an uninterested way:

"Praise be to God, how long has she been here?"

"Many years."

"Whose zenana is she in?"

"Nobody's; she works at sewing and keeps herself, a Nawab gives her a room in his zenana house, and she does some little work for him. She is old."

"She is not an English lady. I think perhaps she is a half-caste."

"No, she is a real lady, sahib. Would you like to see her?"

"Yes, I will speak English to her and find out who she is." For I did not conceal any of my Christian accomplishments; instead, I rather bragged of them and got it believed I pretended to know more than I really did. Whether the old barber wanted to test me with a real Englishwoman, or whether he did it in a kindly busybody spirit, I cannot say; there is no accounting for motives. At any rate, he arranged a meeting at his brother-in-law's house (a Moulvi) at two o'clock next day, saying he was certain to get the woman to come. The old fellow may have seen clean through me and expected a tip from one of us, and, if so, he got one. You may be sure I had but one thing to think about that night. An Englishwoman in Meccah; been here many years; impossible! I have seen a gentleman driving an ox team in his swallowtails, and once met a Cambridge B.A. before the mast in a whaler; but this seemed impossible even to me. Still I thought, "I am here, and I did not find it very difficult to get here either;" and great misgivings came as it occurred to me, I don't know how in the name of the Prophet I could get out if anyone wanted to stop me; and then, to have to spend a whole life as she was doing, in such wretchedness and misery, buried alive in Meccah, I could put up with it while the novelty and the excitement of acting a difficult part lasted, but twelve months of it would kill me. "No," I said, "she can't be an Englishwoman;" and I consoled myself by settling she must be a country-born half-caste, fair enough to be called English. However I should see.

The next day I put on a clean tunic and bright red cumerbund, and paid as much attention to the set and folds of my turban as I ever did to the tying of a white choker, and brushed out my beard with a—Allah, preserve us!—pig's-bristle brush. That brush had got me into great disrepute for a time, for incautiously telling the Amér what it was made of when asked; but no notice was taken of it, as they did not want to believe, and I took care to publicly explain on the first opportunity how hair-brushes were made of elephants' hair, and the old bristles went their round of some two dozen faithful beards every day. Allah, preserve us! Allah, forgive us!

When, having got myself up for the occasion, I hurried off at the right time in a great state of anticipation to the good Moulvi's house, called a boy in the yard, announced myself, and went upstairs into a little room about the size of a small bedroom, very clean; the only sign of untidiness being the usual dust-heap in the doorway. At one end of this room were a number of shelves let into the wall, covered with curious china-ware. This is to be seen in nearly every well-to-do house in Meccah, though how or at what time the china-ware found its way into the Hejaz in such quantities I could not find out. Perhaps it comes directly through Persia; but I heard of no existing import trade.* It is likely to be very old, as it is valued only for ornamental

* I should think it not improbable that some of it represents the remnants of treasure that may have been brought to Arabia at any time during the five thousand years of prosperous commerce carried on from its shores before Vasco da Gama led Europe round the Cape of Good Hope to "far Cathay."

purposes. Some of the vases were filled with artificial flowers; and two French flower lithographs hung on the wall. Representations of animal life are prohibited to Mohammedans. There was also a six-feet by four-feet window, with open teak-wood shutters, roughly carved in an elaborate pattern of very unfinished but substantial joinery. The only furniture in the room was a cushioned ottoman running half round the walls about eighteen inches high and three feet wide, having one or two pillows lying on it; a rough teak-wood cabinet standing against the wall, and, lying on it, the Moulvi's Koran, praying-carpet, and turban. On the floor a good Persian carpet, one or two small mats, and of course a hookah and spittoon.

This may be taken as a good specimen of a room in any middle-class Meccan's house. The occupants were the Moulvi, a kind honest old man with a genial pleasant face. Who could believe he had been a great conspirator in his youth? Yet he is now an exile, and dare not return to his own country; and is said to have been one of the most daring mutineer leaders at Lucknow. I was greatly taken with the genuineness of the old fellow. He may have fought, and fought hard, for his faith and his country, but I believe he never acted other than conscientiously according to his lights—which is saying a good deal for a Hindi. Seated on the ottoman near him, the barber, a most "or'nary cuss," a shiny old black with a straight white beard and a tongue like a Bengali; and the woman sitting on the floor in the costume of the country—a figure squatted down with a sheet thrown over it and the edges well tucked under, two slits somewhere near the eyes with pieces of gauze sewn over them for looking through. Give the whole a convulsive subdued shaking, and you have the "Lady Venus" as I first saw her.

I slipped off my shoes, entered the room, and made my bow and "Peace be upon you," exchanged a few "Take-a-seats," "Don't-stirs," with the Moulvi, then subsided cross-legged on the floor opposite the woman. She evidently understood my real character, and it seemed a painful interview to her. We sat silently for some minutes, the motion of her hand to her eyes under the veil showing she was in tears.

At length the Moulvi spoke to her in Arabic, telling her to ask me some questions in English—as my name, age, country, employment—all of which I answered as I wished the Moulvi to believe; but when she asked, at his instance, how I came to Meccah, and I replied—"God put it into my head," which she interpreted, "God put it into his heart,"

I felt safe and talked more freely. After a time, by her advice, we talked in Hindi on general and safe topics of interest to both. I found that she had been amongst Mohammedans since 1858; and satisfied myself, in the half-hour's conversation, that she was a real, educated Englishwoman. When she rose to go I asked her in English if I might shake hands with her. She said: "No;" and told me the part of the Haram in which she prayed, where I could meet her any day at noon.

Afterwards I stayed to dinner with the Moulvi, his poor relation, the barber, joining us. He improved the occasion after dinner, over a pipe, by giving me a long religious and moral discourse—a fac-simile of the sort of advice we get from our good old God-fearing seniors at home. He made me feel miserably hypercritical and as ashamed of myself as I could be. I believe I blushed when the old fellow said: "Go, and peace be upon you; trust in prayer, and be sure God will protect you;" at the same time slipping a dollar into my hand as a token of good feeling. This is an Eastern custom of simple substantial politeness, very preferable to "What will you have to drink?" though much the same kind of thing.

When I got home I found the Amér had suddenly

made up his mind to start on a long-talked-of pilgrimage to Jerusalem in two days, and that four of the party and myself were to be left to occupy the house till his return. During the next two days it was "all hands and idlers" hard at work at it, getting ready for the road, purchasing stores, and packing boxes. The Amér personally undertook that most important part of the preparations, the confectionery, and had the "third warrior," the head cook, and myself as assistants. We made about half a hundredweight of a new kind of sweetmeat the Amér had just taken a fancy to, intended to last the trip, but the Amér ate so much of it before it was cooked that he made himself sick, so he took an emetic, had a good cry, and would not have any of it packed up. This was of a piece with the whole thing, everybody ordering, nobody obeying, packing up things in the wrong boxes, leaving the most important articles to the last moment. I never expected they would get away at all, and certainly they would not if they had waited till things were in order. However, camels had been engaged and came at the right time—nothing ready of course; still away they went, bundled everything handy on to the camels and started; found they had forgotten something, sent back for it; sent back for something else, and kept on sending back for things till they got too far away. One of the last things sent back for was the Amér's watch, a very valuable English gold one, which was found under the rug where he had been enjoying an opium sleep during the hubbub of the last two hours before starting. All my Hindi friends were addicted to opium, and in any emergency used just to increase the dose a little and trust to Providence. They got on all right in a kind of "good-enough" fashion, by the "help of God," they say, and I suppose that's it. I know they left half the things purchased for the voyage, and took a couple of camel-loads of rubbish that wouldn't be of any earthly use to them. Before they left the Amér's public purse-bearer gave me thirty dollars for the support of my companions and myself while he was away. The four who were left with me were the "third warrior," a boy, the sort of youth you instinctively call Jack the moment you see him, and a couple of old black nonentities, one to cook and the other to eat. The boy Jack's story was rather a characteristic one as to how he came to be with the Amér. He was thirteen years of age, the son of a Hindi small farmer, and had been seized with the desire to rove, which I suppose we are all subject to more or less strongly; it seems to make its appearance at some time in most people's lives, and just as the English youth looks to the sea as a safety-valve through which to exhaust his uncontrollable wandering propensities, so the Mohammedan invariably vents the same mania in a pilgrimage to Meccah. Jack "felt a call," and appears to have had it badly too, for though his father beat him and his friends laughed at him, still he held out for months keeping up the same cry, always having the same object in view—he must go to Meccah. He offered to accompany pilgrims and work, but of course could not get the employment so much coveted, such pilgrims as do take servants confer a great favour on them by doing so; indeed most wealthy pilgrims take their relatives in such capacities. Remuneration is seldom expected by any, more than is sufficient for their subsistence. At last the mania reached to such a pitch with Jack that one night he stole all the money his father had (one rupee) and ran off. He first walked from his home near Hyderabad Scinde to Kotiee, and here his story became rather confused; he seemed to have gone on "fire-ships" (steamers) and "fire-carriages" (railway trains) for the first time in his life; he is only clear that he found himself in

Kurrachee after some days, and knew he was a good step on his road to Meccah. Jack then "stowed away" on board an English steamer for Bombay (how a country boy who had never seen a ship before could be up to this I cannot understand !), and was put in prison in Bombay for doing so. When he got out he told his story to many Mohammedans whom he asked for help, and who thought it very great "kismat," and that he must be "chosen of God ;" but though he received enough charity nobody offered to take or send him to Meccah. Jack's zeal had not spent itself yet; no, his success hitherto encouraged him to go on.

The pilgrim season came round ; crowded steamers were leaving Bombay for Jeddah, and on board one of these Jack managed to conceal himself on the day of sailing. When the ship was about four days out, all the pilgrims were mustered, and Jack, with half-a-dozen others, was found to have no ticket. It is probable nothing would have been done to them really, more than a kick or two, but the officers of the ship made a great fuss, sent them up on to the look-out bridge, and half-frightened them to death. Two of the stowaways were the only two barbers on board, so the other five hundred pilgrims got up a subscription to pay for them ; but the officers would not let these two go without the rest, so they all spent another day on the bridge. In the meantime the Amér, who was a first-class passenger, heard of this, and also heard that one of the delinquents was from Hyderabad, and thinking he was a countryman of his own, at once made up the subscription and had them all released. He then sent for Jack, but, finding he came from Scinde and not from the Deccan, was of course very much disgusted; nevertheless he heard the boy's story, and ended by taking him into his service. The boy is now with us in Meccah, happy as Larry. Not only is the stolen rupee intact, but he has added seven annas to his treasure and has a very good outfit for a nigger. I never could get on with this boy, always had to be giving him mild Hindi slaps, and abusing his female relatives: he was a cheeky young dog. I could not help a certain amount of sympathy—a sort of fellow-feeling—and that perhaps led me to give him too much of his own way.

The zenana was also left, but they lived in another part of the house, and I saw little of them. An old hag (one of those Eastern horrors more hideous than European could picture—a fury with a face like three kicks in a mud wall) used to come down to us to beg tea or anything nice we might happen to have going for her mistress the Begum, the Amér's mother, who was the head of the zenana; for though we lived in completely separate households, our culinary operations were within the range of the old lady's (the Begum's) nose, and she never failed to make her ancient handmaiden swoop down upon any little extra indulgence we might choose to be having. The old women servitors, having discarded the veil, take the place in India of the eunuch in other Mohammedan countries, that is, go-betweens between the men's and women's apartments, acting as spies on both, and are generally chosen for remarkable ugliness.

The first thing we did in the morning after the Amér's departure was to organise a general clean-up. The sleeping apartment had not been swept out since we had been living in it, and was filthy. We removed out of this room, fifteen feet by twelve feet, and threw into the street outside (this being the custom of the country) eight large packing-cases full of rags, spoilt and wasted, fragments of food in different stages of rot, broken pots, bottles, tins, old shoes, straw, torn matting, and sticks. Besides all this, two snakes, a dead cat, a great many rats and mice, both dead and alive, and about five or six pounds weight of maggots out of one corner. I was afraid to raise the carpet, heaven knows what awful disclosures might have followed! All this brought a perfect treasure-trove to Jack in the way of lost trifles, and I found among the rubbish a ball of opium, which I pocketed. Next we cleared out the cooking-room adjoining the sleeping-room. In the middle of this room there was a large sink, a concave circular stone about four feet in diameter, with a round hole in the centre, down which the refuse and offal of cooking and butchering were thrown. Round this stone we used to sit and perform our everlasting ablutions. The aroma emitted from the hole was—pooh! "odours of Eden, myrrh, aloes, and cassia!" Pooh! Its fragrance varied in kind from day to day, but always seemed to be at its worst. What horrible depths of corruption existed below might be guessed from the thick layer of maggots that formed a coating to the inside of the hole as far down as could be seen, constantly writhing and crawling upwards, spreading round at the surface, and developing into flies which filled the air with their black buzzing filthinesses. I formed a plan for the amending of this which was strongly opposed at first; however, I got the "third warrior" and Jack to join me, and we carried the day. We filled the large rice-pan with water, about six gallons, made it hot, and emptied it boiling down the hole. This we did three times, with such beneficial effect that no objection was raised to it on the next occasion when the maggots began to appear, and we very soon saw a sensible diminution in the swarms of flies. I then purchased some benzoin, a yellow gum or resin, which has a very agreeable scent when burnt and is the aversion of all kinds of winged vermin. With this we fumigated the whole place, and so completed the sanitary arrangements of our little household. I am aware the foregoing savoury fragment is not very "inviting," but I think the reader will recognise how scanty justice would have been done to the description had such important factors in the sum of our discomfort been omitted.

During the last three days I had had no time to look for the "Lady Venus," but the moment I was at liberty I set out in quest of her. To such of my readers as may be wholly unacquainted with the customs of the East, I may here explain why in my interview with the "Lady Venus" such great caution was preserved. Our being English, and the subjects of our conversations—which will appear obvious and sufficient reasons—had really little to do with it. If we had been born Meccans we should not have been able to maintain nearly such free intercourse as we did, for we should have had more prying friends to make scandal of our (from a Mohammedan point of view) grossly improper "goings on"—immoral they would have been called, in a society where it is a canon that no woman may uncover her face to any man who is not her father, brother, or husband; and it was chiefly on this account that our meetings had to be of such a clandestine character. Any one familiar with the social habits of Mohammedans—the jealousy, conventional and affected, of the men, and the formal restraint under which the women are held—will be surprised that I was able to walk in public with the lady without attracting notice in the way I did; but in Meccah the women are allowed great freedom. Many of the most ordinary precautions of the harem are relaxed, and it is quite the correct thing for the women of the wealthy to appear at public worship unattended, praying among the men, no part of the Haram being set apart for them as in every other mosque. On the second day after the Amér's departure, I went to that part of the Haram she had mentioned as her place of prayer at noonday. After the prayers I remained sitting, counting my beads. There are ninety-nine beads in a Mohammedan rosary, not counting certain little pendants or stops. As you count your beads, for each bead passed you mention one of the ninety-nine names or attributes of God: the hundred is not complete, as the perfection of God is unlimited. A Mohammedan therefore says, "God is great, good, merciful," etc. etc. etc., through the ninety-nine; imagine the rest—a sort of 99·9 recurring idea: or, as others say, the hundredth attribute is love, which man shares with God, and so is not mentioned.

When the crowd had dispersed I observed a little way off on my left a woman sitting alone. I thought this might be my friend, and looked fixedly at her for a few minutes. She was evidently looking at me, and I thought I noticed a beckoning movement of the hands under her garments, so I rose and walked towards her. She then got up and went out of the Haram, and I followed her at a little distance. We had gone some quarter of a mile through the town in this way, she always looking back at me before turning a corner, when she stopped, and let me come up to her. She at once addressed me in English, telling me to walk by her side, and that we were going to a Hindi friend's where we could talk undisturbedly as long as we liked.

Some two hundred yards farther on we passed through a narrow part of the street, where a Turkish sentry was posted; here she talked loudly in Arabic, and I answered her in the same, making a great display of such expressions as I was master of. Half-an-hour's walk brought us to a little shieling, into which we went and sat down. I found the old Hindi who dwelt in it very well disposed. He made tea, gave me a smoke of his hookah, excused himself, and left us to ourselves. What a talk we had! How we let loose our English tongues! Sometimes we laughed wildly, sometimes she cried. It must have been a strange pleasure to her to hear and talk her native language after so many years. I, who had only been a few weeks away from my kind, felt most foolishly elated, talked all kinds of nonsense, anything that came into my head, just for chattering's sake. We asked one another questions, and asked others without waiting for answers.

We had three hours of this, and then the old Hindi came in, and we thought it time to be going. Before parting she raised her veil and showed me her face, which was as English as my own. We also shook hands, and arranged that a boy Abdallah, a mutual acquaintance, should be our future means of communication. We then parted, and went home by different roads.

That night, as I lay on my rug, thinking over the occurrences of the day, and hugging myself in the anticipation of many such pleasant conversations —for there was a taste of danger and secrecy that added zest and a feeling of having given another pleasure that made me supremely satisfied and contented that night—only one thing troubled me, almost her last words to me had been, "I can't make out who you are, child"—she always called me child, I suppose on account of my light-hearted attempts to raise her spirits—and I could not make out who she was. So there and then I thought over a list of questions I meant to ask her at our next meeting; but "man proposes," etc. Little did I think it would be some weeks before we should meet again, and that then we should have much more interesting matter in hand; and, most incongruous incongruity, a pilgrim fell asleep in sight of the Kaabah repeating those lines of Hood's :

> The other sex, the tender, the fair,
> What wide reverses of fate are there !

CHAPTER III.

IN MECCAH DURING THE AMÉR'S ABSENCE.

THERE is so much room for exhibition of taste in the way of personal adornment about the Eastern dress that I defy the most simple-minded of men to don a turban or cumerbund without bringing into play a little vanity. For my part, I became quite an Eastern swell—my tunic of the whitest, my turban of the largest and brightest; and besides, I felt myself to be rather an important personage, a householder, and possibly entitled to a vote for a Kasi,* though I did not test my rights to any great extent in this way. The idea of any rowdy Arab questioning me as to who I was never for a moment entered into my calculations; I swaggered about the streets anywhere and everywhere, but I was doomed

* Judge.

to be let down in a manner that rather astonished my weak nerves.

One day I was passing a large college on the outskirts of the town under the "Rev. the-grace-of-God-d-his-blessings,—D.D.," when the students, about one hundred and fifty, of all ages from five to fifteen, were out playing. I stayed to look on at their various games, such as marbles—not unlike the English game, as far as I could see. One little group had an old pistol, snapping caps, and altogether I was much amused watching them, when a little Hindi child near me shouted, "Oh, look at the Christian!" I shall never be able to guess what put it into that son of Iblis's head. Perhaps he had seen Englishmen in India, and was struck with a fancied resemblance; or it may have been only for fun, though Eastern children are not generally given to unprovoked mischief. Up to this nothing of the kind had happened to me, and as it was unexpected it took me very much aback. It also collected all the young imps in the neighbourhood, who took up the cry; and one great hulking brute stepped up to me and said, in a blustering manner, "Christian dog, if you are a Mohammedan make the profession of your faith."

Now I am one of the most peacefully-disposed of

men, as "Jack" says, "I would rather run a mile than fight a minute," yet all my life I have been getting dragged into fights. I suppose I must look like a fellow easily put upon, whereas I have a Bedawi aversion to dirt* as an article of diet. This beggar riled me and I did not feel at all disposed to give an account of myself to him. No, I just took the fellow by the shoulders, turned him round and administered a kick in the rear that must have made him see stars. Now, I do suppose I could not have perpetrated a more un-Mohammedan act. Instead of seizing the opportunity to deliver myself of profuse expressions of devotion and faith, as a Mohammedan does on the slightest provocation, I had offered to my very proper interrogator one of the greatest indignities possible to a Mohammedan—I had struck him with a shoe. It brought a yell of "Ya! Christian" from its recipient, taken up by the whole crew. I had put my foot in it, had been taken off my guard, and now saw things could not be mended, so turned round and attempted to make a dignified retreat, when—whirr!—close past my ear flew a blue object (a pigeon I thought), but it lit a few feet ahead with a clatter that showed the kind of blue rock it was, and another

* I have eaten dirt—that is, taken an insult.

followed, fetching me one on the skull, that would have "settled the number of my mess" but for the thickness of my too attractive head-dress. These Meccan youths living, so to speak, on a stone-heap, get, from constant practice, to be able to deliver a stone as straight and almost as hard as a pistol-shot. I looked round an instant, and saw that the whole swarm had entered into the holy work of stoning a Christian to death, with a zeal worthy of first-century Jews. Stones were coming from all directions, I was getting some nasty blows, and had to defend my face with my hands. My probable ignominious fate flashed across my mind—stoned to death by children, the disclosures that would follow, the example I should be held up as. Suddenly one on the knee and another in the small of the back brought me down; when up again I did not know which way to turn. A pretty little Arab child was struggling to heave a rock he could scarcely lift, I made a rush, seized the squalling brat in my arms, and a run up (" Rugby rules") of about twenty yards brought me to a long wall, to which I turned my back and held the kicking little wretch before me as a shield. This bewildered my tormentors for a moment, then on they came again, led on by my kicked friend, to rescue young struggling Ibrahim, as I heard them call him.

Poor little Ibrahim! even when torn nearly limb from limb he looked a very pretty child, and I was sorry for him. The struggle was short and sharp, Ibrahim got terribly mauled, chiefly by his friends. I was somewhat of an old hand at a scrag and managed to keep from under the ruck, watched my chance, bolted off, and got about twenty yards' start before I was missed and the pack set out in full cry after me. A Turkish guard-house was close at hand, into which I rushed, passed the sentry and squatted down behind him out of breath, arms and legs aching with bruises, and completely blown; however, I was safe for the moment and had time to pull myself together for what had become a very serious affair. In the meantime a crowd of Arabs and Negroes were gathering outside and the word "A Christian!" was being passed, and the Turkish guards were giving me very black looks. One of the soldiers went to bring an officer, and returned in a minute or two with a young lieutenant: very spruce and civilised he looked, it was quite a relief to see him in his Paris-cut uniform. He came up to me and at once addressed me in French; but I had got myself all there by this time and artlessly replied, "I cannot speak Turkish," and proceeded on to declare that, "Allah was great, all praise be to Allah! there is only one God,

Mohammed is his prophet," working myself up gradually till at last I rushed out of the guard-house, saw an old friend—an Arab slave-dealer, who in his negotiations with the Amér had smoked many of my cigarettes—seized his stick and went for the promising young crowd with "sons of burnt fathers" and a torrent of similar abuse. The men now all took my side, and the old slave-dealer laughingly apologised for the excess of zeal in the rising generation, though he could not help admiring it; while even the Turkish sentry helped to disperse the boys with a parting stone, and the lieutenant showed me out into a back way by which I could go home without any chance of being further annoyed. On my way home I strayed into a coffee-shop to arrange my disordered robes, explaining that I had been thrown from my donkey which had bolted. After a smoke and a cup of coffee I began to feel a little more myself, and limped off home, getting stiffer all the time from bruises about the back and limbs. I had luckily no marks on my face, so that I was able to lie down as soon as I got into the house without any awkward questions being asked. My chief fear now was that the affair would get noised abroad in quarters where it would lead to my having a visit paid me by some inquisitive gentlemen, whom I knew I should not be able to humbug, if once their suspicions were really aroused and they took to serious inquiries.

The Arab to whom the house belonged came also that evening and gave us a good deal of trouble, trying to get us to turn out into a smaller room, so that he might have our larger and better-situated one till the Amér's return; but I knew that the room had been paid for for two months in advance, so would not turn out. Though the fellow was in an independent position, he was not above taking a luck-penny (a dollar), and I was glad to get rid of him so cheap with a blessing backwards. To guard against this sort of thing I told my companions I was very sick (I really was in a good deal of pain), and that I would go and sleep in a little closet off the cooking-room so as not to be disturbed by noise or visitors. Into this room about eight feet by four I moved my clothes and blankets, and did not stir out of it till the Amér's return—about three weeks, during which there were many friendly inquiries for me. My companions stuck to me like bricks, giving out at my request that I had gone to Jeddah. I heard no more of "the Christian" row, and the "third warrior" was very much surprised and would scarcely believe it when I told him some time after what had happened, and although I insisted I knew more about Christians than he did, he would give me much interesting information about their beliefs and their neglect of certain ablutions. I was much edified to learn that their heaven was an eternal gorge of "that animal's"* flesh and wine.

My assurance and indiscretion had all but done for me, and now I must appear to have gone to the other extreme. It was not so much caution kept me confined the whole time as the ball of opium, a small pill of which I took the first night and continued to take every day, increasing the dose as I found it affecting me. I only ate one meal a day, brought me by the "third warrior" when he came to make up housekeeping accounts. He knew I was under opium and sympathised with me and could recommend nothing better, looking upon that drug as a specific for all maladies. I will not go into the "pains and pleasures of opium eating" more than to say the three weeks passed like three days. I was perfectly happy, everything appeared *couleur de rose.* Groups of devotees sitting under my window in the Haram chanting "La, Illah; ah! Il Allah," over and over and over "in a sing-song

* Pig.

tuneful sort of no tune" which had before been most distressing to listen to, would now transform themselves, in my waking dreams, into some merry English party—a picnic perhaps—and the "La-illah" into "La-de-da," the chorus of some charming unheard air. In short, I did not know a moment's discomfort the whole time.

Our living averaged about one dollar a day. As I kept an account of all the money spent I can give an example of a fair day's expenditure.

PROVISIONS ONE DAY FOR FIVE PEOPLE.

(1 RATL, NEARLY 14 OZ.)	Piastres.	Parras.
Meat—Camel, 5 ratl: Mutton, 3 ratl ...	5	—
Vegetables for Curry—Parsley, Beetroot, Bavish Marrow, Carrot	4	—
Bread, 2 ratl	2	—
Water, 20 gallons.—4 small goat skins brought to the house	2	—
Sugar, ½ ratl	2	—
Dates (best common) 1 ratl	2	—
Wood for fire	2	—
Lentils, ½ ratl	1	—
Milk, about 1½ pint	1	—
Chillies and other Spices for Curry ...	—	20
Sour Milk for Curry	—	20
Tea, ¼ oz.	—	20
Tobacco, ½ oz. Turkish	1	—
Lamp Oil, Paraffin	—	10
Sundries—Shaving, Fruit, Sweets, Pocket Money, etc.	4	10
	28	11

Besides this we had rice, ghee, and tamarinds in the house, of which we consumed daily—rice, eight pounds; ghee, four ounces; tamarinds, half pound. This is very sumptuous living indeed for Hindis; quite as good and more varied than we got at the Amér's table.

I must not omit to mention little Ismail, an Arab boy whose acquaintance I had made at his father's place of business, in the bazaar near at hand, where I had often gone to talk to them. He was a very bright youth, spoke Hindustani well; and I had taken rather a fancy to him. Now that I was laid up I found him excellent company, and admitted him almost daily, amusing him greatly, telling him stories by the hour. "Æsop's Fables" I found a capital fund of the very best material, and after them, other children's stories and nursery rhymes, changed of course to suit time and place, as it would not have done to have let him know the original of—

> This little *sheep* went to market,
> This little *sheep* stopped at home—

or he might not have laughed quite so gleefully at my "rattletrap rhyme." For the opium had the effect of not only enabling me to converse incessantly but sometimes to improvise rhyme as fast as I could talk.

Many travellers in the East, especially lady travellers, have had a good word to say for Eastern boys; and they are very attractive, I admit. This peculiar lovableness, for it is such, may be easily accounted for, as they have generally good features, many of them being remarkably handsome, and fine eyes are the rule; all have a feminine grace of manner and speech acquired in the harem, which is their home for the first seven or eight years of their lives. And there is also a downrightness and freedom from anything like affectation about them, when in the presence of strangers, which contrasts very favourably with the bashfulness of the nicey-nicey stereotyped English schoolboy, who has all individuality stamped out of him at a public school. Mohammedan children owe this to a primitive Hebrew innocence, there being hardly a word in their language which they may not freely use as occasion requires. "To the pure all things are pure." With all this, however, they are intelligent to a degree, their intellectual faculties being very highly developed at an early age, and so far as simple learning and having an amount of knowledge (such as it is) in their heads, goes, they are certainly in advance of European children of their years; but by the time they are fourteen they have attained the limits of an ordinary Mohammedan education. They read and write well in more than one language, do simple arithmetic, are perfectly instructed in all the minutest observances of their faith, and have an immense stock of religious lore, in which they take a deep interest and no little pride. For the manner in which the idea of the One God and antagonism to all other creeds is instilled into their minds goes down greatly with the youthful sinners; their little faces brighten up bravely as they declare the One God, and scowl savagely as they curse and defy the "kaffir" in a "quite too amusing" way.

But after leaving the harem all their former attractiveness is soon rubbed off by rude intercourse with the men; and I know few creatures more unlovable than the Eastern in the transition stage from boy to man. He has all the obtrusive forwardness in the vulgar hobbledehoyhood everywhere, and rapidly cultivates the craftiness, low cunning, and brutal coarseness—those chief characteristics of manhood in the East.

On the day before the new moon in December the Amér returned loaded with purchases—crockery, glass-ware, and cutlery, from Cairo; jewellery, two guns, and a rifle (breech-loading), from Alexandria; ornamental wood and stone, cups and saucers, cigarette-cases, etc. from Jerusalem; altogether about half a ton of flashy French "notions;" and such news! Each one of the party seemed bent on overwhelming us with the wonders he had seen—the Suez Canal, the Opera, the Pachas and their beautiful carriages and horses, the splendid livery of their servants.

"And what did the Pacha wear?" asked an old untravelled one, expecting to hear his dress compared to a rainbow.

They could scarcely bring themselves to say it, but were obliged to confess that he "had nothing on but a tarbouche." They had seen Mohammedans and Christians dressed so that you could not tell but for the hat which was which; they had seen Christians working as labourers. This seemed to give them great satisfaction. They "chewed" over one to another:—"Many beggarly Christians under the Sultan"—much to my chagrin, for I knew they could not distinguish between a Greek and an Englishman. Travel had certainly not increased their respect for their rulers.

I now felt perfectly safe while in the Amér's favour and recognised by him. I came out and began to move about; gave up opium suddenly, and found my nerves much affected in consequence.

A stranger coming into the room would startle me, I dare not let anyone pass behind me, always backing up to the wall, and it was some days before this wore off. On the day of the new moon I was so ill, it being the day after I stopped my opium, that I was unable to pray, thereby missing much; for a prayer at Meccah on this day scores something enormous, though I forget exactly how many thousand rupees given in charity it is supposed to equal. I went about a good deal with the Amér now, and wore a less conspicuous dress, keeping more in the background. We paid a visit to the college, the scene of my unlucky encounter. The boys looked very sheepish, and pretended not to recognise me when they saw me in such good company, and you may be sure I let well alone. While in the courtyard, I heard a great squalling and crying going on in one of the rooms, and could not resist my curiosity to see what it was all about; so separated myself from my party, found my way to the door of the room and looked in, and saw a whole class of about twenty boys being punished. Half had already undergone the bastinado, and were sitting blubbering round the wall, five others were at the time getting it. Two big boys held each one end of a thick stick, with a rope noose in the middle of it; into this noose each of the culprits had to put one foot, then the stick was twisted round till the feet were squeezed up tightly into a bunch, which was then lifted breast-high by the two assistant-executioners, and a big Arab tutor came down on those wriggling toes with a Malacca cane, as hard as he could let out, showing no mercy: it seemed to be a very effective mode, judging by the yells, struggles and brandishings of the disengaged limbs of the youngsters as they hung in a cluster head down. I saw by the unhappy looks of the rest of the class that the same was in store for them, and as some of my most vindictive assailants were there, I must say I did not pity them much; though I did not care to stay and witness their tortures.

During the next few days I visited a number of shrines and holy places, the name of which is legion about Meccah, there being scarcely a spring or hill round, which is not said to be the scene of some remarkable event in the life of either Adam, Eve, Abraham, Hagar, Ishmael, or some other holy personage; while as for Mohammed, the lies that have been fathered upon him (honest man!) would have made him take the dome off his Medinah mausoleum in a great triple somersault, and snort the sides out of his shrine, if he had been there at all, a fact which there are other good reasons for doubting.

"What are you picking up that stone for?" you inquire.

"Oh! Mohammed was fighting infidels, and God sent angels and a shower," etc. etc.

"Why are you eating that shrub?"

"Oh! this is called the Prophet's bread. Mohammed and his companions were starving in the desert and he told them to take this," etc. etc.

Rocks, pools, holes in the ground, she-camels, dogs, cats, rats, mice, Mohammed, Mohammed, Mohammed, Mohammed.

I used to find a quiet place and sit down and say over all the swearing I knew in five languages, and make resolutions that if I ever got out of this and met a white man who said he believed in miracles, I would go and get a gun and shoot him. Why, if Mohammed had been actively employed since the year one of the Hegira to the present day, performing the marvels attributed to him, he would still have a few legerdemain trifles, in milk and mud, on hand. No!—nonsense apart!—it cannot be established that Mohammed ever openly attempted to dupe his followers with one single miracle. All these supernatural wonders are the accumulated imaginings of marvel-craving Eastern minds; the more ignorant the more fertile in the like. Not one of my companions but was perfectly well acquainted with the minutest circumstances of half-a-dozen miracles of yesterday, or who had not been eye-witness to at least one. Only a year before the Amér's uncle had been present when six laden camels were either eaten up by the earth or carried off to the zenith—the work of the devil, who appeared in the form of a dog. We are not living in an age of miracles. Are we not? Come to the East and see, or for the matter of that, not so very far East either, for the genuine article.

Such of these places as I did visit I will now attempt to describe. First, the Haram itself, of which I have already given a view from the top of Jebel Kubays, shall be more minutely described. The Kaabah, in the middle of that enclosure, is called the Centre of the World, the Mohammedan Hub of the Universe: towards this Mohammedans in all parts of the earth face when praying. The whole ground within the outer bounds of the arcades is deemed part of heaven on earth, to which it will return on the Last Day. The architectural design of the whole is such that I know of no other structure or edifice familiar to Europeans with which to compare it.* The same form of mosque may be seen in Cairo and some other places in the East; but if, as I hope, I have already given the reader a general idea of its form, I may now succeed in conveying some notion of its appearance on closer inspection. It is entered from the street by doorways of different sizes: the two largest are on the northern and western sides, the Gate of Abraham in the western being very high and arched, and really fine. There are a dozen or more other public entrances and a number of smaller private doorways and windows into the offices of the Haram and adjoining dwellings. The tower being some ten feet above the level of the square, you descend, at all the entrances, either a steep paved incline, a flight of steps, or an irregular compound of both, into the arcades, which are about fifty feet wide and paved throughout with limestone and a greenish crystalline stone common in the neighbourhood, laid very unevenly and in small oblong blocks, none of them bigger than could be conveniently carried by a man. The roof is supported on three rows of thirty-six pillars on the

* Sale compares it to the Royal Exchange, London. It is true they both are open squares surrounded by colonnades, but beyond that the two have not a single point of resemblance.

longer and twenty-four pillars on the shorter sides, each sixteen feet apart. Every fourth pillar is an hexagonal-built support about four feet thick, the rest are plain round pillars something more than a foot in diameter, composed generally of either sandstone or limestone. The capitals of these are the only ornamental stone-work in the building; they are carved with flower, scroll, or angular devices, respectively and promiscuously. The roof consists of rows of arches, thirty-six on the longer and twenty-four on the shorter sides longitudinally, and all round three arches transversely springing from every pillar throughout, dividing the ceiling into three rows of small domes, except at the corners, where the architect seems to have got confused, tried to round them off, failed, and so bungled them up anyhow, and at the principal portals, where ingenious, bewildering non-uniformity baffles description. From the top of each transverse arch a large globe lamp is suspended by a brass chain, and all round under the inner row of arches facing towards the Kaabah there hang from a cross-bar, reaching from pillar to pillar, five lamps to each arch. The square itself is gravelled and divided by narrow pavements into a sort of "Union Jack" pattern. There are three bronze date trees, about twelve feet high, with lamps hanging to the ends of their fronds equidistant from one another, and midway between the Kaabah and the arcades, across the eastern and western ends of the square. All round on the gravel at intervals are placed stacks of earthenware bottles containing water of Zem Zem for the use of the pilgrims. The well Zem Zem is about eighty feet from the north-east corner of the Kaabah. It has an irregular shambling building over it, roofed by a large cupola, a small dome, and a couple of sections of a pagoda, and probably occupying an area of about seventy feet square. On the eastern, western, and southern sides of the Kaabah, at about the same distance as the well, are three other unimportant erections with rather more than their share of lamps. On the northern side, about thirty feet distant, Abraham's Stone is deposited in a small house ten feet high by six by eight feet square, having a large heavy wooden door on its north side. This is the stone which acted as a stage for Abraham when building the Kaabah, passing up and down to and from the work as required with any weight of workmen or material. I did not see the stone, as it can only be seen by paying very highly, and few can afford it; but it is popularly believed to have Abraham's footprint on it—another of the many like impressions Eastern celebrities seem to have been so fond of leaving. About eight yards off on each side of this building there are two stone pulpits, plain hexagonal pedestals, three feet thick and twelve feet high, topped with a stone railing and mounted by a set of stone steps on the opposite side to that facing the Kaabah. At each of these pulpits commences a row of lamp-posts about ten feet high extending all round the Kaabah about fifteen feet distant from one another, and having between each two posts seven lamps suspended from cross-bars, each post being surmounted by a gilded crescent. Outside this circle the pavement extends about twenty feet, and is the same as that under the arches, while that within the circle of lamps is a pavement composed of smooth flagstones about eighteen inches below the level of the square.

On the western side of the Kaabah is a horseshoe wall four-and-a-half feet high and three feet thick, its ends towards the Kaabah, leaving a passage between, enclosing a semicircular space thirty feet in diameter, in the middle of which is the tomb of Ishmael with an engraved slab of marble over it. The base of the Kaabah is surrounded by a marble rim or "half round" about two-and-a-half feet wide and one foot high, and into this a number of brass ringbolts are let, having a four-inch cotton rope passed through them, to which the lower edge of the Kaabah cover is laced. There are three openings in this cover—one in the east end of the north side is a heavy bullioned curtain before the silver-plated door in the Kaabah, which is of ordinary size, about seven feet from the ground; near this, but right on the corner of the building, is a round hole in the cover about five feet in circumference, and its lower border about two feet above the base rim of the Kaabah, showing a massive silver boss, with ears for securing it to the stone-work; and set so deeply into this that the face is concealed by the silver rim when in the act of kissing it, is the Black Stone. This is about the size of a man's head, of a brownish-black, glassy substance, presenting rounded inequalities of surface, as if from fusion or fracture. There is a piece of obsidium from Hecla in the British Museum, its exact counterpart in shape and appearance, but about three times its bulk. So closely do they resemble one another, that after having carefully inspected both—and I lived for four months in sight of the Black Stone—I have no doubt whatever that the two are identical in substance. If I required anything to confirm the evidence of my senses, there is a belief that the Black Stone will float in water; this most likely means that it is momentarily buoyant after being thrown in, which might be true if it contained a great number of cavities or bubbles, as a piece of obsidium often does. And another general belief is that the stone is white, but that its surface has been blackened by defilement; which led me to break the agate in a ring I wore in order to test it with a scratch, but the result showed it to be white like any other piece of coloured glass. There are two or three versions of the history of this stone, but the most generally received one is, that it is the angel who had charge of Adam and Eve in the garden of Eden turned into stone for allowing them to be beguiled by the serpent into eating the "wheat," and that he will be restored at the Last Day.

In the south-east corner of the Kaabah there is another piece cut out of the cover about three feet high and eighteen inches wide, exposing one of the corner-stones of the building, a small oblong granite block, very much polished by the touchings it receives at the hands of the pilgrims every circuit while performing the tawaf. On the west side from the top of the Kaabah is a gold-plated spout, appearing from below to project about four feet from the building, to be about a foot wide and six inches high at the sides. The rain-water off the flat roof of the Kaabah is discharged through this, and when it rains there is a free fight among the pilgrims to get under it and be douched. Considering the open-air character and the dimensions of the whole, the place is kept in a good state of order and repair, the whitewash and paint all appearing fresh and clean. The colours employed are black, mauve, Indian red, and yellow wash, each stone on the inside and much of the outer walls being painted one of these colours with, as it were, a system of avoiding anything like rule. There are also large whitewashed spaces on these walls occupied with chapters of the Koran, and the stones of the arches are painted like those in the walls, as are the stones in built pillars. The domed ceiling is cleanly whitewashed, and the plaster on the top and front of the arcades and buildings is kept in constant repair, while the whole place is cleaned out by gangs of sweepers twice a day, morning and evening. The reader will not have gathered from all these details the fine simplicity of the whole until reminded that the building occupies within its outer walls a space of eight-and-a-quarter acres.

The behaviour in the Haram is much better than in most other Mohammedan mosques. During the day crowds sit about or promenade under the shade of the arcades until a call to prayer, when all join in the regular worship lasting for about a quarter of an hour, more or less, the noonday prayer being the longest. After sunset the lamps, 2860 in number, are lit, and many groups of pilgrims sit round private coloured lamps, which add greatly to the general brilliancy, until after the last evening prayer, when the Haram becomes deserted, no one being permitted to sleep inside the gates; and all who are not actually employed in performing some act of prayer or devotion are turned out after this hour by the attendants of the Haram.

Jebel Nur, lying about four miles north-east of Meccah, is a steep conical hill rising some nine hundred feet above the sand-level, for the sand in the valley maintains a level of its own as water would. Looking at Jebel Nur from the south, it appears to be inaccessible from about two-thirds of the way up, the upper part seeming to be one solid oval rock, its sides projecting beyond the perpendicular; but in the ascent, having reached this point, you pass round to the north side, where you see that it would have been impossible to ascend so far on that side, but find a somewhat difficult though perfectly practicable path leading to the summit. Half-way up this path there is a rain-pool in the rock, generally full at this season. Here you may perform your ablutions before ascending to the very apex of the cone, where a small dome is erected over a fissure in the solid rocks, some eight feet long by three feet deep, said to have been made by a slip of the Angel Gabriel's delicate instrument, while performing the somewhat nice operation of removing the black spot (sin) from the heart of Mohammed preparatory to giving him his prophet's commission. There Mohammed received his first inspired message. Farther down on the south side are two small caves, in which Mohammed concealed himself at the time of his persecution in Meccah. Into one of these, when being pursued, Mohammed had just time to escape ere his pursuers came up and found a pigeon sitting over its nest at the entrance, and a spider's web woven across the mouth of the cave—a miraculous interposition which led them to believe that no one had entered lately. In the other cave, Mohammed and his friend Abubekr were sleeping concealed, when Abubekr awakening saw a serpent putting its head out of a hole to bite Mohammed. Rather than awake the prophet he put his own heel over the hole and was bitten. When Mohammed awoke he found his friend still keeping the serpent back with his heel, but nearly dead; whereupon he of course killed the serpent and cured his friend by a miracle. Both these events are generally said to have taken place on Jebel Saur, another mountain to the south-east of Meccah, but I and my companions related these stories to one another in the very caves I speak of as having occurred in them.

Umrah lies in a valley, about four miles south-east of Meccah, is a deep pool or janlo, built round, about one hundred feet by fifty feet square. There are steps leading down to the water, in which the pilgrims wash; and it is looked upon as a sort of Pool of Siloam. This is said to have been one of Mohammed's favourite places of resort for prayer and meditation. He is said to have prayed there so long that his knees became stiff and hard and his muscles rigid. Most Arab and Hindi (i.e. stockingless) Mohammedans have a callosity on the outside of the left ankle, the effect of one of the most constant attitudes of prayer—sitting with the left foot tucked under them.

At all these places, and many others, the pilgrim may say a two-prostration prayer, and dole out his charity to the inevitable irrepressible Hejaz beggar. These beggars may be classed under two heads—the pauper pilgrim and the professional beggar. In Meccah the pauper pilgrim falls into obscurity, and so may be dropped for the present. The professional beggar luxuriates simply, and probably forms half the Arab population. "Bakhshish, bakhshish!" they continually do cry. "Bakhshish!" roars the camel; "bakhshish!" brays the ass; "bakhshish!" yelps the cur, till, after passing through a stage where you fancy you hear nothing else, you get so accustomed to it that it costs you an effort of will to hear it. It is encouraged by the pilgrims, who make it a means of carrying out the letter of the prophet's charitable commands; true generosity not being an Eastern trait. A large proportion of these beggars are Hindi; Turkish or Persian beggars being comparatively few; and a Malay beggar is never seen.

Every day all who will take the trouble to go can receive for the asking a bowl of soup, given by the High Sheréf, the hereditary head curl and religious authority of Meccah, who is assisted in administration by the Mufti, Kadis, and a council of Moulahs under the Turkish pacha, or governor, to whom final appeals in all disputed cases are brought.

The Turks can only be said to hold the country in military possession, garrisoning the towns and maintaining order in them. They have no control over the desert men, to whom they yearly pay a reluctant subsidy, which they have from time to time attempted to stop; but the tribes have thereupon become unmanageable and closed the roads, and the Turks have found it expedient to continue payment.

It now wanted but two days to the going out to Mount Arafat. At this time, about six feet of the lower part of the Kaabah cover, which had become very ragged by pilgrims leaning against it, was raised all round and replaced by white calico, adding greatly to the effect by contrast with the black and gold. Pilgrims were now arriving in crowds; all the great caravans had come in, the town was packed till there was scarcely standing room in some of the streets. I have only seen such dense crowding in such places as Gracechurch Street on a Lord Mayor's Show day. The crowd here, however, was very different. Every-one here was all yielding affability. The London rough—who thinks it the height of pleasantry to knock a gentleman's hat over his eyes, or jump on a lady's feet and tender the horsey advice of "Sit hon 'er 'ead" when she faints—had no representative here. Quarrelling of any kind is seldom seen in the streets, which is very creditable, considering the number of different nationalities and sects brought into close contact here, who elsewhere entertain the bitterest animosity against one another.

During the whole of my stay in Meccah I only

once saw serious fighting in the streets. Two Panjabis, tearing mad, were scratching and slapping one another, when one of the Turkish soldiers, who do police duty about the streets, went up to separate them. One of them turned on the Turk and slapped him. The Turk drew his sword-bayonet and smote the Panjabi a swinging slash on the neck, cutting the head half off. Turkish soldiers are never allowed out of barracks without their swords, which are always carried sharp.

CHAPTER IV.

OBSERVATIONS ON THE VARIOUS RACES MET WITH IN MECCAH.

If, at this time, the congregation in the Haram had been shaken together, well mixed, and then one hundred taken out and analysed, different nationalities would have been found in about the following proportions :

* Turks	6
* Arabs	15
* Hindis	20
* Malays	5
* Negroes	10
* Persians	10
* Maghribis	15
* Syrians	6
Tartars	5
Bedawin	3
A nondescript rabble from China, the West Coast of Africa or Russia, and wild Darwaysh-looking savages from God knows where	5
	100

The races marked with an asterisk are mere general classifications, and might be made subject to innumerable subdivisions, as under the head of Hindi I include all the Mohammedan races of India, and under the Turks, Maghribis, an l Syrians, I have allowed the Egyptians to fall.

All these different nationalities brought into contrast in this way give a good opportunity of comparing them one with another, and I may here give the impressions I received, first prefacing with the following stock yarn of the Meccah guide—one of those illustrative stories the Arabs are so fond of. It is told in justification of the bearing of Arabs and Bedawins towards foreigners at the present day, and, like so many of their stories, turns upon what may be called first original characters.

A Bedawi Shaykh, whom we will call Shaykh Salaam, and his whole establishment lived peacefully in the valley of Meccah, worshipped God, performed his prayers and ablutions five times daily, and was proportionably prosperous. When, in an evil hour, there came a Turkish pilgrim to his tent, Shaykh Salaam, with characteristic Arab hospitality, invited the stranger to enter, gave him the best of everything to eat, and allowed him to sleep in his tent. But on Shaykh Salaam's waking next morning he found that his wife had eloped with the Turk.

He had just finished thanking God that matters were no worse when along came a Persian pilgrim. To him the good Shaykh was even more hospitable than he had been to the Turk, and was repaid by the Persian's absconding in the night with his horse, and, the story continues, the Misri * stealing his camel, the Maghribi † his ass; until, what between charity and theft, he is left with nothing in the world but his little son, who falls a victim to the crime of the Sulaymani. Last of all there crawls up to him a wretched begging Hindi, to whom the good Shaykh tells his tale of woe—how he has been imposed on and himself left destitute—to say nothing of his being able to assist the wayfarer. Whereupon the Hindi turned round and blackguarded the good man as none but a Hindi knows how. This is more than even long-suffering Shaykh Salaam can stand, so he sallies forth and slays his reviler; and in the ragged cloth around the Hindi's loins he finds an immense treasure.

Besides the touches of character, the moral of the story is obvious, and I can vouch for the facts related having apparently opened the eyes of the Shaykh to a worldly wisdom which his descendants have inherited in a very marked degree.

* Egyptian. † Moor.

First on the list comes the Turk. He certainly appears to advantage as the most civilised, clean, and sensible of them all; bad as he is, he is as much superior to other Easterns as any European nation is to him. The Turks, as the ruling power, are hated and feared not only by their unwilling subjects, the natives of the Hejaz, but by all other Mohammedans, both on account of their adoption of European costume and their introduction of such Christian innovations as forks, chairs, and, it is whispered, even wine into the holy Meccah; so that none allow them to be Mohammedans more than in name. They do not hesitate to increase their unpopularity, and by a high-handed and bullying carriage freely expressing their contempt for their unsophisticated and more primitive co-religionists. Individually I like the Turk, he is a manly brave little fellow. I never saw a Turkish soldier with his clean fighting uniform, shaven chin, and European accoutrements, but I felt a strong impulse to go and shake hands with him. I once did in English ask a red-haired, blue-eyed sentry: "How do you like the new rifle, old man?" (the Turkish troops in the Hejaz had just been supplied with the Snider) but happily got only a vacant stare in reply. An Arab shopkeeper who professed to be up in statistics informed me that the settled Turkish population numbered five thousand, which is probably near the mark; if so, more than two-thirds must belong to some branch of the military. The rest are merchants and well-to-do shopkeepers, dealing in cloth, tobacco, medicine, and European manufactures generally. This year the pilgrims from Turkey were said to be very few on account of the war, but they have never struck me as being a people likely to mortify themselves for conscience' sake to the extent of pilgrimising much at any time, for the modern Turk shows little respect for the practice of his faith even in Meccah. I have seen a Turkish officer cut across the corner of the Haram from gate to gate without taking his boots off—an unparalleled profanation, for which a Persian would have been mobbed and murdered on the spot.

The next in importance are the Arabs, sanctified Meccans, who honour you by accepting charity. Blustering, "frauds," swindlers to a man, trained from infancy to the rooking of the pilgrim-pigeon, inherited for an unknown number of generations,* they are perfect in every dodge and art of crimping and cadging. I have but one good word for them—they are clever and speak any language they hear.

* See historical accounts of Arabia.

Imagine yourself a perfect stranger in the hands of a population of Cairo dragomen and donkey-boys, only doubly as obtrusive as the first, and doubly as rude and discourteous as the latter, and you would be much in the same situation as a pilgrim paying his way through Meccah. Though this description applies to the great majority of shopkeepers and lodging-house keepers, many Arabs are artisans, since most of the mechanics in Meccah are either Hindi or Arab, the best being Arab gunsmiths, tinsmiths, or carpenters, from Egypt or Syria. They seem industrious, and turn out tolerably substantial work of the elaborately-ornamented and unfinished Eastern description, but preferable to the French "Brummagem" with which the shops are stocked. Imams, muezzins, and nearly all posts of religious and civil authority from the High Sherέf downwards, are held by Arabs. With them, however, I had no intercourse, nor had I any anxiety to make their acquaintance.

The settled Hindi population in Meccah, I was told, numbered thirty thousand; this may be an exaggeration, as my Arab informer would be likely to overrate the numbers to me, coming as I did from India ; still the statement is possible, the Hindi element much exceeding, perhaps even doubling, the Arab, and the pilgrims from India almost equalling in number those from all other parts of the East, except the Bedawin and Arab population of the country round, which must be almost depopulated on the day of assembling at Arafat. Many Hindis are in official employ, and hold lucrative, and a few even important, posts under the Government. There are also a number of wealthy and independent Hindis permanently settled in Meccah, some from religious motives, and a few for political reasons. They occupy also the following positions: readers of the Koran, professors of the law, agents for pilgrims, shopkeepers and tradesmen—for the wily cunning nature of the Hindi is quite able to compete with and hold its own against Arab roguery. In whatever position, they are all beggars from top to bottom—underhand, insinuating beggars; the Arab demands bakhshish, the Hindi cringingly pleads for charity; they form by great numbers the poorest and most miserable class to be found in Meccah: there seems no bottom to the depths of wretchedness and misery to which the Hindi can descend and live.

A good many pilgrims come from Afghanistan and enjoy a very evil repute in Meccah. They are all known by the name Sulaymani, whether true Afghans or of any of the other races inhabiting the country which is bounded by the frontiers of Persia, the Sulaymani range, the Oxus, and Beluchistan. This name Sulaymani is never uttered by an Arab unless coupled with the epithet "harami," a very comprehensive term, which, applied to the Bedawi, means merely "murderer and robber," a character of which he considers himself justly proud, but applied to the Sulaymani it has a different and very much worse signification.

The Malays come in great numbers, considering the long sea voyages from Java and even farther which they have to accomplish. So far as I could ascertain, the Malay permanent residents in Meccah are limited to but some half-dozen. It is known they never set out on a pilgrimage without sufficient funds to ensure their return, and it has become a byword among the Arabs that they never beg, and a common Arab expression, which may be freely translated "No humbug in the Malay," perfectly describes them. Quiet and fairly honourable in their dealings, yet close-fisted, they may be called the Scotchmen of the East, and are the most rational of the pilgrims, the only ones who understand managing the cantankerous Bedawin.

The Negro is to be found here in his proper place, an easily-managed, useful worker. The Negroes are the porters, water-carriers, and performers of most of the real labour in Meccah. Happy, healthy, well fed, well clothed (as such things go in Meccah), they are slaves, proud of their masters, in a country where the slave is "honoured only after his master." Slavery in the East has an elevating influence over thousands of human beings, and but for it hundreds of thousands of souls must have passed their existence in this world as wild savages, little better than animals; it, at least, makes *men* of them, *useful men* too, sometimes even *superior men.* Could the Arab slave-trade be carried on with safety, it might be executed more humanely; and it would, philanthropically speaking, do good to many of the human race, far above that heartlessly cruel coolie trade of India, where the ignorantly credulous natives are deluded by hopes never to be fulfilled into transportation half round the globe, to a country from which but few ever return, as they are led to believe they will by promises—a state of things compared to which Arab slave-trade is humane in the extreme. I have been an overseer on a sugar plantation in the West Indies, where three hundred of these coolies were employed, helpless droves of strangers in a strange land, worked in a manner killing to the feeble Hindi, for the most paltry remuneration out of which they must save enough to pay for the return passage. At the very most, one in ten again saw India, and these only the shrewd, independent and clever ones—exceptional characters among the class of natives from which these coolies are drafted. It is in that country, too, where that abortive production of the *real* slave-trade, the civilised nigger, is met: that objectionable character, the "Wutless Badian,"* might be held up in contrast to his Meccan brother, showing the nigger as he is to be found and the nigger as he ought to be. No! my cheerful, contented slave shall not be seen in such disgraceful company as that depraved shameless creature.

Having been in the heart of the Arab slavery, I may, I hope, be permitted to offer my humble opinion on a rather important point, with all due deference to such of my "most potent, grave, and reverend signiors" as I may have the misfortune to differ from. "Are our attempts to abolish the slave-trade of Arabia likely to succeed?" "Are they at present producing good of any kind?" To both these questions I must answer "No"—most emphatically, "No." While every settled town under Turkish or native rule in all wide Arabia has a slave-market to be stocked, our greatest efforts can but increase the demand and raise the markets. Witness: a strong male adult might be bought for

* Worthless Bardihan.—West Indian patois.

forty dollars four years ago in Meccah, and the same will now fetch sixty dollars. Were our cruisers doubled, the weekly landing of slaves among the creeks and reefs along the coast of the Hejaz could not be prevented. The embarking on the western shore, the crossing and disembarking on the eastern, need be but the work of three days under favourable circumstances, of which the Arab slaver knows well how to take advantage, as some naval men could testify, I think, if tales of more than one successful ruse told me by a Yemen Arab be true. What was before a legitimate peaceful trade has now become a dangerous adventure for the procurers of slaves, even the most unscrupulous and daring of their kind, and the ill-treatment practised on their cargoes necessarily increases with the danger of carrying them. A story told me by a Yemen "jack-tar" will illustrate. A dhow in which he was serving had on board two Negroes, nominally slaves, who had for five months worked on board the dhow, and who, knowing when they were well off, would not have taken their liberty had it been offered them. She was a large Mascat babeela, bound down the Persian Gulf from Aber Shir to Bombay. On the day after clearing the Straits of Ormuz, in a calm, they sighted an English man-of-war steaming towards them, as they well knew with the intention of boarding. The two Negroes would have been enough to condemn their craft, which meant ruin to some and misfortune more or less to every man of the crew, so they killed them and threw them overboard; here my informer regretted the necessity which compelled them to this, mainly because they were both very strong men and very hard to kill, blaming those "Shaitan" English, and barging them in choice Arabic, though they did not confiscate his craft; and I have no doubt the lieutenant and interpreter found everything very satisfactory on board her half-an-hour after what must have been rather an exciting scene.

That there are evils in Arab slavery I do not pretend to deny, though not affecting the Negro, once a slave. The exacting slave-driver is a character wholly unknown in the East, and the slave is protected from the caprice of any cruel master in that he is transferable and of money value. The man who would abuse or injure his slave would maim and wilfully deteriorate the value of his horse. Whatever the Arab may not know, he most assuredly knows what is to his own immediate interest better than that. And the Negro himself, though he possesses the moral senses in the merest rudimentary form, has the instincts of self-preservation from physical hurt most highly developed, and he may through this medium be raised from a savage, existing only for the moment (a state above which he has not capacity for if left to himself), to a profitable member of society, a strong tractable worker, the position Nature seems to have made him to occupy.

I know of the abuses practised in the countries where the slaves are procured, and we must have other Livingstones ere they will cease, but one step towards the abatement of them would be the recalling of our police *de l'univers* from those unhealthy coasts, when labour would again become almost a drug in the Arab market and the traffic assume a more moderate and less barbarous form. We are at this moment opposing the immemorial customs and religious principles of totally distinct and independent races—customs not only almost harmless to all, but actually beneficial to thousands—with a sword worthy of Antient Islam itself. The only effect of this will be to produce permanently a new and horrible form of this slave-trade, if it has not already done so, and the expending of thousands of pounds and hundreds of valuable lives, for a sentiment, in doing so. Let us hope that those in authority will take a reasonable view of the matter, and issue another Slave Circular, applicable to the peculiarities of the case, and not meet the fate of the former rapidly extinguished spark of official intelligence; or, if England must be international monitor, then—as the nigger says: "If you do a t'ing, do a t'ing"—annex Arabia, blow up Meccah, and reform the world; but don't continue to figure a petty plundering pirate to the 180,000,000 of its Mohammedan inhabitants.

I must apologise for having been carried off into this tirade, and return calmly to the proper subject of my narrative.

Besides these slaves, there are many free Negroes, labourers and keepers of stalls in the bazaars. The attendants of the Kaabah are Negro eunuchs, whose duties are to keep order among the worshippers, serve out materials for the trimming and lighting of the lamps to the volunteers who are never wanting to perform these and other like duties. The Kaabah itself is washed out once a year by these attendants alone. They possess a kind of sanctity by virtue of their office, and carry long wands with which they make very free play among the refractory or crowding pilgrims, and are veritable jacks-in-office. There is also a scattering of Negro pilgrims from most Mohammedan countries.*

The Persians move rather under a cloud in Meccah on account of their unorthodox doctrines, keep very much to themselves, and pray together in parties. I believe they nearly all come by land, and many of them on horses which they bring with them. They are necessarily well conducted while in Meccah, and appear to be a quiet and inoffensive lot, and are as good hands at a bargain as any. There cannot be many Persian residents in Meccah, though there are a good many itinerant dealers and speculators in precious stones and hawkers of dried fruit.

Maghribis are the Arabs of the whole of North Africa, a mal-odorous brawling horde, principally remarkable for neglect of the practices of their faith, especially ablution. The Moorish magician exists (but let us hope, for the credit of the Oriental novelist, in a very degenerate form), and a great deal of faith is placed in the charms these Maghribis profess to work, especially by the Hindis. I myself

---

* Especially Jumallis, to whose earnest, childish faith Mohammedanism is fetisch.

underwent an exorcism, for the curing of a large boil on my forehead, at the hands of a hoary old thief, recommended to me by the "third warrior." It consisted in squeezing and stroking my head and shoulders, at the same time muttering incantations with closed eyes and many minor gesticulations, drawing mystic signs and strange devices mingled with the written names of God and Mohammed on a small piece of paper, then soaking it in a solution of common salt (so far as I could make out) with which I afterwards washed the boil; and I must record here either as a coincidence or a curious result, that the swelling certainly did subside without breaking in about three days, when I was obliged to admit it cured and pay one dollar as agreed.

I have given the Syrians a place in the list, but they are only distinct from many others in that they come from Syria. I have not been to Damascus, but should imagine the population there must present almost as heterogeneous a collection, and as many varieties of the human race, as Meccah itself. Among the Syrians I must not omit to mention the sword-sharpeners, numbers of whom are to be seen following their trade in the bazaars of Meccah during the pilgrim season. They bring their somewhat large knife-grinding machines on their backs from Syria, their only "impedimenta."

The Bedawi in Meccah is very much out of his element. He slinks about with a hang-dog, surprised look, and returns the push and curse of the Turkish soldier with a sulky scowl. The mean-spirited Bengali, who would go into a nervous paroxysm if he met the Bedawi in the desert, crowds past him in the bazaar with impunity, though the Bedawi is, I can assure you, a very different customer at home.

Tartars and Bokharans—powerful, well-built races of very large men with Russian complexions and rosy cheeks—come the whole pilgrimage on foot from the most remote parts of Central Asia, some occupying five and six months on the journey. They perform all minor pilgrimages most assiduously, and are never to be seen riding donkeys on such occasions as other pilgrims. They go about enveloped in their thick woollen garments on the most scorching day in the desert, and are as dirty as any others or dirtier.

The last on the list are the nondescript rabble from China, the West Coast of Africa or Russia, and wild Darwaysh savages from God knows where. The Darwayshes are not to be confounded with the professional beggar or pauper pilgrims; they are *bonâ fide* religious mendicants, passing their lives in prayer and devotion, subsisting entirely on charity, and having no home ; to abuse or hit one of these would be a most unholy act. They dress in as remarkable and eccentric a manner as they can, and behave outrageously ; most of them affecting madness. A Negro Darwaysh, with his amulets of talismans and relics, and festoons of knuckle-bones, stones, and rags, would fetch entire the value of his full weight in a marine store-shop. All of them carry a staff, and a half gourd which they thrust forward to high and low for alms; and he would be a bad Mohammedan who would refuse to give at least something, be it ever so small, to one of these when solicited. These with their companions in the list may be disposed of in two words—mangy mongrels.

Having now reached the bottom of the scale of humanity, I will, while my hand is in, pass on to—I am afraid I cannot in justice to the brutes say downwards to—a description of the remaining animal life to be found in Meccah.

CHAPTER V.

THE REMAINING ANIMAL AND VEGETABLE LIFE AND MECCAH ITSELF.

The camel has no hump. Well, not exactly that; but the hard-worked, ill-conditioned camel of the Hejaz has very little hump, a mere slight elevation of the dorsal ridge, more thickly clothed with wool than the rest of the body, over which the saddle fits. The saddle is a long bag of coarse sacking about the thickness of a large pillow and twice the length of the camel's back; when put on it is doubled round above the tail and the ends kept together at the shoulders by a wooden fixture constructed much on the same principle as our pack-saddles. This huge ungainly brute is endowed with a stupidity and helplessness perfectly pitiable, and its temper is diabolical. While being laden it gives vent to spuming, spluttering, bellows and whines not unlike what the roars of an enraged croupous lion might be supposed to be. I never recall to my mind a camel, but I picture it biting, or trying to bite something, an operation for which its peculiar dental arrangement well adapts it. It never loses an opportunity of biting anything it dares bite, and it dares bite anything but a Bedawi: some will even occasionally venture a sly nibble at their masters, by whom they are brutally treated. They are seldom to be seen without saddle sores, raw ulcers as often covering a surface of feet as inches, and they always die in harness. Though the camel if allowed will drink freely twice a day, I have myself ridden them three days from water to water, during which their great sufferings were most evidently exhibited. In some places the road, over an otherwise trackless plain, was literally marked out by lines of their bleached skeletons; many hundreds of which I have seen, and have often pulled the huge bones apart. The camel's pace in caravan is about two-and-a-half miles an hour, and a fair load a quarter of a ton; they may be hired for one-and-a-half dollars a day. This hire varies somewhat with circumstances, and the average price of a camel ranges from thirty dollars to sixty dollars, but there are, of course, fancy prices given for first-rate animals. The Turkish Government use the Egyptian camel, which is a third and much stronger variety than either of the Hejaz camels, though I have been told it has not the same endurance. Altogether camels are more numerous in the Hejaz than in any other part of the East to which I have been. I estimated, so far as such a thing was possible, that there could not have been less than sixty thousand assembled on the plain of Arafat on the day of the celebration there.

The Hejaz can scarcely be called a country of horses at all, as there are few to be found other than those of the Turkish mounted troops. These are the well-known hardy little Arabs, good horses at their worst. They are never groomed, and they are badly shod; their hoofs are not pared, and consequently present some curious malformations—but that Nature has given the Arab an abnormally perfect foot, the coronet or pastern might be the point of contact with the ground. "No frog; no foot" is most assuredly not one of the many saws common to both East and West, for here when the shoe, which is a flat plate of iron with a small hole in the centre, is removed, it invariably discloses the frog in a high state of decay. There are a few horses of the finer Arab kinds belonging to rich Arabs. A good Meccan gentleman's riding - horse can be purchased for one hundred dollars. A few horses—a very few,

I think I saw three—are owned by the Bedawin, and they must be hardy brutes indeed to live at all under the treatment they experience. The marked traits of the Hejaz horse generally are its inability to trot or leap, its even temperament, steady nerve, and a knack of lying down with you like a camel, after having been kept standing for a time.

The donkey of the Hejaz is, I think, peculiar to that country. I am not aware that I have seen the variety anywhere else; it is totally different from the Egyptian. In form it may be said to take the place among donkeys of the Flemish horse among horses; exceedingly powerful to look at, but with this difference—it is a "good 'un to go," and very willing, though, like most donkeys, it "steers aft." Its colour is white, with the black markings very clearly defined. A good donkey may be bought for about thirty dollars. Caravans of them between Meccah and Jeddah start nightly after sunset, and reach their destination before daylight, a distance of over forty miles, either carrying men or heavily laden. Donkeys are said to last three years at this work, and when no longer fit for it, are valued very highly as private riding donkeys, on account of the working habits they have acquired. There is also a small black variety, not nearly so common as the white one. I saw no donkeys in the Hejaz with rough coats, or of the common mouse colour.

The mule, always by large jackasses, is a very fine animal here, and though the mare is seldom over fourteen hands, the mule often stands that height. I was told of a jackass in Medinah as big as a horse, but did not see it when I was there, though I have seen them in Meccah very big indeed.

I saw no cows or oxen of any kind, but was told they existed. I am inclined to account for this on the supposition that they are a transparent description of lean kine, browsing, as they must, on a pasturage of sand, small stones, and dead gooseberry bushes; the more so as the sheep and goats which I did see can be called little more than semi-opaque, and might be driven about the dark lanes of Meccah at night, with lighted candles inside them, to advantage.

There are many varieties of sheep and goats in the Hejaz—close-haired, straight-horned sheep like goats, and woolly, curly-horned goats like sheep, so that the mass of fat round the root of the tail in the sheep is really the only distinguishing mark; this not unusually weighs as much as six or eight pounds. The price of a sheep or goat ranges, according to its size and condition, from one dollar to five dollars.

All the domestic animals are branded, the horses and sheep moderately, but camels and donkeys are sometimes seamed and scarred from head to foot in all manner of fanciful devices most painful to see, reminding one of periods of torture through which the animals must have passed. I have seen a Bedawi engaged for more than an hour on the skin of a camel with a red-hot iron.

Canine scavengers are as numerous and interesting in Meccah as in Constantinople or anywhere else in the East, and notwithstanding their numbers, the great heat, and scarcity of water, rabies is almost unknown. I heard vague rumours of a hunting-dog to be found in the country, but never came across it.

Cats abound, and are lank, large-eared, and small-headed.

The monkeys in this country are, without exception, the most grotesque, quaint little creatures of their kind. I once came upon a pack of about five of these doglike little monkeys on Jebel Nur, and found them very tame, though much too wide-awake to allow themselves to be caught. Stories told by the Arabs of their thieving and imitative propensities entirely lack point, unless you grant the beasts, as a matter of course, great reasoning powers. I know it is universally accepted as a fact that monkeys can talk, but will not, for fear they should be made to work; though I believe this to be but badly authenticated by the unsupported evidence of only one sailor, who stated that he roasted a live monkey in an oven till it cried out, "Could any mortal man stand this?" However, be it known, on the indisputable authority of an "intelligent native," that a sage Shaykh of Arabia satisfactorily settled that question ages ago when monkeys could talk, which they cannot do now. One Shaykh Ali brought twelve monkeys into a yard—you are to suppose these a primal Shaykh and primal monkeys, the progenitors of all Shaykhs and all monkeys: (this is a very favourite groundwork to any piece of thoroughly reliable Eastern history). Well, Shaykh Ali went up to the first of the dozen monkeys and pointing to a stone, addressed it something in this style: "Now then, I want you to move along that stone, or, much as I may regret it, I shall have to make a decapitated ape of you; come, walk round, exhibit, show the ladies your agility, Alhamdulelahe Hurryup Alak Akbar." But the artful beast remained inattentive and apparently preoccupied—a way they have. Quoth the Shaykh: "My conviction is that that's altogether too logical a lie. Bismallah!" and whipped off its head, and so on through the lot till he came to the twelfth, an *enceinte* lady he had considerately spared till last, which got up and walked away with the stone without being asked; explaining that now it was the last of its race it did not mind confessing it could talk, but swore that the accomplishment should die with it. "May dogs defy your great-grand-mother's beard!" said the Shaykh. "Certainly," said the monkey; but it taught none of its progeny the faculty of speech. I wonder if it is true! There are a great many of these little baboons kept as pets in Meccah; sometimes they are tied in the doorways and make very good gatekeepers; there could be few things much more amusing than to see one of these little men objecting to a stranger. I can understand their having been quite "the rage" at Jerusalem in Solomon's time.

Rats and mice swarm.

There are eagles in the country, as a Bedawi once tried to sell me a large pair of wings; and hawks of many species are numerous.

Vultures and kites wheel in circles over all inhabited localities, or share the carrion, of which there is no lack, with the ravens and crows.

Fowls are plentiful, though eggs are rather dear, seldom being less than a piastre for four.

Desert grouse, partridges, and quails are brought to the bazaars by Bedawi children, who snare them and knock them over with sticks.

Blue-rock pigeons are to be seen here in large numbers such as are probably not to be met with elsewhere. I amused myself for some time by counting smaller flocks and comparing them with larger, so estimating the number to be seen at one time in the Haram, which could not have been less than between five and six thousand. They are so tame that they feed freely from the hand. The reason of this extreme fearlessness is that they are held to be almost sacred, more so than any other Meccan animal (unless, perhaps, the swallow). They are considered the property of the Haram, and are, I believe, never killed.* I have occasionally gone out into the

* I heard no reason given for the special favour shown to these birds, and suppose that they, sharing with all other Meccan creatures a common immunity from harm, have by their nature merely accommodated themselves in the way they have to the favourable circumstances.

Haram to feed these birds, after the manner of the pilgrims, who purchase baskets of mixed and damaged grain sold for the purpose. The moment you leave the pavement you become the vortex of a revolving storm of pigeons, the air taking a leaden hue above and about you, while the view is completely obscured by the cloud of birds, and the grain is whisked out of your basket, and your clothes whirled about by the wind from their wings. The noise is deafening, and you are glad to empty your basket and escape. Or I have sometimes sat down in the middle of the turmoil, and let the birds light on me and struggle over me, the ground for yards round paved two or three deep with their fluttering bodies; when the grain is finished they disperse over the square or to the neighbouring bazaars. I observed among these birds a number of interesting varieties curiously like our commoner domestic varieties. My attention was called to this, shortly after my arrival in Meccah, by seeing a jacobin-looking specimen, which I afterwards saw always in the same flock, as I knew by the number of birds composing it. This bird I at first supposed to be distinct, but I afterwards ascertained that no pigeons were to be found in the district other than wild ones; and indeed where every house has its sitting bird in some room or another (in one room I saw as many as five nests with eggs or young ones in them, on niches placed high up in the wall apparently for that purpose); any attempt to introduce a permanent variety would be a failure, as it would soon be absorbed into the more numerous stock. I saw many in which the bars on the wings and tail were single, reduced to a mere blotch on one or two feathers, or absent altogether; while a strawberry tinge across the back is not at all uncommon. The tumbling peculiarity of one of our pigeons is to be seen, and appears to be used as a means of suddenly stopping to alight during swift flight. As these birds have existed in their present state probably for centuries, such varieties can scarcely result from occasional temporary introductions of distinct kinds, and are more likely to have been developed naturally in the condition in which the birds live.

The swallows are held in the greatest regard, and are allowed to build in the Haram. The beautiful Saracenic arch, about fifty feet high, forming the Gate of Abraham, is completely disfigured by the masses of mud composing clusters of their nests. This respect for the swallows is held on account of a belief that they were the instruments by which Meccah was saved from an Abyssinian army in the same year as Mohammed's birth. The tradition is that God sent these birds with three small stones each, one in the beak and two in the claws, which they dropped on the heads of the Abyssinians, and which miraculously penetrated the bodies of men and elephants to the ground till only one of the invaders was left alive, who fled back to his own country, and had just finished telling the news to his king when one of the swallows, which he had observed following him overhead from Meccah, dropped its stone and killed him.

It occurred to me, as a possible explanation, that if a swallow had been seen to drop one of the particles of mud they carry to make their nests, this, together with a sudden panic, might have given rise to a fiction that would have been quite a solid foundation for such a piece of history in the East, but I have since come across the subjoined note in Syed Ameer Ali's "Life of Mahommed" (Williams and Norgate. London, 1873).*

To the statement in the note at the foot of

* The account of this event exemplifies well how legends grow among uncultured nations. The invaders were destroyed by some pestilential epidemic, probably small-pox; and the word *al-hasabat*, which signifies "pustules," also signifying "small stones," the origin of the legend that the army was destroyed by stones showered from heaven can easily be traced.

page 116, I may add that if a Sepoy army were to encamp in the valley of Meccah to-morrow it would be quite in the ordinary course if a week hence it had not a man capable of doing "sentry go" from pustules—the Meccah disease which I have already alluded to.

The above tradition had matured into its present form, and was recorded during the life of Mohammed as a fact.

The cosmopolitan little house-sparrow twitters on your window-sill here, as where does it not?

A few small birds of the fly-catcher family are to be found in the desert.

Snakes are all over the country, though nowhere very numerous or large; some are very venomous indeed. One of our party was bitten on the toe by one which had escaped; by the man's description of its appearance it was a yellow-and-black spotted slender snake, about eighteen inches long, and he almost succumbed to the bite, remaining insensible for about three hours, nor did he recover the shock for some weeks.

There are a few large lizards among the rocks; and a little yellow fellow who frequents the houses amused me for what would have been many a weary hour, watching him hunting flies on the ceiling.

Scorpions, tarantulas, spiders, centipedes, and all creeping creatures, abound.

Cockroaches an inch-and-a-half long may be brought to bay in any corner, or stalk past you with a contemptuous wave of a three-inch antenna.

Clouds of locusts cross the country at times, and are always more or less abundant. The Arabs eat them, the children looking upon them as a great treat, buying halfpenny-worths of the men who hawk them about the streets in baskets very suggestive of "sh-r-imps," to which they do bear a distant resemblance, both in the shape of their bodies, their great percentage of legs and spines, and in taste, which is rather fishy and very oily. I gave them a fair trial, but could not bring myself to like them, apart from the idea they are not good eating. I was told the Arabs caught them by setting fire to the dry vegetation over which they were flying, or among which they had alighted, and so suffocating them by camel-loads. When caught in this way they receive no other cooking than the slight scorching and smoking of the light fire into which they fall.

The honey of wild bees is to be bought in the bazaars for about five piastres a pound.

A few butterflies are to be met with in the

sylvan (?) districts, and moth doth corrupt "the worst kind" in the urban.

Carrion flies of every description are a pest in Meccah, though not equalling the perpetual fly plague of Egypt.*

Mosquitoes are troublesome, but there are many worse places than Meccah for mosquitoes, so I will not ask my most incredulous reader to "strain at my gnat."

All other carnivorous, man-eating invertebrates infest the place, and rare feeding-ground they find it.

This finishes the somewhat limited fauna of Meccah, nor do I think I have omitted to mention a single creature that came under my notice.

The flora is not quite so limited as the fauna.

Though the general appearance of the country is bare rock or sandy desert, there is no part absolutely without a little vegetation. In some places there are large savannahs of coarse grass like long stubble, and in others small jungles of gorse and broom-like growths (not in the least like gorse or broom on close inspection, only presenting the same appear-

* Probably the flies inoculate the stranger with the Meccah disease, as the sores only appear on the skin of the uncovered parts of the body.

ance in the landscape)—all good grazing for camels, for the camel munches greedily large mouthfuls of desert thorns, the spikes of which make stilettoes used for embroidering, and compared to which a white brier in December would be a luscious morsel, a birch-broom a delicate tid-bit.

In the most arid and rocky parts small stunted shrubs crop up here and there, enough to support a few sheep and goats; among these an absynthine plant, one of the favourite adornments of the filthy fakir, deserves mention for its remarkably sweet scent and delightfully fresh greenness. The whole of the surrounding country is dotted over with widely-dispersed spots of most thorough fertility where almost anything can be grown—wheat, dates, apples, or oranges. These places are assiduously cultivated, and send a great variety of fruit to the market.

The water-melons and pomegranates are perhaps the best in the world. One kind of pomegranate has the seeds so soft that they may be eaten with pleasure. A much-worn green dye is procured by a simple process from the skin of the pomegranate. This colour in Meccah is not worn exclusively by the Kuraysh,* nor is it looked upon as the mark of

* Descendants of the family of Mohammed.

a three-pilgrimage pilgrim, as has been said by some writer.

Vegetables are dear, though nearly every kind but potatoes and cabbages is grown.

The thorny acacia and tamarisk supply firewood and small timber. Beams and rafters are made of the split trunk of the date tree, and laths for roofing from its fronds.

I suppose I should be doing something unprecedented were I to write a book, however small, on Arabia and say nothing about dates; and I admit myself rather puzzled to think of something to say about them that everybody does not know. Dates are the staple article of food in Meccah, though bread runs them very close. Still I have scarcely ever seen bread eaten without dates, and I have often seen dates eaten without bread; so dates may be allowed to be the staff of life here. There are many kinds; but of whatever quality, they are a trifle dearer than the same would be in London. At times, and in places, the streets of Meccah are almost laid with date-stones. Painful-looking old women and miserable Hindi beggars gather these and sell them, for they have, in quantities, a considerable value, being about the most nutritious fodder the country affords for milch-camels or sheep; a few hours' soaking in water softening them so as to be easily masticated. The largest and best-coloured stones are carefully sorted out and sold to be turned on the lathe into rather pretty beads. Meccah producing nothing itself depends on external sources even for its dates.

Most of the gardens are said to lie in the direction of Tayf, a town three days' journey east of Meccah, which I did not visit. It is the sanatorium of Meccah, where many of the rich Meccans spend the months of August and September (the season at Tayf), "living on grapes and honey among cool breezes," as I heard it put. Besides the produce of Arabia great quantities of fruit and vegetables are imported from Egypt, and timber from Burmah.

Though I do not know the mast from the gun in geology, so to speak, a man must indeed have gone through a country like this blindfold not to have observed the wonderfully rapid changes in the surface of the land so palpably in process under your very eyes. If the reader remembers, on our way to Meccah, we journeyed over some twenty-eight miles of sandy plain, from the sea to the beginning of a rocky region. This border extends up and down the entire coast of the Hejaz, and is, on a fair average, about thirty miles across.

I have at different times travelled over probably

four hundred miles of this part of the country, and found it everywhere of the nature of a dry sea-beach. On entering this most unpromising desert from inland, before you are five miles past the last ridge of rock, you will pick up a decayed fragment of the shell of some flinty old bivalve, and ere long you will find yourself passing over beds of bleached and rotten sea-shells. Turn your camel from the beaten track, and there will be a crunching under foot as though walking over "afternoon-tea" cups. As you advance over this all but perfectly barren waste, you will find everywhere similar indications, immense tracts of large water-worn pebbles, or ditto of small shingle and tiny shells set to a hardness like conglomerate rock; and, overlying these, another feature will be miles in area of dusty shifting sand, stirred up by the lightest breeze; or at the bottom of some gentle long undulation you may come upon a crust of fine light clay two or three inches thick—a greasy yellow slough yesterday in the shower, and in the solar oven of to-day baked hard as pot, cracked and seamed like the enamel on old china, with all the little segments loosened from their beds and some of them curled up into positive drain-pipes. In such places the camels have "a hard road to travel," for, when it is wet, they slip and sprawl about on it and often sprain themselves badly, and when dry the hard curled-up cakes break under their weight and cut their feet. In either case, if lamed so as to be unable to keep up with the rest, "their throats are cut to save their lives." As you draw nearer to the sea the shells become noticeably harder and have not the mother-o'-pearl scaled off them, and you may traverse hard black marly patches covered with a white saline efflorescence like hoar-frost. Even here something will grow. Every two or three hundred yards a little green plant, an inch or two high, or small bed of violet-flowered vetches, quite startling as seen beneath your camel on the eye returning from glaring painfully over a hot waste of glittering plain with nothing more substantial to obstruct the view than a few curling sand-pillars flitting about an uncertain horizon in little whirlwinds. These are always most numerous on the hottest days, when the discomfort is too great to admit of your taking any interest in them; but if seen towards evening their rapid movements and changing forms may be watched with great interest, and you may chance to see the description of the poet realised:

Before my dreamy eye
Stretches the desert with its shifting sand,
Its unimpeded sky.

And, borne aloft by the sustaining blast,
This little golden thread
Dilates into a column high and vast,
A form of fear and dread.

And onward, and across the setting sun,
Across the boundless plain,
The column and its broader shadow run,
Till thought pursues in vain.

LONGFELLOW.

I cannot swear that I ever did reach the sea, except at Jeddah, not having actually felt the water elsewhere; and at the other points on the coast, where I came nearest to it, sandpits and growing reefs blended into shallows and retreating creeks in such a way that there was really no defined junction of land and water; and besides, in places like this, the mirage is so constant and plays such extraordinary freaks that a man would be a fool to believe his eyes.

So much for the superficial deposits of the coast, a good deal of which is not geology, I am afraid, and has led me wandering from Meccah. The nature of the strata!—save the mark!—its rocks are about as much stratified as are the various components in a bowl of Scotch broth. For the materials of which the hills about Meccah are composed, I suppose there is not a possible mineral combination, plutonic, metamorphic, or eruptive, of which a specimen could not be procured from the hills of Meccah. How a geologist would revel in it! A mangled limb of old mother earth, compound comminuted fracture, bones protruding, exposing the very marrow of the world; or better, call them skeletons of mountains, around you on every side pile after pile of naked rocky ribs falling apart, crumbling to pieces as you look at them, burying themselves in their own *dêbris*, fantastic ruins, the sides clothed with fragments of themselves, to be cast off only to make room for others, and help to swell the level plain, creeping steadily up like an ocean tide. Of all the countries in the world in which I have been I have beheld not conditions so favourable for rapid disintegration of rock as the sudden extremes of heat and cold of this part of Arabia, and I never (not even in an earthquake) so fully realised having seen Nature at work as when I felt I had caught her in the act, reducing those iron rocks. I have slept at night on them: I may here mention in passing that I should be very much surprised if it had been recorded of Jacob, that he, similarly situated, did not have a bad dream, "pace" of the serious reader. I have lain on those rocks on a chilly night and heard them crack and felt the dust from them fall on my face.

Sitting one day on a hill about one hundred and fifty feet high, perhaps a mile or so to the west of Meccah, half round the base of which passes a road called the Sultan's Road, I noticed on the plain below a formation which struck me as very curious and set me speculating. All along the side of the road opposite to the hill, from the point where the road first touched the hill to the point where it left it—a distance of about four hundred yards—extended as symmetrical a stone-heap as ever lay by the side of an English highway, but of Brobdingnagian proportions, about fifteen feet high and fifty feet across; between it and the hill ran a smooth beaten camel-path wide enough for two laden camels to pass one another.

I soon guessed the way in which this stone-heap had been made. Bedawin, as they walk along leading their camels, throw out of the path all stones over a certain size which would be likely to hurt the feet of the camels if trodden on by them unexpectedly, and in this way this vast heap had been formed. To prove it I took the trouble to push a few stones down into the road, and the very next Bedawi who came past gave me the satisfaction of seeing him do a share in a public work of collecting all the pieces of stone larger than a walnut that fell from the hill, and depositing them in a heap by themselves. If, as its name seems to imply, this road has been made since the Turkish occupation of the Hejaz, the hill, other things considered, looks to have shed about one-tenth of its entire bulk in three hundred years.

Of the many other interesting workings of Nature on an unusual scale in this country, I have seen a sand-storm, by forming drifts, alter a landscape in a few hours ; and the triturating action on the rocks of this sand—with which the air is so loaded during any fresh breeze as to give the appearance of a yellow fog—is very considerable, as all the harder nodules of stone lying in the valleys are rounded on their upper surfaces, as though water-worn from this cause.

A rain-storm raised the valley of Meccah six inches (of which a description will be given in due course). I have seen a mound of sand one hundred feet high in the open desert, for which I could not account, unless it were a tenable theory that it had accumulated round some such nucleus as the growths over a spot fertilised by a dead body.

But now I think enough has been said to illustrate the extraordinary rate at which geologic change goes on over the surface of this country, and possibly to prepare you to agree that "Araby the Blest" may not have been quite such a fabulous country after all. Say five thousand years ago, after having passed through the first stages of natural change in which, as geologists tell us, the finer soil forming particles from the rocks would have been brought down to the well-watered lower levels, might it not be in accordance with scientific principles if Arabia had been a country of richly fertile valleys?—how much so may be judged from the almost rank productiveness of any place where the water is not too deeply buried under sand and stones even at this day.

I will not say how rich I believe the Hejaz to be in metals, because, understanding nothing of mineralogy, my opinion would be worth little. I know, however, as a matter of fact, that gold is procured by the Bedawin, and that there is in Meccah a large sale of precious stones which are found in the country; moreover, the Arabia of the ancients is also the Arabia of the Scriptures—then why should these concurrent testimonies be doubted? For my part

I think it most likely that the gardens and lakes of Arabia have, in the course of nature and during the historic era, been buried under the ruins of its mountains. The often-quoted explanation, which accounts for the difference between the Arabia of to-day and the Arabia known to Solomon, and described by the ancients on the supposition that they were designedly misled by the Egyptians and Phœnicians, who themselves traded only in the wealth of India, seems to me to be utterly feeble.

The dollar called "riyal," in which I have given all the prices, is, with the English pound (called "jinni") and the Turkish piastre, the standard currency of the country: though every gold and silver coin known can be readily changed. The most common and most preferred dollar is the Austrian Maria Theresa, and I noticed that although they were all dated about 1790, such a great proportion of them looked new, that I fancy they must have been struck since that date, if they are not now being coined somewhere. The only copper coins current are the Turkish piastre and parts of a piastre, so that as pilgrims bring only gold and silver, they find a great scarcity of small change, and the shopkeepers can refuse to sell if you offer to pay with a coin worth more than three times the value of the article to be purchased. The money-changers charge an unvarying rate of a half piastre in the dollar.

The shops are of the ordinary Eastern description. A low platform facing the street, on which samples of the wares are exposed, behind which the dealer sits in a room containing the bulk of his merchandise. The bazaars do not follow the rule, as in other Eastern countries, of all shops in the same line of business being collected in the same locality; the order being oftener—a dealer in European commodities, a fruiterer, a baker, and a gunsmith, or anything else, the butchers being the only dealers who stick to a particular market-place. All things considered, order and honesty are kept up to a wonderful degree in Meccah, theft being not nearly so common as might be expected. No indications of female profligacy are publicly observable, and, apart from existing legislative prohibitions, would not indeed be tolerated by the pilgrims. Spirits or wine are not to be procured by the uninitiated outsider, though I did meet with one adventurous Egyptian speculator, who was making a good thing out of Eau-de-Cologne, selling it as a "medicine for head or heart ache," to be taken internally; until it was discovered to be a spirit, when all his stock was thrown into the street and his bottles smashed by the mob, the owner only escaping with his life. The water, which is very bad, is plentiful—that is to say, can always be got for a price.

The sanitary condition of the place is wonderful, considering what a cesspool the valley of Meccah really is, there being no outlet whatever from the valley for the sewage, which must percolate down into the wells; and I strongly suspect that the water of the well Zem Zem owes much of its virtue to ammonia, it being in the centre of the city and at the lowest level in the valley.

Notwithstanding the general squalor, unhealthy condition, and indescribable filthiness of the place, I believe no very great plague is known to have visited Meccah. This might be accounted for by the exceeding dryness and clearness of the atmosphere, in which dead flesh generally dries without decomposing, and the facts that the majority of the population are men who have been in a physical condition which has enabled them to perform a long journey—consequently much-enfeebled constitutions among the great mass are rare; and that the pilgrim frame of mind is such as to render him not liable to disease, for, if faith works the wonders accredited to it, there should be few sick men in Meccah. Another, and perhaps the main, reason is that famine, the usual precursor of pestilence, cannot reach Meccah, since there is no great lower class in absolute destitution; the thousands seen begging are "beggars at a fair," reaping the yearly harvest of supplies and wealth brought by the pilgrims. It is not surprising that Mohammedans attribute the comparatively small rate of mortality among the community to a perpetual miraculous interposition of Providence in behalf of "Meccah the inviolable." The climate is subject to occasional heavy downpours of rain in the winter months, seldom lasting longer than a few hours. The temperature is extremely variable. I have sat at night shivering, fingers blue and teeth chattering with cold, and have been on the afternoon of the same day scorched by the dry heat till my lips cracked. I often wished for a thermometer, which would have shown some curious fluctuations. I am convinced that the shade temperature would at times have ranged from 40° to 100° Fahr. in twenty-four hours.

The history of Meccah shows it to have passed

through fully its share of the exigencies of flood, fire, and sword. The pilgrimage to Meccah and almost all the ceremonies connected with it were ancient customs of the Arabs at the time of Mohammed, and were believed by him to be of Divine origin, and so adopted into his faith.

CHAPTER VI.

THE PILGRIMAGE.

FRIDAY, December 14th, 1877, was the day of standing to Arafat. The pilgrimage coming off on Friday is called the "Greater Pilgrimage," and is attended by far greater numbers than in an ordinary year. On December 13th, all the gathering of nations which had hitherto loaded almost to bursting the small valley of Meccah was shot out, discharged —I can give no better idea. In twenty-four hours this army of two hundred thousand strong, everyone his own general, everyone his own commissary, evacuated Meccah almost to a man, marched about eleven miles east, and camped on the plain of Arafat, near Mount Arafat; this march must at least have been confused, but with every man doing his worst to make a rout of it (for it is intended to be figurative of Mohammed's flight from Meccah) confusion was no name for it. Our preparations had as usual been of the most casual and desultory character. The camels were at the door shortly after morning prayer, yet it was eleven o'clock before the tents, baggage, and provisions could be hurry-scurried together on to their backs. Some of the most important articles had been forgotten, such as water-bottles, new pilgrims' garbs, etc., which had to be purchased at the last moment. The pilgrims' garbs in which we had made our first entry into Meccah had been mere lengths of calico; we now found there was a fashionable pilgrim's garb, this being nothing more or less than a couple of rough bath towels. We mounted the camels at the door, and it took us two hours to get over the first mile through the streets, so closely were they thronged with camels; sometimes the shugdufs would get entangled and be torn nearly off; the inmates, if women, would scream and pray; if men, curse and pray, notwithstanding the guard which they are supposed to keep over their tongues on this so solemn an occasion; and predominant over all rose the oft-repeated shrill "labbayks," to which I added my quota of discordance, entering into the thing gleefully. In the narrow streets, the shugdufs would get jammed together, and no advance could be made for some minutes; but as the crush all tended in one direction, we were at last carried out of the town into the open roads, and passed on with the current—one continuous stream of men and animals flowing out of Meccah towards Muna, a village some five miles east of Meccah, at which we arrived about three P.M. Two rooms had been engaged for us on the ground-floor of a house near the middle of the village, facing the main road, passing through it to Arafat, and here we put up for the night. The road towards Muna had been a gradual ascent. We passed over one or two stone viaducts and some cuttings between the hills; altogether it was the best attempt at a made road I saw in the country. We also met with one or two reservoirs well supplied with water.

The village of Muna lies in a pass rather than a valley, some two or three hundred yards across and half-a-mile long, between two abrupt rocky ridges about two or three hundred feet in height. A good many low houses are built along the pass at the sides of the Arafat road, which is about eighty feet wide. All along this street rows of provision, tea, or tobacco stalls had been set up, and the place for the time had become a fair. In one of the windows of our room I took up my post to watch the crowds passing in their uniform white dresses, for although the women do not wear the pilgrims' garb, they must dress in white. I had not been looking out long when I became aware from the greater commotion and a general pressing from the middle of the street that something was going to happen; so I inquired from the keeper of a date-stall outside the window, and was told the "Sheréf" was coming, and in a minute or two the head of the procession appeared. As nearly as I can remember it passed my window in the following order: First came the Sheréf's vanguard, about one hundred bare-backed camels, each ridden by two armed Bedawin, a spearman in front and a matchlock-man behind, the choicest collection of Bedawi rags and filth I ever had the pleasure of contemplating. Their animals were huddled together like a flock of sheep, filling up the whole street, forcing the crowds before them and into the shops and stalls; though the raga-muffins exerted themselves madly, and appeared to be riding furiously they made little headway, their very hurry and confusion retarding their advance. I never saw a more barbarous, savage exhibition than these excited ferocious-looking warriors, with their long matted locks and the twenty-five foot spears surmounted with tufts of ostrich feathers which some of them carried. In rear of these mingled with and close behind came other camel-riders, playing on reed instruments like short flageolets, keeping very good time and producing much noise: the music was in keeping with time and place, and was not at all bad to listen to: an Irish keen played merrily on half-a-dozen Highland pipes would perhaps be as much like the Sheréf's band as anything. After them followed a led camel in crimson cloth and gold ornaments, said to be carrying something belonging to the Kaabah: what was visible was a piano-case-shaped structure about four feet high, covered with red cloth, and a lot of bells hanging on its front side which made a great jangling at every step of the camel. Behind this followed a rabble of armed functionaries on foot, carrying breech-loading and revolving guns and rifles, spears, swords, and anything to kill with, from a Deringer to a battle-axe. After these came twelve led horses in gold and silver trappings following one another in line—light bays and chestnuts in rather too good condition for work, but compact, muscular, pretty little animals, each one handsomer than the last; and if they had gone on following one another all day, you could not have taken your eyes off. Then came the Sheréf himself, riding an iron-gray horse somewhat higher than the led ones, with exceedingly slight limbs and neck, giving the idea of light weight and great speed, but pacing quietly and unconcernedly through the mob without as much as turning its lovely little head. The wonderful docility of these evidently high-mettled animals was good to look at. The Sheréf's horse was "the model" of them all; it seemed to be diligently persevering to carry its burden easily and not to have a look or thought for any other object. The Sheréf himself was dressed in the costume of a Bedawi Shaykh; light blue mantle* worked in gold about the shoulders and collar, fastened in front with a thick gold cord and tassels; on his head the ordinary silk head-dress† of the Bedawi, kept on by a camel's-wool ring‡ round the top of the head. He is a slight, wiry, well-made man, below the medium height; his complexion would be considered very dark even for a Bedawi, almost black. He has a small round bullet head, and that peculiar cast of countenance which provokes

* Aba. † Kufiyah. ‡ Aahal.

you to say he has a face like a monkey, notwithstanding his very shrewd intelligent expression. His beard and moustache are short and scrubby, and I should guess him at under forty years of age. His years, however, are hard to judge, and he might be any age from twenty-four to forty, or older if he uses hair-restorer, as is the custom of many Meccans. I have only one little matter to add: the High Sheréf, the first Mohammedan in the world, was mounted in an English saddle, doing the Great Pilgrimage in the pig's skin, happy and unconscious! The soul of that porker, wherever it is, must be grunting triumphant hallelujahs. It does not require a profound knowledge of the East to appreciate the awful portent to Mohammedanism in this. At distances of about twenty yards respectively followed his nephews or sons—(I was differently informed). The elder came first, a rather good-looking, bamboo-complexioned youth about fourteen, and after him the younger, evidently a brother of the first, about eight years old. Both were mounted on chestnut horses, and dressed like the Sheréf. At this part of the procession were a great number of followers, bearers of wands and insignia of office, mounted and foot armed attendants, some in pilgrims' garb and some in ordinary gala-dress. At a distance of some fifty yards behind these rode a number of Turkish officers in uniform clearing the way for the Pacha, the Sheréf taking precedence of him, I believe, in consideration of the religious nature of the ceremony. A line of Mamelukes (all Turkish horse-soldiers are called Mamelukes in the Hejaz) in uniform, armed with sabres and "Winchester" repeating-carbines, were drawn up on each side of the road; this line was kept advancing by the rear-man trotting outside to the front, where he would draw up until he again became rear-man. This kept a line of some fifty horses stationary on each side of the road: between them the Pacha passed in an open carriage, which was a new shiny barouche drawn by two European chestnut carriage-horses, with coachman and footmen dressed in civilised livery, and the Pacha, a gray old gentleman, in a well-cut suit of black cloth —a spick-and-span turn-out that would have shone in the Park. Imagine the contrast between them and their surroundings! I had become to think of such things as belonging to another state of existence; the barouche and pair quite carried me back with a revulsion. Close after the carriage followed two brass twelve-pounder field-guns drawn by mules, and a regiment of infantry, carrying their arms sloped and bayonets fixed, all the officers being in uniform, but the privates in pilgrims' garb. This ended the procession, which encamped about a mile farther on. Then the same crowd of men and animals, with now and then detachments of Turkish troops, kept sweeping by till two A.M., when I lay down on my blanket in a corner of the room where the Amér and nine or ten more of his principal servants were sleeping.

In the morning I did not get up till the stir of rolling up rugs and carpets awoke me. I found bright sunshine, and the morning prayer long over. So taken up had my companions been with peace-making and forgiving one another all grudges, as they were to be absolved from all past sins on that day, that I had been overlooked. So I said a great many "God-forgive-mes" with all due contrition, and after my ablution and prayer, joined in the general reconciliation that was going on. We fell on one another's necks, recalled and confessed all little petty offences one to another, certain of being forgiven in tears. I at first relied on my imagination for items, but my companions soon reminded me of numbers of ways in which I had offended them unconsciously or otherwise. They seemed sincere though, and made very clean breasts of it themselves. I found where numbers of little articles had gone that I had missed from my bundle. This one had appropriated a penknife, another a pair of socks. I, of course, gave and forgave with the best grace possible. We were now supposed to be at peace with all the world of True Believers, and might with clear consciences appear at Arafat. Though the crowds had been pressing past all night, their numbers did not seem in the least diminished.

I remember feeling very uncomfortable on that morning, the morning of the day on which I was to acquire the honoured title of Haji, and witness a scene, which it is given to few Europeans to see (probably not more than one in a generation). I felt a sort of depression, as though I required to be brought up to the sticking-point. Perhaps I had not quite got over the opium. I tried to wear this off by extra exertion in assisting at loading the camels; and while passing to and fro from the house, with bundles of gear, I twice fancied a woman in the yard tried to attract my attention, and the next time I passed I heard her pronounce my name. The "Lady Venus" at once dawned on me. I had been living in such stirring times lately that she had quite escaped my memory, and you may be sure my "Peace be upon you!"

and "God be praised!" came from the bottom of my heart, when she now appeared on the scene so opportunely. She told me that she was staying in the same house as myself, with a lady friend, who was treating her to a seat on a camel for the pilgrimage. She also said the boy Abdallah had been twice to my house in Meccah to inquire for me, but had been told that I was gone to Jeddah. We had not much opportunity to talk, but I hastily got her to give me a programme of the forthcoming events of the next three days, and we agreed to meet in the Haram on that day week. Coarse remarks soon began to be made by the men standing about, and we were obliged to part quickly.

About eight A.M. our party started. In a shugduf you are so shut in by the cover that you can see little outside but your own animal's head and the preceding one's rear; so as I had been considerably freshened up by my meeting with the "Lady Venus," I preferred to walk by the camels, and mingle with the throng, giving my mount to one of my companions. As we passed along the valleys between, the rocky hills became more open, and the crowds were able to disperse themselves over wider roads, so that the press was not so great as on the day before.

About an hour after leaving Muna, I recognised in a dead horse on the road one of the fine carriage-horses I had seen the day before drawing the Pacha. Its throat had been cut, as is the custom when an animal is thought to be past recovery; and though it could not have been dead more than three or four hours, its skin was fast becoming like leather, so quickly does the dry sand and air of the desert absorb moisture. The road from Meccah to Arafat cannot be more than ten or eleven miles, yet many animals had fallen by the way. Between Muna and Arafat I counted fourteen dead camels, and also saw many fresh graves of the last night, probably those of men who, having travelled thousands of miles, had died at the very threshold of their goal.

The camel-shaykh, who was conductor of our caravan, and from whom we had hired the camels owned by him or some of his relations, spoke a little Hindustani—a very unusual accomplishment for a Bedawi. He was an exceedingly good specimen of his kind, though not by any means a fair sample of that light-hearted murderer; far too good for that. The ordinary Bedawi is slightly made, wiry and short, and you may see a better leg on a crutch than his any day. This man was tall, muscular, and full-bearded, but a thorough Bedawi in manner, active and seamanlike. He gave his orders to those he considered under him with all the confidence of an efficient officer, and a good deal of the "hop along" air of a Yankee boatswain. So much of the "nautical touch" was there about him and his companions, that I at once christened him "Shaykh the Bow'sen," and would have quite expected to see him give his pants a hitch if he had worn what he and all Bedawin consider such a very unnecessary and effeminate article of apparel. He walked for some distance by my side, mounting his little son, about nine years of age, on his riding camel. After bandying a few Eastern questions and compliments, he asked me for one of the cheroots I was smoking, and then went on to ask me about India, a country where he had heard the inhabitants were not quite all Mohammedans. I noticed one of the weapons in his girdle, a long straight knife which struck me as being somehow familiar, so I pointed to it, and said inquiringly, "Good?" He at once drew it, and holding it out in admiration, exclaimed, "Rodgers!" Well, come, I thought, this is worse than my not knowing the "Lady Venus"—an unmistakable large Rodgers carving-knife, clean and bright, calling to mind more than one cut off a ham. "Rodgers!" I said. "Where's Rodgers?" He was astonished at my ignorance. Did not I know a Rodgers blade when I saw it? And he pointed out the mystic characters and explained that all knives with that mark were——and here he gave the steel point a significant spring with his finger and thumb, and went through the motions of cutting a throat with, "In the name of God!" "God is great!" and "Infidel!' I did not care to continue the subject.

A Rodgers blade in the Hejaz I afterwards found need not necessarily have been made by Rodgers, but any blade with English characters on it, or even a native-made blade of well-proved metal obtains that name, the word having been generally adopted as a synonym for good steel; and I suspect you would have some difficulty in finding a Meccan who could explain the derivation of the word or tell when it was introduced.

There are many other words of the same kind current. The term "Anglais" is applied to all wares of well-known or evidently good material, without any reference to the place they were made; the merchants themselves, either by courtesy or from ignorance (it is difficult to say which sometimes), calling all European manufactures Egyptian or

Turkish, utterly oblivious to glaring Manchester or London brands and labels; and a Bedawi will pronounce an article to be Français or Anglais at a glance, without in the least knowing the proper significance of the terms.

About eleven A.M. we reached the plain of Arafat, a large sandy open, appearing to be somewhat below the level of the approach, and occupying an area of some four or five square miles. In the north-east of the plain is "Mount Arafat," a small hill, about two hundred feet high, composed of large masses of gray granite, at the base of quite a respectable little mountain, the "Mount of Mercy."

We pitched our tents (one for the Amér and men, another for the Begum and women) about a third of a mile south of this hill. As soon as this work was completed, I took good bearings, marked the tents well, and went off alone to the top of Mount Arafat. The scene from here was. . . . I shall not be surprised if it flits across my mind on my death-bed. The depression of the plain gives an amphitheatre-like appearance, and you could almost believe yourself on the stage of some mighty theatre, miles of audience before you, and the sombre scenery of the black "Mount of Mercy" behind you. What a time and place for a sermon!

We had all come out into the wilderness to hear a sermon on this day; and I had determined to hear it, so sat down on the hill to wait till noon, when the "Lady Venus" had told me it would begin.

As I looked down on the great throng, a gray rippling sea of black heads and white bodies, extending from the sides of the hill, thickly clothed with men to a mile and a half off on the south, and half a mile across, and remembered the distant countries from which they came, and what brought them, it was impossible to help a feeling almost of awe. It set one thinking. Could all this be of no avail, and all this faith be in vain? If so, it was enough to make a man lose faith in everything of the kind.

At noon I left my post on the top of the hill and pressed my way about to try and find where the preacher would stand, and see what was to be seen. The practice among the pilgrims seemed to be to come up on the hill, say one or two prayers, remain a quarter of an hour or so, and return to the plain. At noon there was no general call to prayer, the pilgrims praying in parties near their tents and judging the hour for themselves. I said no noonday prayer myself, but spent the afternoon looking about on Mount Arafat.

On the top there is a small colonnade, an obelisk

about fifteen feet high, and some low stone walls separating one little irregularity of the surface of the rock from another. Inside and outside these enclosures, and, in fact, all over the hill, the crowd was so great that it was very difficult to get from one place to another, even by climbing walls and jumping from rock to rock. On the sides of the hill are a number of platforms, built up or hewn out of the rock, and a winding road, cut from the bottom to the top, much of which is composed of steps in the rock. At the bottom of the hill is a gravelled terrace forming a road between the hill and a large reservoir of water at its base, and there is another of these built "tanks" (as they are called in India) about one hundred yards south of the first. The sides of both these tanks were occupied the whole day by pilgrims performing the "lesser" ablution. I only saw one man enter the water bodily, and he slipped off the stone edge, I think, as I noticed those near him laughing. Though I stayed on or about the hill until nearly time for afternoon prayer I heard no sermon, saw no preacher, unless a very old and dirty Arab, not in pilgrim's garb, sitting with his legs across the top of a six-foot wall, haranguing the crowd in a voice that could not be heard ten yards off, was the orator we had all come so far to hear; but this I doubt. The probability is, seeing the crowd and noise was so great, the Mufti and his sermon escaped me, more especially as I did not risk inquiring of strangers whom I did not know and who might be anybody short of "Our Special Correspondent," even in the Hejaz nowadays.

As the afternoon wore on the press on the hill became greater, the crowd so dense as to literally bear you up, and those on the top had the greatest difficulty in forcing their way down. Many women had got on the hill and were being much crushed, some people were trodden under foot and forced into the crevasses of the rocks. I managed to battle my way out of it, and began to make for our tents. I had been pushing across the plain for a quarter of an hour or so, and was well out of the thick of the crowd, to where the ground began to be occupied more by tents and hobbled camels, when I was "brought up all standing" by a confused roaring behind me, and, on looking back, saw all the men taking off their upper pieces of cloth and waving them over their heads, shouting at the same time the names of "Allah!" "Mohammed!" and other exclamations. It seemed to begin at a preconcerted signal, whether the afternoon call to prayers or the end of the sermon, I did not know. This shouting would last for a few minutes at its height, then die almost out, and the cloud of waving white cloths almost all subside, then rise again, beginning at Mount Arafat and spreading over the plain. These intervals of great noise and almost silence continued regularly for about half an hour, and then lapsed gradually into roar and tumult.

The whole multitude was now worked up to the highest pitch of excitement, individuals expressing the greatest emotion, while some were quite frantic, and the scene had become a perfect pandemonium. There was something eerie, almost horrible, about it to me, an unimpassioned observer. I felt like a sane man among three hundred thousand lunatics. However, I shouted, flourished my cloth, capered about, and conducted myself like my uncanny mates, till the firing of the Pacha's two guns, which was the signal for decamping, reminded me that I had better return to my party. All the tents at once began to be rased and camels moved, completely changing the whole appearance of the great camp in a few minutes. I had much difficulty in finding our people, and only reached them when they were on the point of moving off. They were not at all surprised that

I had lost them, and congratulated me on my luck in finding them as I did. All was ready for starting, but the Sheréf and Pacha, together with another procession of the same kind from Medinah, passed near our camp, so we waited to follow behind them, spending the time firing off all the firearms we had, and sending up rockets. The breechloaders were fired without taking the trouble to remove the balls from the cartridges; the Amér alone expended fifty rounds of ball cartridge, impartially distributed over the thickly-peopled plain; but as he fired high and the guns had a long range, I cannot give a return of his killed and wounded, though I have no doubt he winged a great many in remote parts. The two field-guns, as they were being drawn along, were fired, round after round, as fast as they could be loaded with small charges of loose powder without being sponged; they were laid point-blank, and at every discharge cleared a lane through the crowd, which immediately closed up, nobody seeming to be hurt. One fellow repeatedly exploded an old matchlock, with a bend in the barrel that could be distinctly perceived twenty yards off in the dusk! Immense Congreve rockets and coveys of smaller ones rose from all parts of the plain, whose sticks as they fell could not but have hurt some one. For though the fall of a small rocket-stick is an indirect wavering flight and so harmless, still I think a twelve-foot rocket-pole, after a descent of nearly three thousand feet, might hurt a man, if it did not harpoon him clean.

Though I know every man there was living through a succession of narrow escapes, I must say I did not see a single accident. I afterwards heard of a good many who had been privileged to win (when a Mohammedan dies he is said to win or gain) on the field that day. One dead man was carried past me, who was curiously enough said to have been killed by the *kick* of a camel. That night we camped about a mile and a half before we came to Muna, at a place called Muzdalifah, and here we gathered the sixty-three small stones to be used during the next three days stoning the devil-stones at Muna: these pet stones ought to be gathered on this spot, and ought to be of a certain size (about that of a buckshot). Some were very particular as to this, and spent the greater part of the night gathering and sorting out such as they supposed to be of the proper size.

This site, like every other pilgrim site described, has innumerable minute observances connected with it, which the pilgrim performs more or less punctiliously according to his strictness, and differently according to his knowledge or belief. We spent much of the night praying and listening to a stranger Moulvi giving us a long extempore prayer, in which he prayed literally "that all who profess and call themselves" Mohammedans, "might hold the faith in unity and peace," that "the God who conquers by many or by few," might "give us victory over all our enemies," and much more to the same effect straight from our Church Service, we responding "Amen" to every approved sentiment.

It was piercingly cold next morning, and about two hours before daylight we started for Muna, being among the first of the great mass to get there. I said my morning prayer at Muna, using warm water for the ablution, and went off immediately after to Meccah on a donkey, in company with the boy Jack, as I was anxious to reach the town, which had before been such a scene of life and bustle, in the deserted state I knew it would then be. There was nothing out of the way in this, and my haste to go before the morning meal was only put down to a little superfluous religious zeal, it being the proper thing to go into Meccah as soon as possible after the pilgrimage, and perform the same rites as on your first arrival at the "Holy City," discarding the pilgrim's garb. The road to Meccah was not yet thronged by returning pilgrims, and the few who were on foot so early we soon passed on our donkeys, reaching Meccah shortly after sunrise. On the outskirts of the town a few coffee-shops had already been opened, and we passed two or three groups of Bedawi and Negroes; but as we came more into the town the streets were entirely deserted, not a living soul to be seen, all the shops being shut up, and the house-doors and windows closed. It had a most strange aspect, after the appearance which I had been accustomed to for months. As we approached the Haram we came upon some beggars sitting and lying at the roadside, who had been *in extremis* or too feeble to join the pilgrimage: such as were alive, for some were actually dead, greeted us most piteously, imploring us for food—and a hungry time they must have had of it. It was not so with the dogs, as they had been making horribly free with the legs of the defunct. I soon got rid of a handkerchief of bread and dates I had brought as a snack for myself, and prolonged the existence of one or two exhausted wretches. One of these held our donkeys while we went into the Haram.

I found only a party of half-a-dozen Maghribis who had returned straight from Arafat during the night, and who were the only pilgrims that had been beforehand with me. Some of the Arabs who officiate in the Haram, and who had remained behind to change the cover of the Kaabah, which is renewed at this time yearly, were giving the finishing-touches to their work. This cover is sent from Cairo, and is supposed to be made there by seven hundred virgins. After our prayers and tawaf, we did El Sai on our donkeys, which is allowable to the weak, and we easily reconciled it to our consciences, seeing we had made such haste to do it, and might be supposed to be at least very tired. After this we roamed about the dismal streets, letting our animals go as they willed. There was a kind of fascination about the lonely, lifeless lanes and passages lately so thronged, and my companion seemed to share the feeling with me, for he made the original remark, which I quote from him and not anyone else : "It is like a city of the dead." While going along a narrow out-of-the-way passage I had not before been in I came across an object that nearly brought me off my beast. Overhead, projecting straight out over the lane was a large black board, and painted on it in yellow these letters—LODGINGS.

"Jack," I said, "let's go back." I felt as if I had seen a ghost. However, I recovered the shock sufficiently to note the locality for future investigation, and returned thoughtful and meditative along the road, now thronged with returning pilgrims, to our headquarters for the time at Muna. When I got back I was glad to get out of the pilgrim's garb, which I had found very inadequate against the cold of the night and the sun in the day, which struck painfully on my bare shaven head. Most of our party had gone into Meccah, but returned before noon to purchase and kill the animals of which every man, who can by any means afford it, should kill at least one on this day, and which the country supplies plentifully for the occasion. This ceremony partakes more of the character of a feast than of a sacrifice, though all the sheep and goats killed are young males: I do not think even this is essential, but rather a custom resulting from the necessary practice in the country of always preserving females for breeding and milk.

I purchased a little black ram for two dollars, and killed it at home in the usual way, except that the head was carefully turned towards the Kaabah, and saying, " In the name of God the most merciful and charitable," while cutting its throat. There ought to be something soothing to the feelings about this short prayer, which in the mouth of the Mohammedan operator sounds a fervent hissing curse, as all who have heard it know. Besides a good many rams and goats, the Amér had two young camels killed to be given to our Bedawi followers and the poor. They were killed at the east end of the village, where a level square space of about half an acre had been set aside for butchering, with a deep trench dug round it for the blood. Here the greater number of the pilgrims brought their animals to be killed, as most of the flocks were stationed at that end of the village. The mode of killing the camels was this: The animal was made to kneel down close up to the trench, and its legs were then tied in a position which made it absolutely incapable of moving them. One man then held out the head, and another drew a short knife, like a sailor's sheath-knife, round the neck, close up to the shoulders, then a rotation of the head and the neck falls, severed clean from the body. The cutting up is done without moving the carcase, the skin being opened down the centre of the back. This work went on actively all through the day.

We also on this day got rid of the first twenty-one of our stones, seven of them being thrown at each of three places in the village. The first place is at the eastern extremity, and is a small obelisk about nine feet high, with a low circular wall round the base, inside which the stones fall after striking the obelisk. The second is in the middle of the village, like the first, but rather larger. The last is at the west end of the village. This is a high stone wall on the right-hand side of the road looking west, and a particular stone in this is the object to be hit.

It was very difficult to get near them on account of the crowd. Many pilgrims less robust than others had to throw their stones from a distance over the heads of those in front, making very wide shots. This rite is to commemorate Abraham's stoning the devil at the advice of the Angel Gabriel, when tempted by Satan at these three places. We repeated this throwing of stones on each of the two next days. I estimated that about three tons of shingle ballast had been deposited in the receptacles round the bases of the obelisks before I left Muna. These must be cleared out every year, or they would be filled in a couple of pilgrimages. The popular belief is that they are conveyed back to Muzdalifah by angels.

Little occurred specially worthy of remark during the rest of our stay in Muna, except that we revelled in butcher's meat, of which hundreds of carcases were wasted, while gorged vultures could scarcely flounder out of your way, and flies became a great nuisance. Water was very dear, having to be brought some distance to the village.

CHAPTER VII.

IN MECCAH AFTER THE PILGRIMAGE.

On the fourth day after the pilgrimage we returned to our old quarters in the walls of the Haram, and next day early I set out to look for—LODGINGS. As I wended my way among turbaned and scymitared Syrians, Parthians, Moguls, and Arabians, I began to think it must have been a dream, and when I came to the place and saw the veritable notice, I was almost as much surprised as on my first meeting it. There was a little tobacco-shop opposite the house, to which I went and began making small purchases, getting up a dispute about the change of a rupee, at the same time taking stock of the premises opposite, for I fought rather shy of the place. I had just come to an amicable conclusion about my change, purposely making a mistake on the right side for the shopkeeper to put him in a good humour, and was asking him who lived in the house over the way, when a tall heavily-built man, whom I at first took for a fair-skinned Arab, slouched out of the door and came straight over to the shop, whistling merrily. That was enough.

"Good morning," said I.

"Well, I be d——. Do you speak English?"

"Yes."

"Good morning."

We stood for some moments looking at one another, and I thought I had taken the fellow's measure to be the right sort, and was just on the point of opening out and declaring myself when he said:

"You are not an Englishman, are you?" with a gravity that gave me my cue.

I replied in the vilest Che-che* I could muster, "Oh yes, I am Englishman. I am speaking the English very well."

This and a happy unconscious air banished any suspicions of such a possibility he might have had for the moment. Though he said: "Englishmen turn Mohammedan and come here and see what

* Half-caste Indian.

we do, and go back and write books. There are three here now with iron collars round their necks chained among the hills."

I did not tell him I thought that was a lie. He walked about with me the greater part of the morning, I talking broken English to him. He was a Cape of Good Hope Malay, one of an English-speaking Mohammedan community, who yearly send their half-dozen pilgrims to Meccah. He had been living some years in Meccah, and said his people had been very ill-treated when they began to come the pilgrimage. The authorities had only allowed them to live in Meccah on condition that they spoke no other language than Arabic, of which few of them knew the meaning of more than a dozen words. If an Arab had heard them speaking any other language, he was at liberty to beat them, and they dared not retaliate. This was in the days of a strict old Pacha of the good old school, who had administered the law of the Koran to the letter.

In evidence of this he pointed out to me what a number of beggars were to be seen minus a hand or a foot, the result of the said old Pacha's summary justice. This lopping-off of limbs is a great idea, by degrees practically incapacitating the old offender.

However, such severity is seldom resorted to under the present milder *régime.* The Cape Malays have now outlived all prejudice, and my new friend told me that he was very comfortable in Meccah and making money. He had in his youth been to an English school, could read and write English well, and he confessed he missed his beer and potatoes. He then began to inquire into my antecedents and what I was doing. I told him I was the servant of a rich Hindi, giving him a wrong name, for the fellow knew a great deal too much to be pleasant company, and the worst Mohammedans at heart often for appearance' sake act as the most bigoted and truculent where there is no danger to themselves.

So to get rid of my friend I put in practice a dodge I had never found to fail—begging. I began by guessing the value of his watch-chain very high, admiring his rings, and flattering him up into a little Crœsus. I then, in contrast, represented my own poverty and dependent position. After this it did not require great 'cuteness in an Eastern to see what was coming. He recollected he had business to attend to, and went off suddenly, with a hasty "Upon you be peace."

I saw him several times after, but he never granted me an interview long enough to allow of my following up our last conversation. On one occasion he told me he had lately imported a sewing-machine, which some Moulahs had viewed and declared to be the invention of an English devil, and he wanted to know whether I could put him up to a likely purchaser.

On this day the Kaabah was opened for those who had not been in Meccah during the Ramazan, and the Haram was crowded. Every part of Meccah was always crowded. I might have given you to understand this at the beginning of my story, and that when I ever did come upon a part of Meccah that was not crowded, I should mention that remarkable circumstance; however, as it is, the reader must understand that when I say crowded, I mean crowded.

Every part of the Haram was crowded with men, but no women, as the Kaabah was to be opened for them on the following day. It took me two hours to force my way up to the steps to await my turn, for the pilgrims were let in by parties, the steps being wheeled up to the door and drawn away by the eunuchs of the Haram, who laid about them with their sticks as we pressed for admission. At last I got in. There is no opening into the chamber but the door into which

I was carried in the rush. The heat was intense, the atmosphere unendurable. I instantly plunged my way out as a man struggles to the surface after a dangerous dive. Inside I had just time to give a good look round and glance up. Nobody is supposed to look up while in this chamber. You are told that the only man who ever did so was struck blind. All that could be seen—for the place was very dark—were the red hangings of the walls and ceiling embroidered in gold, and the three pillars supporting the flat roof, between which a number of dim lamps hung suspended from metal cross-bars.

On the day on which the women were admitted I heard the Arab cheer to great perfection. This is given by the women, or sometimes by boys. It was often repeated by hundreds of voices all through this day. They give a prolonged cry in a rather high note, with the right thumb inserted in the left cheek, which they shake rapidly; or a vibration is given to the cry by means of the tongue. Some of the women seemed almost to warble in their throats, giving to the cry a tinkling sound which was really musical.

Then came my meeting with the "Lady Venus." This time we had arranged that she should, after the noonday prayer, walk backwards and forwards in the arcade under my window, where I was to sit and look out till we recognised one another. This was easily managed, and I went off under her guidance. The crowd was so great that we were able to keep close together without appearing to be in company till near the shop of a Hindi binder of Korans, where she told me to wait while she went in. After waiting a few minutes a little child came up to me and invited me into the shop, leading me through to a small room at the back, where I found her sitting alone: the child then left us to ourselves. We talked for a short time about our lucky meeting at Muna, about her health, which had been very bad during the last year, almost as bad as on her first coming to Meccah many years ago (I think she said twenty). She threw her veil back and exposed her face for some time—a scandalous impropriety, which if witnessed by anyone, the least I could have done would have been to declare her my wife on the spot. I had time to observe her features closely. She was rather short, and appeared about forty. She must have been good-looking in her youth, nor was she by any means ill-favoured now. She looked healthy, all things considered. Though her complexion was somewhat sallow, her skin was fair. She had an animated and pleasing expression. I can at this moment see her in my mind as distinctly as if she were before me in the flesh—the same sad, indulgent smile with which she greeted my little attempts at Anglo-Arabic jokes, saying: "Speak English, child."

I really felt the deepest pity for her, an Englishwoman existing in the way she had been doing for years; and I must confess to a very soft moment when I saw the poor creature smiling, with her eyes brimful of tears before giving way and having a good cry, which relieved her. I had found in our very first *tête-à-tête* that any reference to her past had a painful effect, and hesitated to broach the subject, and so began to tell her about myself, my *christian* name, why I had come to Meccah, and the like, in the hope of getting her to give some such account of herself, when a noise outside made her draw her veil, and a boy entered with some tea and sweetmeats sent by her friend the master of the house. This took our attention for the moment, and we both had tea, and I asked the boy to get me a smoke: first, because I wanted a smoke; secondly, because when I had done, returning the hookah would be a good excuse for going out of the room and having a look round. This little interruption over, I asked her if she knew the Cape people. She said she had made friends with some of their women a year or two before, and had sent letters by them to the Cape to a relation whom she had seen there on her way out to India, and whose address she remembered, but had heard nothing of it since.

Having brought her to talk about herself, I now kept her at it, and pumped her as dry as I could, but it was very hard work. As well as my memory serves me, she told me that her name was "Macintosh," her father a doctor, and that she had lived in Devonshire in her youth, that she was at Lucknow at the time of the siege, and had been taken from there by a leading rebel. She avoided going into particulars, so that I did not ascertain whether she went willingly or as a captive. She said she had lived a year or so in India with this man, and that he had been hunted out of the country by the English, who set a price on his head, and had found refuge in Meccah, taking her with him; that he had died eight years before, leaving her in poverty, and that she now made a living by embroidering skull-caps, which she sold to the dealers in the bazaars.

A rich Hindi merchant, who occasionally received

letters written in English from his son, who was managing his business for him in India, and knew that he could get them translated by her, gave her a little room in his zenana-house to herself. All this I got from her only in replies to my persistent questioning, till at last I was obliged to desist out of pure compassion, she seemed so cowed and bullied, and was getting quite incoherent. After this I got her to repeat a few chapters of the Koran, pretending I wanted to learn the Meccah accent, so interesting her. I found, besides Hindustani, she could speak and read Persian and Arabic, though not Turkish. She regretted she was not in a position to be acquainted with any Turks, for whom she seemed to have some respect. She mentioned the names of a number of men living in Meccah who she said had been rebels or mutineers, also telling me the prices set on their heads by the English Government, and appeared perfectly up in everything connected with the siege and relief of Lucknow. She also let drop that a young Frenchman had lived eighteen months in Meccah, and had died about six months before my arrival. I asked her what he died of. To which she replied in Hindustani, with the usual "God knows; God giveth and God taketh away. Blessed be the name of the Lord." And then told me the following story:

"That about two years before a young Frenchman had come to Meccah with whom she became very intimate, and had often seen him just as she was now seeing me. He had told her that he was a Mohammedan from conviction, and that he had at first gone to Constantinople to live, but that his father, who was very wealthy, had made such efforts to get him back that he was obliged to remove to Cairo. Here he was again found out by his friends, who did everything that money and influence could do to make him return to Christianity. He seems to have been a mere lad, for some attempt was made to get him off from here by force to France; however he escaped and fled to another place in Egypt, where he was again hunted out by his friends, who drove him to Meccah as a last refuge from them. It must have been 'preserve me from my friends' with him, poor fellow! In Meccah he took service in the house of a wealthy Turk, and was thought a very clever youth, 'learned in all the learning of the Egyptians,' so much so that he was looked upon with great jealousy by the Moulahs (most likely on account of the peculiar views he would be likely to have held), and, as the 'Lady Venus' said, 'made many enemies.' He repudiated the Frenchman, always calling himself a Turk."

I asked if he was known to be a Frenchman, and she replied:

"He was a True Believer," implying that beyond that nobody knew or cared what he might be.

She laid great stress on his extensive reading and the fluency with which he spoke Turkish and Arabic, and on the fact of his being well known and much disliked by a certain set who made it so hot for him that he was on the point of going away, and had seen and said good-bye to her when he suddenly died, and she had no doubt but that there had been foul play, darkly hinting at a cup of coffee.

This was the sum of all I heard from the "Lady Venus" on this our longest interview. On parting she pointed out to me a peculiarity in the make of the upper part of her veil by which I might distinguish her from any other woman, and we appointed a rendezvous in the Haram, where we could meet on any day at a certain hour, in order that we might see as much of one another as possible, and that I might consult her about my prospects of getting away; for I was becoming very sick of hearing every day of ships leaving Jeddah, only a matter of some forty odd miles off, yet seeming to be almost in another world—ships I knew well, and whose officers were old shipmates. Often when I with difficulty recognised under the disguise of Arab mispronunciation the mutilated name of some well-known old craft, and pictured to myself scenes "so near and yet so far," in which iced beer and table-napkins figured prominently, I would have given five years of my life for a few dollars to carry me over the little strip of desert to Christianity and cleanliness. The "Lady Venus" could not help me, and there was nothing for it but to wait with my eyes open. Sometimes I would think of "humping my swag,"* taking the road for it in the true "turnpike-sailor" style; but the Hejaz is not the Colonies, and a "sundowner"† here runs the risk of being potted at from behind every rock, as a Bedawi would not think of letting a solitary wayfarer pass without at least the little attention of a casual snapshot; not that he would hit or expect to hit, but then nothing is impossible, and though the boast of the Hejaz Bedawi is that he never robs a

* (Colonial) Shouldering my kit.

† Colonial name for a tramp; so called, from their way of going from farm to farm, timing it so as to arrive at sundown, in order to ensure a supper and bed.

living True Believer, he has a knack of asking said True Believer to give him something, at the same time playing the curved point of a short sharp sword about the pit of his stomach in a way that generally influences even a True Believer to be charitable; or should he prove ungenerous, our Bedawi has not the slightest hesitation about stripping him *dead*, and, to insure his not feeling deprived, generally makes his children with careful kindness relieve him of his head and hands. Also my position with the Amér, though solid enough at present, might have been very delicate had I shown any wish to desert him or failed in an attempt to do so. No! I decided that as I had a whole skin as yet, it would be a pity to risk it when I might do better by waiting.

I think it was on the eighth day after the pilgrimage that the inundation occurred. Such a flood had not visited Meccah for seventeen years, on which occasion the water had risen seven feet in the Haram. This time the day opened very black indeed to the eastward, the clouds having a sandy, smoky appearance I had noticed before on one or two occasions when it had been followed by a heavy downpour of rain. These black days were very marked as a great and sudden change from the usual blue clearness of the sky. It did not begin to rain in Meccah till about eleven A.M., though it must have been raining for some time towards Muna and Arafat, for the stream from there into the valley of Meccah had overflowed, and already the streets at the east end and in the centre of the city were flooded with several inches of water. Still no serious inundation was anticipated, the flooding of the streets being the usual result of an ordinary shower, and the stalls in the bazaars stood at the sides of streets, down the centre of which people were wading in little torrents.

As soon as it began to rain I returned to the house, and saw through the window that it shortly after set in to blow hard from the east, accompanied by heavy tropical rain—not exceptionally heavy for the tropics, but much harder than would be likely to be seen out of them. As the rain continued, all our people and a number of friends not belonging to our party, dripping wet, came in for shelter and filled our two rooms. In the Haram a few inches of water quickly gathered, and the attendants were employed, as I had often seen them before, in keeping the pavement round the Kaabah clear by sweeping the water down large holes in the pavement.

Another hour, and the rain still continued to come down as hard as ever, the wind blowing half a hurricane, flapping and bellying out the cover of the Kaabah as though it would blow it away, which it certainly would have done had it not been new. At this time the Amér sent some of his under servants out to try and get a little of the water that flowed off the Kaabah for us to drink, and, as they went in and out, they told us that the water was rising rapidly in the streets, and shortly afterwards came in and said it would soon be flowing into the Haram.

Some of us went out to see; I among the rest. The water had risen so suddenly and unexpectedly that there had been no time for the most ordinary precautions. Those who had seen it said it had come in like a wave from the direction of Muna; if so, and it had passed over the scene of the late slaughter, it must now be simply a poisoned flood. It was now flowing in turbid muddy streams, three or four feet deep, down all the streets.

Across every entrance to the Haram there is a raised stone parapet, apparently built for the purpose of keeping the water out during these floods. I took my stand on one of these and watched the strong steady stream flowing past laden with the floating wreck of the bazaars, cages of fowls, all kinds of fruit, flocks of bread loaves, empty baskets, the legs and tops of wooden stalls, dogs swimming about, and being forced whining back wherever they attempted to land, Negroes and Arabs standing in the stream seizing whatever was best worth picking up as it floated past.

Most of the shops were already flooded, and the water had risen so quickly that there had not been time to remove much of the stock, which was being floated out into the stream, the owners piling it back manfully. Such of the shops as were not already flooded were crowded by as many as could find standing room, as were all steps and isolated dry points.

The depth and strength of the stream continued to increase visibly, and it became a business of swimming for those who plunged in after salvage. The flood had not yet reached the Haram, where thousands had taken refuge and shelter under the arcades, but in a few minutes the water trickled under our feet down into the Haram behind us.

The larger gates of the Haram were now shut, but these had little doors in them which were left open till the rush of water became so strong that it was found impossible to close some of them. This was about noon. I then went into the house out of the storm, put on dry clothes, and spent the rest of the day looking out of the window.

The rain showed no signs of easing, and the wind continued to blow with great violence, and in the same direction. The water was rushing into the Haram at every gate, the badly-made and loosely-jointed doors scarcely offering any obstruction and merely filtering it of the coarser *débris*. At this time a sailor might have described the Haram as taking in green seas fore and aft, except that the water was bright pea-soup colour.

About two P.M. the wind suddenly shifted to the west, taking the cover of the Kaabah "flat aback," only giving it time for a couple of tremendous flaps and bangs before it settled into fluttering and bellying in the opposite direction. It continued to rain and the water to flow in until about three P.M., when the wind fell away with a few parting gusts, and the rain took off with one or two parting gushes of large drops.

After this, the water ceased to rise in the Haram, and stopped flowing in from the outside very quickly. During the whole storm pilgrims had been performing the tawaf and kissing the Black Stone in greater numbers than usual at this time of the day, and now, when the water was at its highest and the Black Stone immersed, many continued to swim round the Kaabah, and put their heads under to kiss the stone. The temperature throughout the storm was uniformly cool, though not more than normally so, and it only remained overcast until sunset, the storm passing away to the north.*

The whole of the large square was now turned into a lake, the water lying about three feet deep in the western arcades, six feet round the Kaabah, and a few inches in the eastern arcades, showing that though the square looked a plain when dry, it was considerably inclined in these directions.

---

* Notwithstanding that storms of this nature are rare in the neighbouring sea, erratic whirlwinds of any dimensions are daily occurrences in the Hejaz. The one above described, however, will have been seen to have been a true rotatory storm of moderate cyclonic violence; and acting on the known laws it travelled up from the south-east in an indirect course, at varying slow rates, averaging about four or five miles an hour, which would give it a diameter of some twenty miles.

There was great rejoicing among us when the water ceased to rise, for it was beginning to be feared that it would put out the lamps as it had done in the last great flood; and this is looked upon as unfortunate or ominous in some way. The water subsided almost as quickly as it had risen; by the time of sunset prayer it had retreated from the arcades on the three higher sides of the square, and at the evening prayer (nine P.M.) there remained only a couple of feet of water near the Kaabah, and the arcades were left dry all round.

The next morning opened with an azure firmament, and when we got up for early prayer there was hardly a pint-pool of water to be found at the surface anywhere in Meccah; but in every place where the water had been it had left a layer of about six inches of tough springy earth, cutting like clay—in many places it was much thicker: round the Kaabah this deposit was eighteen inches deep. In the morning before the traffic began the lumpy uneven roads looked smooth and clear as though freshly laid with asphalt, and the whole square of the Haram like a sandy beach at low water. It was pleasant to the bare feet—soft and smooth. I did the tawaf several times that morning at a good run—sharper exercise than I had taken for many a day. I had a walk after daybreak in the streets, which were soon trodden slushy, for though the layer of earth left by the flood was pretty firm at first, there was a good deal of water in it, and the feet of the passengers soon kneaded it into a tenacious black mud, from which the beggars and passers-by unearthed all kinds of little articles of property. Here and there the leg of a drowned dog protruded, perhaps side by side with a prettily-worked broken cane basket, or a squashed melon. It was curious to reflect what a number of strange odds and ends must have been buried side by side under that layer of mud, the productions of almost any age or state of art, from a piece of worked gun-flint or Bedawi pottery to a four-bladed penknife, perhaps in some future age to be brought to light together in bewildering variety. Three old tottering ruins in the east end of the town had received the last shake to their foundations and fallen, killing, I was surprised to hear, only four persons. I heard of no other human lives being lost directly from the inundation. Much destruction must have been done to all damageable property on the ground-floors throughout the lower arch of the valley, still I heard very little complaint about losses except from the beggars and people who had nothing to lose; these of course made a great pretext of the flood.

Next day the bazaars looked the old style, and business flourished as if nothing had happened. With their "all's-for-the-best" indifference to fate, these people barely made the events of the previous day the subject of a morning call's gossip. The mud defiling the Haram was another matter though, and great numbers of volunteers were soon at work removing it, many of the wealthiest pilgrims carrying baskets or fishing-mattocks, together with working-parties of soldiers from the barracks. In spite of the great supply of labour it took three days to clear it all out, and place it in the streets in the immediate vicinity in large heaps blocking up the way, till the mounds were trodden out and hardened down, still leaving some of the roads so hummocky and uneven that camels could not travel before the soldiers had done a little towards levelling off the tops of the steepest hillocks; for notwithstanding the soft, I was going to say catlike, feet of the camel, it can neither go up nor down a very steep hill.

For many days after the flood the water in all the

wells was brown and muddy, and if left standing all night would not be more than half settled in the morning. The taste of all the wells was altered, the ordinary water tasting like Zem Zem, and the Zem Zem itself much weakened. For a couple of days there was some moisture in the air, and bread left on a shelf uncovered for a few hours did *not* appear to have undergone a second baking, and have a metallic ring from hardness. The worst result of the flood was the great amount of sickness that prevailed after it; cholera, small-pox, and typhus epidemics broke out and raged wildly together for about three weeks.

Mohammedan burial rites differ a good deal in different countries, and of course vary with circumstances—from the dancing howling wakes of Egypt and Syria, to the mere laying of the body straight and placing a few stones over it in the desert. In Meccah it is usual to take the bier to a part of the Haram near Abraham's Stone, so that the soul may pass out of it through the door of the Kaabah, and the noonday prayer is recited by the Imam before interment of the body under a few bushes and a couple of feet of earth, with its face towards the Kaabah. A coffin is never used by Mohammedans, though voluminous swathings and wrappings are, the grave-clothes being sometimes made of fine material, white being the common mourning colour.

Within three days after the flood I noticed the number of funerals increasing; and at one time, about ten days after, the quantity passing through the Haram was so great as to form almost a continuous procession for an hour before noon. One day I counted sixty-three funerals.

No idea can be formed from this of the number of deaths which really occurred daily, as probably by far the greater majority of those who died had no friends, or were not thought worth the trouble of carrying to the Kaabah on the way to the burial-ground. Men in the agonies of cholera might frequently be seen lying at the sides of the streets, and never a good Samaritan went near them. Small-pox and typhus cases, in all stages of the diseases, walked about in public, almost arm-in-arm, no one avoiding or seeming to think it the least out of the way. In one house I visited there were eight small-pox cases down at the same time, of which five died, and yet five other healthy men continued to eat and sleep in the same room!

If there is any foundation at all for our English notion about contagion, how Meccah escaped decimation does seem a miracle. Somehow I did not apprehend anything myself; I don't know why exactly, but I had not the slightest fear, though I certainly expected some of our party to be laid up, so many of us being crowded into the two rooms, which had become revoltingly filthy. Still, though we moved about amidst infected localities and among infected people in the most reckless manner, none of us were taken seriously ill. This was attributed to the Amér's energetic precautions, he having, regardless of expense, provided his whole household with a new and infallible charm. I wore mine round my neck till it got entangled with my beads, so I broke the string and threw it away, first opening it out to see what it was made of. It was a ball of bees'-wax, about the size of a No. 12 bullet, with a little pellet of paper inside on which something had been written; but it was now so crumpled and torn I could make nothing of it. The run on the graveyards soon began to take the pilgrims off, and the town was getting less crowded, the pilgrims leaving by thousands; and we now began to make our preparations for starting with the first caravan to Medinah.

I met the "Lady Venus" three or four times in

the Haram, and had conversations with her for intervals varying from the mere exchange of a few words during a moment's opportunity to a ten minutes' talk walking together under the arcades. Once she asked me if I had a book or any English printing to give her, saying she had part of an old almanac, ever so many years old, which she had come across in Meccah, and hoarded up ever since to read. One day she showed me her much-thumbed treasure—only five pages, one month on each page. I did not notice the year, but saw the sort of thing it was—"Coronation Day," "Battle of Waterloo," etc. etc., and then returned it to her carefully, telling her that it was not bad reading under the circumstances, though it did occur to me how she would value a more substantial and interesting volume, poor beggar! I wrote in English my christian-name and address in England on a little bit of blue paper and gave it to her, and heard her read it straight off. I told her if she wrote a letter and could get any returning pilgrim to give it to an English officer in one of the ships, it would be sure to be forwarded. She had little hopes of being able to find anyone she could trust, or who would be likely to do such a thing even if they promised. The last time but one that I met her she was very queer, slightly hysterical I thought. She kept repeating: "Ah, child! you don't know what it is to me to see you," and then, "I would not hurt you," "I would not do you any harm," stopping me and catching hold of my arm as we walked along so excitedly that I expected a scene every moment: certainly in London the expression of half such emotion would have found us the centre of an admiring throng. I looked as unconcerned as I could, talking in Arabic to her and trying to calm her; till at last I lost my temper, and said: "Do you want to raise a row?" and then told her that I should meet her on the day of my leaving for Medinah, if she would keep cool and find a place where we could be alone. I then hurried home, for I had distinctly heard a sly-looking Arab make use of the nasty word—Christian.

In view of our desert journey to Medinah, the Amér began to curtail his retinue: he disbanded quite a little army of spongers and loafers, who had attached themselves to us on one pretence or another. These hangers-on were very useful, always ready to oblige or do any little thing, getting in return only what they could beg or steal, which is not much really. However, they have an innocent weakness for new boots, which they have a somewhat inconvenient habit of mistaking for their own, often accidentally slipping their feet into the best pair on the threshold (where all the boots are left) when they go out of the house. My boots seemed to be especially coveted by them. I lost a couple of pairs a very short time after I came to Meccah. If that sort of thing had gone on it would have been disastrous, so I was obliged in self-defence, whenever my boots were changed, to put on the old pair left, make a call where I knew there would be a crowded "At home," leave early, and mistake some other gentleman's boots for the ones I came in. In this way I seldom went about in the same pair for more than a fortnight. They were loose red leather slippers, turned up at the toes and worn down at the heel, and there was no difficulty about the matter of fitting if they were only big enough. I gave up the sandals I had at first taken to, as my feet got so dirty, and would soon have been so deformed that I should have found it difficult to return to European boots.

I had some hopes about this time that the Amér would give me "the sack" and a few dollars, as he was doing with others, and indeed I did not think it at all unlikely, as he seemed to have forgotten my existence since our return from Arafat, and I had kept a good deal out of the way, merely coming in to eat and sleep, neither making myself useful nor amusing. Some of my companions, too, had got hold of a story that I had been trying to join the Sultan's army. The fact was that a fanatic Moulah had raised a band of about four hundred men to go to Turkey and fight the Russians, by preaching a jehad and proclaiming that miracles would be performed for us if we fought with swords only, and gave up our lives with proper cheerfulness; and I had secretly enrolled myself under the good Moulah in the hope of getting away with him. But as the Turkish authorities discountenanced all this sort of thing, and as the Moulah met with only half-hearted encouragement from the pilgrims, the scheme fell through for want of funds to carry us to the far-off scene of action. I was told that on the outbreak of war between Turkey and Russia, the Pacha of Meccah had made a call for volunteers, which had been responded to by thirty thousand untrained men. They were all immediately put into training, when orders were received from Constantinople to tell them that the Sultan was grateful for their offer, and would not ask them to endanger their lives, but that any little trifle from their purses would be most acceptable: I suspect this call was not so readily responded to. I believe some rumour of Turkish reverses must have got abroad to cause this second war fever, which appeared just after the pilgrimage, though the only talk I ever heard about it was the everlasting "By the help of God the Sultan wins," and no further interest seemed to be taken in the matter.

Well, I let this story of my wanting to enlist pass without contradiction, as a sort of feeler to see how the Amér would like it (I never knew whether he heard it or not, but think he must). I then invalided. I had noticed all my companions took turns at a rest, pretending to be suffering from what they called "cold fever," another term for an opium booze. It would not have done for me to take opium, the symptoms were too well known to my companions, and so to make myself thoroughly useless, I had to get a "cold fever" which they could not cure. I lay on my blanket, got off my feed, and did *not* sleep all day and say *good* when every one else said *bad.* The giving up of my regular meals made no great difference to me, as I had lately become so tired of the dietary that I could eat nothing with pleasure, and felt a craving for a slice of white bread or salt beef almost as badly as the gnawings of real starvation.

In the meantime our preparations for the road were going on in earnest, making immense tins of sweetmeats (at which I would not assist), cleaning and burnishing up of arms. How those niggers and their arms did tease me, to be sure! Four months before their humanlike movements might have amused me; and now, when the Amér struggled the bayonet on to the end of the rifle, and displayed his skill in the use of it by making swinging slashes at an imaginary adversary in the top of a cocoa-nut tree or in a balloon, if I had not been able to resist a very powerful impulse, I should have jumped up, whipped the rifle out of his paws, clubbed him with the butt till he made a new joke, and forced all the rest to sing "God save the Queen" at the point of the bayonet. I suppose it was because I knew that if I had offered to explain that five rounds in fifteen minutes was not consid (c sharp practice with the Martini-Henri, I should have been told I knew nothing about it, and the Amér would have condescended to explain the action of the breech in this "invention of the Sultan of Turkey's for the benefit of the Russians!" as he called it.

I had been living so long with these people as one of them, that I had actually come down to being annoyed by the airs of a nigger. It's time I was out of this, I thought, and no mistake.

Their own weapons are murderously dangerous to look at, and ingeniously harmless to use. Take the swords for instance.* The blades are so much curved, and so badly balanced, that in real work it would require half your attention to prevent them turning in the hand. The hilts are like old-fashioned brass door-knobs, or paper-cutter handles, about large enough to admit of being grasped with three fingers on a pinch, and the idea of giving points has yet to occur to the mind of an Eastern swordsman. For all the rest of our impossible

* Only Indian swords, as some of the Persian swords, might be trusted for work.

armoury, a similar collection may be seen in any museum of antiquities.

The only one worth description here is the Arab knife or jambiyah, with one of which most of our people had provided themselves. Jambiyahs are slightly different in make in different parts of Arabia, and are known by the names of the places that most affect the particular shape. The Meccah jambiyah is the broadest and most bent; the Mascat jambiyah is nearly straight, and about half as broad as the Meccan. The iron of the jambiyah is exceedingly soft, and sharpened by beating out the edge cold on a small anvil, shaped for this purpose only, the sharpening of jambiyah being a trade of itself. This gives the best edge I know for severing skin and hair, though of course when applied to anything hard it instantly disappears. With a newly-sharpened jambiyah a rolled-up sheepskin may be divided at one stroke.

At this time if a gunlock was out of order, I would not mend it; for though systematically snubbed for my general ignorance, I had established a bit of a reputation as a mechanic. I was too sick to pray, or if I did, I would only perform the "jumo," that is, going through the motions of the ablution without water, which is allowable to the very sick, or when there is no water to be had. I lay on my blanket night and day, scarcely speaking to anyone, but taking in everything going on around me most keenly. Tales of robbery and bloodshed committed by the Bedawin were being brought in every day by kind friends who were not going with us, and long stories of past adventures in the desert would be recounted by comforters who dropped in to cheer us up, generally putting the Amér into half-an-hour's passionate weeping and praying, to pass off in a second when "Shaykh the Bow'sen" (the same who had conducted us to Arafat) appeared on the scene, to bargain and arrange about the number of camels we should require; then the Amér and all his uncles and relations composing his suite would smile, cajole and "brother" the Shaykh, to whose tender mercies they were going to entrust themselves for a month in the desert, only to curse and abuse him and all "Shaitan" Bedawin after he was gone.

Some of our people, the "first warrior" among them, "funked" the Medinah journey altogether, and set to work to persuade the Amér that the best thing he could do would be to send them home to Hind with the bulk of his purchases and all the baggage he was unable to carry across the desert with him, and, above all, that his letters home might be carried by safe hands. This settled it, and he decided to let them go. I could quite understand his anxiety to communicate with his friends, for he and all his party most fully realised the dangers of their next undertaking, even I—who certainly did not, being very sceptical as to the amount of peril, putting down the Hindi exaggerated accounts for what I thought they were worth—would have liked to have left some traces behind me before starting three hundred miles into Arabia.

As soon as these last arrangements of the Amér were settled I put on foot another scheme, which promised to answer perfectly. I told the "first warrior" that if the Amér proposed retaining my services, I should like to go at once to Hind to the Amér's home and wait there without wages till his return; but that when he did come back I should insist on pay beginning. I explained that though the hope of my life was to perform the meritorious pilgrimage to the tomb of the Prophet of God, I was now so sick that I should only be an encumbrance to the Amér if I went with him.

As I expected, this came at once to the Amér's ears, and he called me to him the same evening and asked me whether I would prefer to go to Medinah or return to Hind. It would not have done to have appeared too anxious; so, after stating whys and wherefores, I asked him to allow me not to decide till the day before starting, when finally the number of camels required was to be fixed, and when I hoped, please God, to be well enough to go with him to "Medinah the Honoured;" if not, then God is great, and I am ill-fated. "Good! Go," said the Amér, and I already almost fancied myself eating ham and eggs in the Bombay Sailors' Home.

When the day for giving my answer came, I told the Amér that I was worse, "my blood was dry," "my brains were wet," "my stomach twisted," and "I was not as strong as a chicken;" but by the help of God, once at his honour's house, the "Diamond Gate," its world-famed air and water would soon restore me; "Meccah the fortunate" was undoubtedly heaven-sent, "its waters!"—here raptures; "its climate!"—here outbursts of admiration. Still I declared I was afraid I was too bad a sinner to derive full benefit from these great gifts, and my own poor climate of Hind would suit me better. He soon cut my blarney short with, "Good, you shall go to the 'Diamond Gate;'" and I had to sustain my part by expressing proper grief and having to be forced back to my blanket greatly excited.

Next day by noon the Amér and all his party had gone to a place outside Meccah, "Waddy Fatima," where the Medinah caravan was to assemble before starting. There had been most gushing partings between us—we that were going back to Hind had innumerable messages to kith and kin given us to take. I felt I was parting with them never to see any of them again most likely, and they believed in me, so that I must say I felt a certain amount of regret. I was sorry to lose the "third warrior," with whom I had really struck up a friendship. We were to start the same evening for Jeddah. I soon tied up my bundle, which was not a very big one, and now as I might consider myself booked, I thought there would be no harm in going out to make a few little purchases of relics and other reminders of Meccah, as my companions had done; this is what I told the "first warrior," but I of course went at once to the Haram to meet the "Lady Venus," as I had appointed with her. I had not been sitting long when she came up to me, and we went off together as we had done on other occasions. This time we walked about two miles into the country on the Muna road, to the house of an Arab; here she went in, and shortly after came out and told me that the man had disappointed her and was not at home, and as there were only women inside I could not be admitted. This was a disappointment, and poor "Lady Venus" was extremely sorry; however, we walked about together among the hills, always walking fast, as if we were going somewhere, and had a talk. I told her how I had worked it, and the luck I had met in getting away on that day, and I asked her point-blank, "If I come back for you will you go to England with me?" to which she replied "Yes," much in the same tone as the little boy answered the lady who asked him, "Could you eat a bun?" I said to her, "You, understanding so many languages, could easily make a living in England," and I mentioned the "Asiatic Home," not that I knew anything about it, but it occurred to me at the moment as a place where she would be likely to find work. I also told her that there were many rich people in England who would, if they knew of her existence, soon provide money or means of getting her released. To this she replied :

"How you talk!" (events have shown how I did talk, to be sure! Yes, I am afraid I was a great deal too hopeful), and so on; I promising her she would be in England in less than a year, and she very much doubting the chances of such a thing till we got back to the Haram, when she again became as excited as on our last meeting, and behaved so foolishly that (I am ashamed to say it) I doubted her for a moment and remembered the fate of the poor Frenchman. Three times I said "With you be peace" and left her, but she followed me to the gate of the Haram, and I had to go back and speak to her and tell her that people were noticing her strange conduct. The last time I went back I led her to the opposite side of the Haram, and then said "Good-bye" and ran out of one of the near gates. As I passed out I looked out and saw her sitting down against one of the pillars and a number of children standing round looking at her. This was the last time I saw the "Lady Venus."

As soon as I reached our house and passed in through the outer door, I heard the "first warrior" in the inner room protesting loudly that something was not at all "the cheese," and then met "Shaykh the Bow'sen," coming out, who told me he had brought a letter from the Amér recalling the "first warrior" and myself to go with him to Medinah. In half an hour more the letter would have been too late. The first thing I did was to run back to where I had left the "Lady Venus" to tell her what had happened and see if she could not help me. When I got to the place where I had last seen her she was gone. I looked out in the crowded street and could see nothing of her. What was I to do now? My chance of getting away knocked on the head at the last moment by the whim of a nigger! I was savage. A good rule for a man who smokes is, whenever bothered, take a pipe. I went across the street to a little coffee-shop, called for a chillam, and sat down to consider. At the third whiff I found myself laughing at my own awkward fix, and by the time I had finished my smoke I had fully decided to start that night for Jeddah and run with the donkeys. Arabs did it, and why should not I?—though I certainly was not in good form for fifty miles in twelve hours. I then went into the Haram and walked round the square and changed my mind. I should like to see the tomb of Mohammed, I thought, and two months more of this would not kill me, and then I changed my mind again, felt how sick I was of it, and thought I had seen sights enough for one while. Jeddah or nowhere !

When I got to the gates of the Haram nearest to our house I took out my little bag, which I kept hung round my neck, to look at my money, one dollar four piastres: the sight of the dollar determined me. Bird for Jeddah—Christianity, cleanliness, and something to eat; cap for Medinah—the tomb of Mohammed and discomfort the worst. Up went the dollar—cap—there was no getting out of it. Oh ! twice out of three times, of course ; up again—bird. The people about must have thought me mad. I moved off a short distance, dropped my dollar on the pavement and picked it up—cap. Medinah it is.

And now, reader, I must take my leave of you for the present. The rest of my career in the Hejaz became one of such incredible adventure that I hesitate to publish an account of it ; but should the reception of my present effort encourage me to do so, I can promise to put before you a narrative of hairbreadth escapes and strange incidents which appear marvellous even to me, who has lived a life of the wildest adventure from the age of twelve to twenty-five in every quarter of the globe.

CONCLUSION.

"THE LADY VENUS."

I HAVE been withholding my MS. from the publisher for the last eight months in the hope of being able to add, in conclusion, the story of the "Lady Venus;" or, at least, to be able to assure the reader of her release. But I now find that there is no likelihood of her story ever being divulged, which is to be regretted, as it cannot but be one of intense interest.

She has had an opportunity of escape offered her, of which she has refused to take advantage; so that there seems nothing more to be done on her account, as I think the reader will see when I have shown him something of what has already been done for her.

On my return to England, in the winter of

1878, I told my story to a number of gentlemen who had been either long residents in India or were well-known travellers in the East, and through them the fact of an Englishwoman being in Meccah was brought to the notice of the Government authorities. The Foreign Office then sent instructions to their Consul at Jeddah to send a Mohammedan agent into Meccah and make inquiry for the supposed captive. The inquiry found my statements of her existence and locality correct; but she had left Meccah a short time previously for India, accompanying the family with whom she had been living in Meccah. As she was now no longer within the range of the Foreign Office (Consular), the India Office was moved to go on with the necessary inquiry, and with some difficulty the lady was traced in India and at last found.

Whether she is really an English lady, now unwilling under her sad and painful circumstances to disclose her real identity, is open to doubt. The English magistrate, whose lady had two hours' conversation with her, seems to have some suspicion of the truth of the story now told by her. And as I have been given an opportunity of reading that gentleman's semi-official communication on the subject, I hope I shall not transgress in quoting the following from it:

"*Semi-Official, from the Magistrate in whose District the lady was found, to the Foreign Office Authorities.*

"I beg to say that I acted on your suggestion to continue my inquiries through my wife; but finding that the required interview was on one pretext or another put off, I sent for Mohammed ——— myself on the twenty-third instant from D———, which is about twenty-four miles from the station, and he came next day. I at once told him what I had heard about an Englishwoman being under his protection, and if so I required an interview between her and my wife. He frankly admitted the fact, and while he said he knew nothing about her he made no objection whatever to bring her to the station and let my wife converse with her. Accordingly, nine o'clock last night was appointed, and the lady duly came to my bungalow, where my wife conversed with her in privacy for more than two hours.

"I enclose herewith the substance of her own story.

There is no reasonable doubt that this is the lady referred to by Mr. Keane; for except the material point (which she here denies) that she is an Englishwoman who was ravished from her friends during the Mutiny, forced to turn Mohammedan and marry her ravisher, all other details of Mr. Keane's description are found in her. And as I have carefully kept all the correspondence sealed and concealed from native view, it was utterly impossible for her to have been prompted in telling any set tale; and, moreover, as she conversed without reserve, no suspicion could arise as to the truth of her own story—except, perhaps, the main point, which she may be loath to divulge, and which certainly she positively denied to my wife.

"The facts referred to are these. She went to Meccah soon after the Mutiny. Her husband died there, or at Medinah, about seven or eight years ago. She supported herself at Meccah by doing small needlework. She was always known as an Englishwoman in Meccah. She speaks Hindi (i.e. Hindustani) and Arabic, and used to translate English letters for a native merchant. She is about forty years of age (probably nearer forty-five). She was in straitened circumstances in Meccah. She appears to be an intelligent and educated Englishwoman. She lived in Meccah in the house of Mohammed ———. She had interviews with Europeans at Meccah. She was known in Meccah to be an Englishwoman turned Mohammedan.

"Finally, Mr. Keane's impression that 'she was certainly an European, though bronzed from long exposure,' he judging from a momentary view of her face when she raised her veil and shook hands at parting, is corroborated by my wife, who had a very long *tête-à-tête* with her in strict privacy, as she has the appearance of nothing so much as a reduced gentlewoman. In the face of her repeated and unreserved statement it is difficult if not impossible to believe that she is an Englishwoman, although fair enough to pass for one. And yet her English accent is hardly at all East-Indian, while her speech is so fluent and natural that it is not easy to suppose that she could ever have acquired English, which she seems to have learnt as her mother-tongue. Could I have had five minutes' conversation with her, I should probably have satisfied myself as to her race; but I had promised Mohammed ——— that I would not see her, and she herself shrank from seeing me, a suggestion which my wife made to her in order to settle the matter.

"Be she whoever she may, there is no doubt she is very well content where she is. She is under no restraint whatever, beyond such as is imposed on females of her creed and country (supposing she is, as she says, a native), and has nothing to complain of; has neither friends nor relations according to her own account, and is treated more as a companion than as a dependant by the members of Mohammed's family.

"My own impression is that her father (of whom she says she knows nothing, and about whom her mother would never disclose anything to her) may have been an Englishman, and her mother, as she says, a Kashmirin; that she was brought up to speak English from infancy until she became an adult, and that in a way which her own story does not account for; that, after the Mutiny, by some vicissitude of fortune over which a veil still hangs (her own story to the contrary notwithstanding) she was taken to Meccah, where she lived ever since till the beginning of this year.*

* 1879.

"It is only just to Mohammed to say that, barring his putting off my wife two or three times, for which probably the ladies of his family were more responsible than himself, he has given every assistance in his power. I believe, what he says, that he never conversed with the lady herself till I asked him to introduce her to my wife, and that all that he knew about her was that the Shahzadi, his stepmother, was a kind of patron of hers, and called her a Feringhi * in Meccah, and an Angrezin † in this country. Of course I have in no way intruded on the privacy of the family, the lady in question, according to mutual accounts, being no connection. But the fact that the lady was sent for alarmed the family, and only this morning Mohammed begged of me to take charge of the lady, whose residence with him would at any time, he thought, expose him to suspicion. I assured him that there was no occasion for any alarm, as he at least had done all that was required of him, and I requested him to let the lady live on with him as she had done for years past, which he consented to do for the present at least.

* Frank. † Englishwoman.

"DESCRIPTION OF THE LADY.

"Complexion light olive, eyes of a light colour, middle height, medium size, hair short and thin, face slightly pitted with small-pox; manner quiet and self-possessed; general appearance that of a reduced gentlewoman; speaks English remarkably well, with an accent slightly East-Indian; reads and writes English and Arabic; is said to speak Hindi with a foreign accent; age about forty-five."

Either her present statement is true, or, as some think, after her sad and painful captivity and degradation of more than twenty years, and the uncertainty she may feel about finding a home and maintenance open to her, she prefers to remain in her present obscurity and seclusion. If not really English, it is difficult to account for her accurate knowledge of English—a language to which she has been a stranger for twenty years—her manner and appearance. At all events, I have fulfilled my promise made to her in Meccah.

THE END.

CHARLES DICKENS AND EVANS, CRYSTAL PALACE PRESS.

MY JOURNEY TO MEDINAH.

MY JOURNEY TO MEDINAH:

DESCRIBING A PILGRIMAGE TO MEDINAH,

PERFORMED BY THE AUTHOR DISGUISED AS A MOHAMMEDAN.

BY

JOHN F. KEANE

(Hajj Mohammed Amin),

AUTHOR OF "SIX MONTHS IN MECCAH."

There were men with hoary hair amidst that pilgrim band:
Why had they come to wither there, away from their childhood's land?
There was woman's fearless eye, lit by her deep love's truth;
There was manhood's brow serenely high, and the fiery heart of youth.

What sought they thus afar? Bright jewels of the mine?
The wealth of seas? the spoils of war?—No——.

—*Hemans.*

LONDON:

TINSLEY BROTHERS, 8, CATHERINE STREET, STRAND.

CHARLES DICKENS AND EVANS,
CRYSTAL PALACE PRESS.

PREFACE.

On concluding my account of the Mohammedan pilgrimage to Meccah, in my work "Six Months in Meccah," I promised that, should the reception of it by the public encourage me to do so, I would continue the narrative of my travels in the Hejaz. I am happy to say that the book has been most favourably received, and therefore I now fulfil my promise, by publishing the following account of my pilgrimage to Medinah.

I trust that the series of uncommon adventures met with will make up in interest for what the book may lack in information. For the truth of the narrative, I pledge my name and faith.

JOHN F. KEANE (Hajj Mohammed Amin).

CONTENTS.

MY JOURNEY TO MEDINAH.

CHAPTER I.

THE DEPARTURE FROM MECCAH.

Faith, fanatic Faith, once wedded fast
To some dear falsehood, hugs it to the last.
LALLA ROOKH.

WITHOUT interrupting the sequence which is intended to be maintained between this volume and "Six Months in Meccah," I may introduce myself as having now lived for some months disguised as a Mohammedan, and acting as the servant of a rich native of India, known as the "Amér," whom I am now about to accompany on a pilgrimage from Meccah to Medinah, and then to return by Meccah to Bombay.

Of the whole of this journey, and of the many and strange adventures met with by my companions and myself, I shall now proceed to give an account. Though at first I shall find it necessary to go accurately into many apparent trifles, I feel pretty sure that, as the narrative opens out, the reader will be rather thankful that he has plodded through much of the dry minutiæ of the earlier chapters.

The Mohammedan pilgrimage to Medinah is not, like the pilgrimage to Meccah, commanded in the Koran. It is a purely gratuitous tender of respect to the memory of the Prophet who is buried there, and is in no way an obligatory religious duty. Those who perform it, though aware that it is theologically a work of supererogation, do look forward, as a reward for their meritorious penance, to some slight return of superexaltation in the next life.

The distance, by the shortest road, from Meccah to Medinah is only three hundred and seventy-five miles, but by the roundabout way known as the Sultan's Road, which was followed by us, the distance is reckoned to be five hundred miles; and from my own observation I should say that it was fully as much.

After the "Great Pilgrimage" to Arafat, the pilgrims who intend to go on to Medinah remain in Meccah for a time, to organise caravans and make preparations for the journey. Each of the caravans is composed, as far as possible, of individuals speaking the same language. An interval of four or five days is allowed to elapse between their different departures, so as to avoid there being too great a demand for supplies on the road at any one period, and to allow the wells of the desert time to replenish themselves between the passing of the caravans. Though this arrangement is generally said among the pilgrims to owe its origin to Bedawin influence; and it is greatly to the advantage of the Bedawi, for the comparatively small parties of pilgrims are much more at their mercy than were the immense well-protected caravans, consisting of many different nationalities, in Burton's day.

Every year the Malays are the first to be ready, and this year they started nine days after their return from Arafat. The Hindi caravan is invariably the last to leave Meccah; and not till a month after the pilgrimage did we begin to collect in the Wady Fatima, a valley about four miles north-west of Meccah, and the point of departure for the Medinah caravan. To this camp I walked with one of my companions on the evening of the day before our final leave-taking—the Amér only then making up his mind to take me. In passing out through the streets of the town I purchased a few private stores, such as tobacco, pipe, matches, and a good strong pocket-knife. When my companion and I reached the camp we went into the Amér's tent, and he received me most graciously, telling me to make myself comfortable in the tent, and saying that if I had forgotten anything, or wished to purchase anything for the journey, there would be plenty of time to-morrow. It had been dusk when we reached the camp, and all those who were allowed to sleep in the tent with the Amér had chosen their places, and there was left only room for one, in a very inconvenient place near the entrance. There I shook down my blankets on the carpeted sand, placed my bundle for a pillow, and after a last pull at the hookah, as it was being passed from one to another, rolled myself up to try and sleep. My tent-mates seemed tired, and their conversation and tobacco began to die out; but when the final muttered prayer had ceased I still found myself wide-awake. The night was very cold, and my blanket, though thick enough for the house, I found would never do for the desert. The tent walls were single, and the tent badly pitched, so that the wind entered freely under the lower edge of the canvas. I got up and shut out the draught at that point by building a little bank of sand along the outside, abreast of my stretch. I then tried again to go to sleep, but it was no good; the unintermitting scratchings of my bed-fellows fell on my ear in the "stilly night" so distinctly, that I all at once found myself guessing from the sound what part of themselves they were scratching; and then I got so interested and curious about it that I asked my next neighbour the seat of his irritation, but found he was doing it in his sleep. After a time numerous entomological specimens began "to work their wicked will" on me, and I took to scratching. Hitherto I had not been troubled much in this way; instinct in the various varieties of the insect "faithful" had taught them to avoid defilement through me—my companions said it was a sign of bad health. But whatever it was, I had gone for days without a "strange bed-fellow," while the Amér had two or three skilled "shikaris"* to beat over his person every day, and his covers never failed to afford the liveliest sport. But now all the noxious creatures which Mussulman flesh is heir to, seemed to have been seized with a sudden rage for christian blood. I suppose I must have scratched myself to sleep at last, for the morning call to prayers transmuted me from the Russian army retreating over the Balkans, after a crushing defeat by the Turks, into a very flea-bitten, stiff, unrested pilgrim, who had to perform his ablutions and go cheerfully about his daily devotions.

* Hunters.

On our falling-in, outside the tent, for prayers, I was introduced to two distinguished strangers, countrymen of the Amér's, who had now been added to our party, and were living in the tent. The Amér described me as a great traveller, who had been in many countries, and mentioned a number of services I had rendered him, some of which were founded on fact, but most of which, I am sorry to say, were pure invention. Among other accomplishments of mine, he told them that I could cut a rope in two and put it together again, so that the minutest search would not detect the joint.* This showed me that I had risen in favour with the Amér for some reason—probably my seeming ready compliance with his wish that I should go with him to Medinah, contrasting as it did with the sullenness of my companion, whom, like me, the Amér had intended to send off to India at once and not to take to Medinah with him.

The first of the strangers above alluded to was a thin little old Tallukdar, reputed very rich, and a great

* Common long-splice.

miser. The other was a native gentleman, who lived by his wits, and was able to dress richly and curiously out of what he made. He was a universal genius, his imitations of the trumpetings and screams of an infuriated elephant being such as might deceive the head-keeper of the "Lord of the White," and was only to be equalled, in its way, by his bul-bul song. Add to these accomplishments, that he was a deep politician, an advanced scientist, a devout "true believer," and one of the most powerfully-built men I ever saw. I need scarcely say he turned out to be a great acquisition to the Amér's suite. After the morning meal I went to the Amér's steward, or Dirvani, and asked him to get me another blanket and a Bedawin camel-hair cloak* with a hood to it. He tried to satisfy me with a blanket only, so after a good deal of shilly-shallying I went to the Amér himself, and told him what I wanted, and he ordered his Dirvani to send into Meccah at once for them.

This practice, usual all over the East when a long journey is intended, of going out for a short

* Aba.

trial-trip, and living for a day or two within easy reach of your source of supplies, under precisely similar circumstances as will be necessitated by the road, has its advantages where rapidity of transport is only a secondary consideration to indulgence in lazy habits, and among people who regard the exerting of a particle of foresight as contravening Providence.

I almost despair of being able to describe our setting out from Wady Fatima in any kind of order. From our tent-entrance the scene on every side presented a massed inextricable chaos of tents, camels, and men, distributed by chance over the ground in about equal bulk. But, as my habit was, I will take my readers to some elevated standpoint, from which we will look down together on the movements of this disorderly camp.

This way I had of frequently ascending elevations from which to observe, had become a standing joke against me among my companions. If at any time I was not to be found when wanted, someone would facetiously remark: "Oh! Mohammed Amin has gone climbing;" or sometimes one of them would point derisively to any little mound we might be passing, and say: "Sailor, why don't you go up aloft?" I was frequently told to fancy the tent-pole a mast, and climb up it. For my part, I thought this was as good an explanation of my little eccentricity as they could have conceived.

About two hundred yards from our side of the camp there rose a rocky hill, some hundred feet high; towards this I went after noonday prayer, and clambered to the top. Just at the summit I rose a brace of partridges, and remembering that we had two double 12-bores and five hundred cartridges in the tent, it looked like the promise of a little sport by the way, which was very cheering. The plain below, as seen from this standpoint, was an almost circular valley of a mile across, bounded by low rocky hills. Most of the surface of the valley consisted of loose yellow sand; but here and there grew patches, of an acre or so in extent, of coarse brown grass, a couple of feet high, among which a number of camels were grazing. From this large valley narrower valleys wound off among the surrounding hills. All over the plain, leading towards every outlet from it, were beaten camel-tracks: these last look exactly like a beaten footpath in England. The town of Meccah was hidden behind the hills, but the road to it might be easily known by the number of passengers going along it, to and from the camp, with occasional half-frantic Bedawin riders, on swift camels, flying backwards and forwards on some almost forgotten important commission. Close under the hill upon which I had posted myself, and not more than one hundred yards from the nearest tents, were the wells—three round pits, about thirty feet deep, having stone walls, about four feet high, built round the mouths of each of them, with a number of stone troughs placed near each well for the camels to drink from. The water is brought up by means of a hide draw-bucket. The above describes the well we shall come to at nearly every halt on our journey; perhaps we may find a rough post and pulley, for the bucket-rope, where the well is very deep, and we may have to pay a toll for the water at some of them, but all the wells in the Hejaz are very similar in construction. At this time our wells exhibited a lively scene of squabbling between the Bedawi, whose camels were "laying in water for a voyage," it seemed, and the pilgrims who were filling their skins, pots, and bottles with a supply to last them until the next halt.

It was impossible to judge how large our caravan would be from the size of the camp, for a great proportion of it was not going with us, but would return to Meccah after seeing us off.

About three P.M. the watering of the camels appeared to be nearly finished, and the bustle in the camp increased. Here and there a few tents were being struck, or a nucleus in the tumult, which had looked in the distance like a "free fight," would gradually dissolve itself into a string of some half-a-dozen laden camels. In a short time, noticing our tent was about to be struck, I took a stroll down the opposite side of the hill to the plain and gathered a few flowers, some of which were very pretty and sweet scented, and returned with them to the Amér, as I knew he was very fond of flowers. The tent had been taken down over his head, and there he was sitting on the tent carpet, with four or five others, smoking hookahs and placidly awaiting events.

It was very tickling to see them so calm and unconcerned in the midst of such excitement and uproar as the remainder of the scene displayed. I handed him the flowers and he began to play with them as if he were at home. I then looked for an old friend of mine, the third warrior, junior member of the Amér's bodyguard, who told me he had put my new blanket and cloak on a camel on which he and I were to ride, and which was ready. He led me off to look at it. It was a very high camel, and it turned out to be the highest and worst in the whole caravan. After seeing our camel we went back and took the tent-carpet from under the Amér, to roll it up, and left him sitting on the sand, perhaps more indifferent to results than before, and then we rushed recklessly into the heat of the action, and I have no doubt that, together, we performed prodigies of obstruction. I know that more than once we came near being slain by exasperated Bedawi. But there must have been some method in all this commotion, for Shaykh the Bo'sen,* our Bedawin conductor, whose tall form, heavy iron-shod mace, and hoarse curse appeared ubiquitous, ultimately succeeded in evolving order out of it.

Towards dusk the camels began to form themselves into lines and straggle about the plain. Then an ugly, truculent, little, old Bedawin rushed at the third warrior and myself, as though he regarded us as his long-sought prey, and drove us before him to our camel, which it seemed we had been expected to mount as soon as it was ready.

Our camel was one of a string of some twenty others, connected head-and-tail by their halters, which allowed about two fathoms drift between each camel.

* I gave him that name in my mind from his seamanlike bearing.

The tow-ropes are made of small cocoanut-fibre line, about an inch in circumference, and not so strong but that it will part if the camel falls; though with a terrible jar on the animal. The halters of such camels as are inclined to lag are fitted with an ingenious spurring-curb, formed of two small plates of iron with serrated edges, and these edges are turned in, and their sharp points pressed against each side of the lower jaw by the tightening of the halter.

We now had to mount our camel without a ladder. This is done by first pulling the animal's head down to the ground with the left hand, and then quickly placing the left foot in the hollow of the back of its neck, at the same time catching at the rise of its shoulder with the right and letting go with the left hand, the animal then throws up its head, and with a slight turn of your body you find yourself placed deftly in the saddle. After some practice, and by hopping along a few steps, a camel can be mounted in this way while going at considerable speed. But in getting into the large cumbersome "shugduf," or covered-in litter used by pilgrims, the platforms of which are on a level with the top of the hump, great care must be taken to land in the centre, or you may overbalance and bring down the whole concern; and after getting in you must wait until your partner is mounted, so that you may deposit yourselves carefully and simultaneously on your respective sides. Then, after a little trimming of ballast from one side to the other, you may stretch out at full length, with your feet to the open or front end of the shugduf. Both my companion and I managed this without much difficulty, considering it was our first attempt of the kind, and then remarked that we were very hungry. This was a bad look-out; we had neither of us eaten anything since morning, and there was no knowing when we should get our next meal. Soon we both noticed a most disagreeable smell, and after some conjecture concluded it must come from the camel.

CHAPTER II.

DEPARTURE FROM WADY FATIMA.

We made a great many false starts and long stands —not *still*, for laden camels cannot stand still, it appears to give them pain to do so, and they constantly shift the weight from one leg to the other in a most distracting manner, completely throwing out all your balance adjustments. But at last we fairly got off. The moon was young, and the night soon became very dark. What a miserable night that was! The awful jumpity-wabbledy gait of Mabarak* (for that was our camel's name) soon jolted us into utter despondency, wriggled our blankets off our bodies, and tied them up into great knots under us, and at every jolt I felt a certain conviction that some piece

* The fortunate.

of my property was being shaken out into the desert and lost. To add to our wretchedness, a sand-hopping little "preparation" of a Bedawin camel-driver glided along by our side, shrieking curses at us to "Sit forward," "Sit back," or "Sit in the middle," without ceasing for five minutes the whole night, accompanying himself by an incessant "rub-a-dub-dub with a club" on the hocks of Mabarak that sounded quite close to one's ear. I afterwards ascertained that he had no object in thus belabouring the poor brute; it was only done from force of habit—perpetual absence of mind, in fact. I had been made altogether too sick by the shaking I was getting and the horrid smell we carried with us, to "turn and rend" that Ishmaelite, otherwise it might have been pretty bad for him before morning.

Several writers have made observation to the effect that few things recall lost recollections like the "greeting of the nostrils by a long-forgotten odour." I quite agree with them. Mabarak reminded me perfectly of a scene of my boyhood. It was a visit to a Hindoo burning-ground in Madras, when I got on the lee-side of an active cremation. The smells were identical. We did not suffer so much from hunger that night as we had anticipated. The hours and the camels dragged themselves along with equal tardiness till towards dawn, when Mabarak created a little diversion by lying down a couple of times and breaking his halter. Then the camel following us was detached, and the remainder went plodding on past us, while we got out and prized our weary brute on to his legs, drove him back to his old position, and strung him on. The second time we came down the day was breaking, and I took the opportunity of having a good look at our camel-driver, who owned the beast we rode, and of seeing what kind of vile thing it was that had been making our lives a burden to us all night. He was, as I had noticed before, a very small, thin, old man, with a large and quite abnormally-developed Roman nose. And I now perceived that he possessed the power of giving this last the most pronounced and vigorous wag; and that, I believe, to have been the only expression his features were capable of, though it did not convey half as much intelligence as the wagging of a dog's tail. He was barefooted, and wore the dress of all his class—a cotton shirt reaching down to his knees, bound with a hide girdle round the waist, and having loose sleeves; about a square yard of thin dressed sheepskin, doubled from corner to corner, was laid on his head, with a rope ring pressed down over it to keep it in its place; and all of him was filthy. He was armed with a short heavy throwing-spear and a cudgel with a hooked end. The usual heavy Bedawin knife was in the front of his belt.

We were now some distance behind the caravan, and as I might not have another chance, also being a firm believer in the old nautical adage that "You should always begin as you mean to go on," I made up my mind to take this fellow in hand, and give him a lesson at once. So I went quietly behind him and let him have one with the right, between the shoulder-blades, which knocked him flat on his face on the sand gasping. My companion looked perfectly astounded by what I had done, and more so when I burst into fits of loud and jovial laughter. The poor camel-driver stood up, and first looked after his companions retreating in the distance, and then looked at me; whereupon I, laughing, lifted my hand as if I meant to repeat what I had intended for a good-humoured pleasantry; but he raised his spear, and I felt I had gone far enough. I don't know what he thought of me, but I must say I approved of the civil and cautious manner in which he approached me from that time until we parted.

When we got Mabarak on his legs I suggested that we should not remount, as we had fallen some distance behind, and would have to hurry forward. To this my companion readily assented, for a walk after the first seven hours of your journey on a camel, means little less than absolute repose. We indicated our plan to the camel-driver, and he evinced the greatest satisfaction, at once jumping up to ride himself. This was not so much to Mabarak's advantage as we had intended, but we thought it best to say nothing after what had just happened. On coming up with the caravan, I was surprised to see what a number of people were accompanying us on foot, not counting the pilgrims, who were now dismounting for morning prayer. We shortly met the Amér and a good many of our party as we went along, and together we pushed ahead on the track about a quarter of a mile in advance of the leading camel. One of the servants followed us with a skin of water from our water-camel, and we performed our ablution and prayer, finishing before the last camel of the long line had passed us.

We always performed our prayers in this way without stopping the caravan. The country in which we found ourselves resembled in a general way the whole country through which we passed—except the open plain afterwards to be spoken of. Sandy valleys between irregular fantastic black rocky piles, varying in height from a boulder to a thousand-feet cliff. Vegetation, more or less, was to be found everywhere, but in no place except near the water was the ground as fertile as on an English grouse moor. I could not identify a dozen of the shrubs that grew in such places, and often regretted that

I had not got together a little of the right sort of knowledge; promising myself that if ever I got out of it, my shortcomings should certainly be rectified. One plant, extremely common in the desert, I must say a word about—the wild melon. The largest of these are about the size of an ostrich's egg, and in colour are exactly like the cultivated water-melon. They are so bitter as to excoriate the mouth; but camels will devour them greedily. The only other use to which they are put, is to make playthings for children. When they have been hung up for some time they become hard and light, and are used as balls, the seeds inside them making a loud rattle as they are shaken or thrown about.

After the chilly nights in the desert, the heat of the early sun is felt quite as strongly as its midday rays, and we were soon glad to return to the shade of our shugduf, notwithstanding its discomfort otherwise.

Not long after this we heard a noisy quarrel going on, a few camels ahead of us, and then Shaykh the Bo'sen came galloping past us to the spot. The noise increased, and a few minutes later the whole caravan came to a halt. We both dismounted, and found that a man whom the Amér had hired, just before leaving Meccah, to go with him as a sort of courier, had got himself into trouble. He was a Meccah-born Hindi, a tall wiry man, about forty years of age, who was said to have made seventeen pilgrimages to Medinah, and it was expected he would act as a "Greatheart" for us. Part of his agreement with the Amér had been that no seat on a camel was to be provided for him, it being privately understood that none of us would object to his making a third on our camel, if the Bedawin in charge did not find fault. On the very first night he had managed to get up and ride all night, without the driver being aware that his camel was carrying three; but he had not been able to dismount without being found out—hence the disturbance. When I came upon the scene, Greatheart had so far forgotten himself, in the heat of a profane argument, as to threaten to strike Shaykh the Bo'sen, who was rushing off to his camel for his sword, although he had lethal weapons enough about his person to call forth a proclamation of disarmament if he had been seen in South Africa. Anyhow, before the Shaykh returned with his drawn sword, looking very much as if he meant mischief, Greatheart bolted off and disappeared among the rocky hills. The last that we saw of our man was about two miles off, scudding over a sandy ridge towards Meccah. It may have been a "put-up thing"—indeed, I think it was, for he had been paid half of the ten dollars he was to receive for the round trip in advance. Shaykh the Bo'sen pretended to be in a great state of disappointment and wrath, and declared that the caravan should not stir until he had hurled vengeance on the offender. The Amér offered the usual salve—money! How much? "A lack of rupees,"* cried the Shaykh. To offer less would only have been to insult him. The Bedawi were delighted with the prospect of a row, and sat about in groups on the rocks discussing the matter quite cheerfully, while some of the heads

* 100,000.

among them held a council. We also held a debate The Amér, a number of graybeards, and wealthier pilgrims assembled in a group, and deliberated several measures of advance towards the Bedawi, which, however, when tried, were scornfully repulsed.

At length, after about an hour's halt, a Bedawin, who had almost as much influence among them as the injured Shaykh himself, came up to the Amér, in the character of a wellwisher and just friend of both sides, and advised him, as it was one of his servants who had committed the offence, to try and appease the insulted Shaykh with a little present of five hundred dollars, offering to do the thing himself for the Amér in a nice delicate way, so that the Shaykh could not possibly be offended. But we had wary old birds on our side too, and he who will in future be known as our "conspirator," whispered to the Amér to put a bold face on the matter and offer him ten dollars. This the poor Amér, in great trepidation, whispered to his steward, who at once gave the Arab to understand, with his master's authority, that the above were our terms. That Arab's glance of proud pity was well done, showing a man capable of a very superior order of dissimulation.

But he came back again and again, and after about another hour's delay consented to take fifty dollars, which settled it, and we were soon in motion again. We had had a nice experience to profit by; but I did not gain anything by it. There had been no blood spilt, and so far as I could see, had not been any chance of it. It only confirmed me in my opinion that most of the blood-curdling stories I had heard belonged to times past, and that most of the dangers of the road were imaginary.

About noon on this day we reached our first halt. It was in another level valley, similar to the one we had left the day before, but not more than about a quarter its size. There was only one well, and near it a dozen or so of Bedawin huts, standing in two rows, facing each other, with a road between them. These huts are generally about twelve feet by twelve feet, and seven feet high. They are built of upright stakes driven into the sand, which have horizontal poles lashed across them, and to these, on the outside, a thick covering of interwoven grass, reeds, or date-fronds, is tied. On one side the hut is left completely open. Shaykh the Bo'sen and the other Shaykhs who owned camels to ride themselves, had ridden on to give notice of our coming at the village, and to lay out the camp, for now the different parties of pilgrims were to be brought together, and each Shaykh to take his own charge. As the long string of camels came in, the Bedawi directed them to different parts of the camp, and in a short time we found most of our party united, and we set to work to unload the camels and pitch our tents. Our women were not allowed to dismount until their tent was ready for them, and then their camels were led close up to the entrance, and they made a little rush into the tent. After this our next duty was to pitch our own tent, and then to place the baggage, shugdufs, and shibriyahs round each tent, enclosing an open space of about fifteen yards in diameter, opposite the entrance of each;

outside this enclosure the camels were made to lie down. There were several of these little "laagers" in the camp, and dozens of smaller parties or families who had only one or two camels, and hundreds of people who had set out to walk the whole way with us to Medinah.

The camp being put in order, our cooks at once set about preparing a meal for us. They were able to carry all their simple cooking utensils with them, and a fire lit on the sand between a few stones, to stand their pots on, differed only in its open-air character from their arrangements at home; so that department experienced little inconvenience in its own particular line from travelling. While the fires were being lit and the provisions unpacked some went off to the well to fetch water. I joined the dirvani (first warrior) and an under-cook, who were going to the village to make purchases. In each of the huts we found a Bedawin family, with a store of one kind or other of supplies for sale. One hut exposed three or four dozen fine water-melons, and in another hut lived the family of a dealer in camel-feed; while some sold dried fish, dates, and such other supplies as the country affords, or as would be likely to be required by the pilgrims. We were some time haggling and bargaining over our shopping, and then returned heavily weighted to the camp. I went into the tent, and enjoyed four or five large slices of water-melon, which were very refreshing, and did a great deal towards banishing my seedy feeling. Cooking operations were proceeding actively, and straight columns of thin blue smoke rose up into the bright clear sky from all parts of the camp. There was a tired subdued air about everyone, which added an earnestness to the scene, and that made things look more like business than on the day before. Good-looking young Bedawin girls and boys from the village moved about the camp hawking milk, dates, firewood, and water-melons, and crying, in rather pleasant voices and quite intelligibly, the names of the articles they were vending. About an hour and a half after we came to a halt our meal of curry and rice and chupattis was ready for us, and most of us did ample justice to it. Our Bedawi—

whom we had stipulated with to pay thirty dollars for the hire of the camel for the round trip to Medinah and back to Meccah, besides two dollars for the driver, whom we were also to supply with one meal a-day, of a mixture of equal quantities of boiled rice and lentils, seasoned with a fair proportion of rancid mutton grease—received their allowance. Although there was more than they could eat, and they were allowed to help themselves to the grease, they were compelled to be dissatisfied and grumble on principle. They complained that there was too great a proportion of rice in their mixture. The beggars, too, were disappointed in our leavings. The chief cook told us that, what between the revilings of the Bedawi and the reproaches of the begging pilgrims, he did not get a wink of sleep during the halt. When the meal had been cleared away I lay down in the tent, and soon fell into a sound sleep, regardless of my position, which was made one of extreme peril by most of my companions handling and loading firearms in a dangerously inexpert manner all round me—arms about which most of them knew as much as a camel does a holiday.

CHAPTER III.

HARDSHIPS OF THE ROAD.

About two hours before sunset we were roused up by Shaykh the Bo'sen, who came to the entrance of the tent and excitedly bawled out: "Mount, mount!" as though he expected us to spring on to our camels immediately. But a look round the camp showed dozens of muffled forms lying on the sand, and still snoring in the bright sunshine or reluctantly waking themselves up. It took the Bedawi half an hour to thoroughly rouse our people and shriek a little activity into them. The third warrior and I went to settle our shugduf, which we found being used as a bed by a couple of assistant cooks, whom we quickly pulled out and sent off to pack their pots and pans.

First, we secured our blankets with twine, so that they could not possibly ruffle up under us, and then we sorted our effects and fastened them in convenient places about the inside of the shugduf, and put our smoking materials in a handy bag, also hung on the inside. I found that during the night I had lost one of a pair of spare slippers which had fallen out into the desert. I made an Arabic observation on the inscrutable ways of Providence, and gave its fellow to a beggar who wanted it badly. The camels were still munching away at their hay, which they eat while they are resting themselves. The hay carried for them is twisted up tightly into two-stranded ropes, and before it is put down as fodder it is threshed loose with a stick. This is a very convenient way of carrying hay when there are no means at hand of effectively compressing it into bales.

We also interviewed Mabarak and discovered the secret of the smell. He was, indeed, in a sad plight. On both sides of his back, extending across the spine, he carried a raw corrupting sore, resembling somewhat in form and size the part covered by the saddle of a horse, and his driver was at that time leisurely engaged cauterising its thick callous rim with a red-hot bolt of inch iron. The operation gave out a loud hissing crackling sound, and quite a little cloud of smoke, all the time he was applying the iron. Horrifying as this spectacle was, we became accustomed to seeing it done to some camel at every stage. But Mabarak had an almost more serious trouble—his teeth. He could not masticate his food, so had to be fed by forcing large moistened balls of chopped hay and pounded date-stones down his throat. We told the Amér about our camel, and he represented our case to Shaykh the Bo'sen; but we could get no remedy. We told him the camel was not fit for the journey, but he only laughed, and said it had just come from Medinah, and had done the same journey a hundred times; and he finally clenched the argument by saying it would be impossible to get another camel till we reached Rabigh, two stages farther on, which would take us four days to accomplish.

Our start to-day was much more intelligently

conducted than on the day before, each man attending to the packing of his own property or particular charge. Shaykh the Bo'sen devoted his energies to us alone, independently of the other parties, who had their own conductors. Just as darkness set in the caravan was prepared for starting. Our portion of it, consisting of sixty-two souls, fifteen camels, one horse, and two donkeys, was placed well in advance on the line of march, which was now marshalled into the order it would proceed in for the future. On starting, a few torches were lit and carried by those on foot, while in many of the shugdufs hung lighted lamps.

The district we were now to pass through had the reputation of being peculiarly infested by robbers. As we went along, many were the oft-repeated stories of the methods and cunning of these robbers, with which my companion entertained me—how they would stalk among the rocks and shoot a camel or two out of a caravan, just as you would "shoot an antelope out of a herd;" how they had been known to come down unobserved in the darkness and mingle with a caravan, and then, in league with the driver, untie the camel of some wealthy unsuspecting or sleeping traveller, who would know nothing until he had been dropped far behind his fellows and his camel was being made to lie down, when he would be dragged out and his throat cut, "just as you would cut a sheep's." Many were the false alarms of that night. Now and again some nervous woman or timid old man would be startled into crying out, "Thief! thief!" The cry would then be taken up along the whole line, and immediately would ensue such a fusilade, fired into the air and echoing among the hills, as suggested a regimental feu-de-joie under the dome of St. Paul's. A little past midnight, however, there occurred one of these alarms that appeared serious. The camels were brought to a standstill, and there was a general rush of foot-passengers to the rear, where the commotion had first arisen. A half-dozen of our Bedawi conductors, who were lighting the fuses of their matchlocks at a torch near me, the fitful red glare shining on them, and revealing in a murky indistinct way a rugged background of black rock, made up a group I have seldom seen equalled for barbarous picturesqueness. Their bright piercing Bedawin eyes, under the overhanging eyebrows, looked even more piercing than common, and they wore a sinister half-amused expression, that portended anything but pleasantly for whoever they might contemplate favouring just then. The news soon came up from the rear, passed from camel to camel, that the two last camels on the line had been swept off in a sudden rush of about a dozen men from an ambush, and that they had driven the camels rapidly off into the darkness, one of the riders, a man, having been able to throw himself out of the shugduf, and escape, leaving two women and a young lad in the hands of the robbers. It appeared that nothing could be done to help them, and shortly after the caravan was put in motion. The affair gave me and my companion an animating new topic of conversation. If the man had not escaped, the third warrior, who believed the whole story implicitly, would have found me more difficult to convince. As it was, I scarcely believed the whole thing. I could not bring myself to realise that two women and a boy were being murdered in cold blood within a mile or two of me. After daybreak Mabarak, who had providentially kept his legs all night, began to stumble about desperately, and took to his old game of lying down. We got him on his legs again and again, but the intervals between his falls became shorter every time, till at length it was evident he would never accomplish the remaining three hours of the march in company with the rest. Sick and weary, Mabarak lay down for the last time. Shaykh the Bo'sen examined him and pronounced him incurable, and after a short consultation advised the one relief left the patient. Mabarak's owner savagely drew his knife, and the brute made a movement that looked almost like presenting its throat, anxious to meet the welcome blade. Exasperatingly deliberate was the cut, as the knife passed steadily and deeply into the neck without causing a flinch.

So the end of his longer journey had come
In its own good time at last.

And "good time" it was that it had come. When the long neck fell supine on the sand I had worked myself up to such a pitch of compassion for the brute and contempt for the man, that I believed I saw the bright eye turned to its heartless master with a look of deep deep gratitude for the last and only act of mercy it had ever experienced at his hands.

"His end was pieces," as someone observes. The first gush of blood from the huge gash had hardly reached the sand ere the fakirs* fell upon him, and soon all the tramps in the caravan were scrambling round the carcass, stripping Mabarak's gaunt emaciated frame of such tough tissue as labour and starvation had left upon it. Those men who succeeded in securing a few strips or shreds of the flesh hung them over their backs, and the dry heat in a couple of hours converted them into light, brittle, and easily portable provender. The caravan halted for a few minutes so that our shugduf and effects might be placed on a pack-

* Religious mendicants.

camel, and then Mabarak's bare bones were left behind for the vultures to polish, as had been the case with the bones of hundreds of his family on the same road, there being no part of it where bones are not to be seen either of men or animals.

I received a message from the Amér to mount one of the donkeys. The donkey I chose turned out to be a very hard puller, so, as the pace of these large caravans is provokingly slow, even to a man on foot, I allowed my donkey to trot on ahead until we came up to the leading camel, and then got off and sat down on the sand and waited for the last camel on the line to reach me, when I would start off again, and so on.

As it was now daytime, and the ground was more open, it will be a good opportunity for describing our caravan in its entirety. There were seven hundred and thirty camels, and these extended in a long line, one behind the other, for about three-quarters of a mile. These camels carried about nine hundred pilgrims, with all their baggage. On both sides of this line walked a wretched company of perhaps one thousand or so of men, women, and children. Many of these were possessed of funds to support themselves by the way; but far the greater number had set out quite unprovided, trusting altogether in the charity of those they accompanied. Although only our second day out, it was said that two of these people had dropped behind, which meant certain death to them; for if they succeeded in avoiding the Bedawi they must perish from thirst. Numbers already began to show signs of giving out. On the whole, it put one in a violent passion to think of the infatuation which could have led not only strong men, but delicate women and young children, to undertake a walk of five hundred miles in such a country, relying for subsistence entirely on what chance might put in their way. Yet such things are—and yearly take place in the Hejaz. To every one of our camels there was a driver, man or boy, and they, together with the Shaykhs and other Bedawi, brought our escort up to only about eight hundred *murderers.*

As the day wore on, the Amér got down from his camel and mounted the horse, a pretty iron-gray, bought in Meccah for eighty dollars. It was led with us and used only for the Amér's convenience. The only signs of game we came upon were a couple of coveys of partridges and a few small flocks of blue pigeons; but we were as yet too near to holy Meccah to think of sport. There was a difference of opinion among the seniors of our party as to whether we were right in hunting at any time during the journey; but as the Amér affected to be a bit of a sportsman, this was over-ruled, and we afterwards blazed away at every-thing that came along. The first day the breech-loading smooth-bores were brought out, Shaykh the Bo'sen was asked to give his opinion on them. He considered them flimsy gimcracks, wholly untrust-worthy, by the side of his old heirloom, with its four-foot iron barrel and cotton fuse. Before we reached the camp another camel broke down, and was treated in the same way as ours had been. After having been nineteen hours on the road without further accident, we reached our camping-ground. When the camp was righted and the evening meal over, all of us who slept in the tent took up our quarters, and the first part of the night was spent in long discussions on the hardships of the next three days of continuous travelling that was before us. The place in which we were now camped was deemed specially liable to the attempts of robbers.

At sundown sentries were posted all round the camp, we providing seven, four of whom were posted at our portion of the camp, and the others to the right and left protecting the sleeping pauper pilgrims near us. After sunset, if the report of a single pistol was heard it would be followed by the explosion of every firearm in the camp, and the night was about as noisy as gunpowder could make it. Sleep was out of the question with me, though most of my companions dropped off in time. Then the old "moonshi"* got quietly up and went out of the tent; there was nothing surprising in that, but shortly after I saw a hand

* The Amér's tutor.

pushed gently under the canvas and begin to draw out the moonshi's bundle. I stepped quickly over to the tent-pole and drew a sword that I knew to be sharp, and if I had not recognised the rings on his fingers I should have amputated our moonshi's right hand. As it was, I called him in and told him what he had risked in testing his security by an attempt to steal his own bundle. The old man looked startled, but his shock was nothing to the "awful caution" I received myself on this night.

Though no sentry duty had been allotted to me, two hours after midnight I still found myself wide awake, so I got up, and after removing a file of heavy dragoons from the nape of my neck, and dispersing a little army of flying artillery that had been hanging on to and harassing my rear, I set out for a stroll and a smoke. I remembered once hearing a fellow enlarge eloquently on the difficulties of returning from mess through certain sepoy lines. On this occasion I thoroughly learnt to appreciate the position. The shortest cut to the outskirt of the camp was between our tent and that of our women. I soon recognised the curious affinity existing between the human ankle and the tent-rope, and discovered by two most conclusive and separate experiments—which, however, had been differently directed—that the human os frontal was not adapted to driving tent-pegs. I reached the cordon of feeding camels that encircled our camp, and ran the gauntlet of them, leaving only about half my tunic to be masticated, and with a "God bless you!" to the nearest sentry, went off twenty or thirty yards into the night, and sat down on a recent grave to smoke my cigarette. I then noticed two Bedawi follow me out of the camp; but as they disappeared in the darkness to my right I paid no more attention to them.

The camp presented a very wild and wide-awake appearance; numerous fires were burning throughout it, and a circle of fires, about fifteen yards apart from each other, all round the camp, were kept going by the sentries. A good deal of motion was going on from cooking and other preparations for starting at daylight.

I had been sitting some time and had just finished my cigarette, when I heard a gentle scratching sound on the ground close behind me. I thought so little of it that at first I was inclined not to turn my head round to look; but as my cigarette was finished, I just threw the end away and gave a glance over my shoulder. It was perhaps as well I did. There, close behind me, on his knees, one hand on the sand and the other in the act of lifting a broad-bladed curved knife, crouched the form of an old graybearded Bedawin. In less than another second the knife would have been driven deep into my back, and I should have been "wiped out," probably without as much as an "Oh!" I don't ever want to get into a "tighter place." I have no recollection of the process by which we arrived at the next stage, but I know I found myself standing up facing the Bedawin, who was also standing up, at short arm's reach, with knife still uplifted. The string of my trousers had come adrift, and I was obliged to hold them up with my left hand, and if I had closed with my man I should have had them down round my feet. I wondered why he did not strike, or do something. We must have remained in these attitudes, without either of us moving eye or hand, for fully two minutes. I cannot describe my feeling at the time as altogether *fear*. I felt the terrible disadvantage of my position—defenceless and encumbered as I was—and stood in a state of high-strung expectancy. Otherwise the feeling was one of intense wonder and disgust, at seeing before me a man who would take a fellow-creature's life as a mere speculation on the most paltry profit. My white face and unexpected actions seemed to have completely paralysed the Bedawin. I felt that I must do something to put an end to this state of things. Hard I doubled my right fist, as hard as I could squeeze it, then a quick sharp cut up, landing my man well under his long nose, bowled him over on his back and dropped the knife out of his hand into the sand. Just as he fell I saw another Bedawin, about five yards behind him, get up from the sand where he had been lying and race off into the darkness. It was well I had no pistol, or I should have taken both their lives. As it was, I now secured the knife and then tied up my waist-band. The Bedawin lay on his back groaning, evidently thinking himself badly hurt. I gave him a hard kick in the ribs, and he then put his right hand up to his mouth and from it to his eyes. "Oh Allah!" he grunted, when he saw the blood from his nose. He could not make out what, in the name of all the prophets and patriarchs, he had been hit with, and he probably thought, judging from the blood, that his head was half off. Then it occurred to me to call out for assistance, and I wondered why I had not had the presence of mind to do so at first, when the fellow would, of course, have taken to his heels at once. Dragging him to his feet by his rather long beard, I called out to the nearest sentry that I had got a thief, and in a few minutes was relating my story to an admiring crowd of armed pilgrims who gathered round, and who looked upon the blow I had struck with "the empty hand" as almost incredible.

We led our prisoner into the camp to be dealt with by the Amér and Shaykh the Bo'sen. In the light of the tent the dogged old wretch certainly did look a little alarming, with the blood flowing down his white beard, and smeared all over his hands and bosom. He was recognised as one of our camel-drivers. He made no excuses whatever for his conduct, and would not reveal the name of the Bedawin whom I had seen with him. The sentence passed was two hours' law, then to be shot at sight; and I promised him that I would keep a sharp look-out for him.

As we were now a camel short, it was arranged that some of those who had seats should take turns of an hour or two at riding the donkeys, so that I and my companion could ride first on one camel and then on another. Before leaving our present encampment, we filled up every vessel we had that would hold water, as we were to be two whole nights before we reached the next well, nor were we to halt until we came to the water. That half the begging pilgrims on foot would ever get over the next stage, I could hardly believe. It was tolerably certain that we, who had a camel loaded with skins of water, besides about three gallons apiece in each shugduf, and probably thirty gallons more in the cooking-pots, would have to go very short for the last part of the march. Yet most of the pedestrians who set out to walk with us carried only a little pot of water, that would have been exhausted by evaporation in the time they required it to last them. One could not feel any real pity for these people. They expected no pity from you. *They have no word in their language to express gratitude to a man.* They regard death under torture (the form in which it would inevitably come to many of them) as an event, if not to be actually courted, certainly not to be strenuously avoided because it might happen to interfere with a few other temporary arrangements made for this life. The knowledge of this sort of thing threw a considerable damper over one's sympathy. I have given a dying creature the draught of water that has saved his life, and heard him thank God in accents of the most heartfelt gratitude, without so much as a "Go to!" for me. If I had not given it to him he would have died; but he would have thanked God all the same!

For the first fourteen or fifteen hours we wended our way through narrow passes between high cliffs. Sometimes we passed over bare rock, up and down gentle inclines, or through ravines so narrow that two camels could not have passed. One of the camels of another party, descending a slope just in advance of us, got a fall on the rocks. Now a real fall to a laden camel is a very different thing from a lay-down: it generally means total wreck, a smashed shugduf, and often broken bones both to riders and camel. Several of us gathered round to see what damage had been done. We found the camel on its side motionless; it had sustained some injury that compelled its being abandoned. The shugduf had been knocked into a cocked hat and the cocked hat knocked into ribbons. The two old Hindi occupants crawled out of the ruins, luckily unhurt. It was very amusing to hear the complaisant self-gratulatory way in which one of them remarked: "God takes care of good people." Some of the cliffs between which we passed rose upwards of one thousand feet, and the sky-line of some was so rectangular and the lines of fissure and stratification so parallel, that it was difficult not to fancy that you saw gigantic works of human architecture. Towards evening we entered a pass where it was said that three years before a caravan of three thousand Maghribis had been massacred by the Bedawi. This place certainly was more thickly strewn with bones than any other place we had come to as yet, and in the evening it was indeed a most gruesome scene. At daybreak I found myself on the donkey, and as the sun rose it showed us that we were leaving the rocky region and approaching a great glaring dusty plain. Every yard into that dead barren waste, with its constant flitting mirage phantoms, made you feel more dismal and insignificant than one hundred miles into the bright, sparkling, living ocean even the Red Sea itself, with a temperature of one hundred degrees in the shade, is nothing to the desert for downright misery and helplessness. The suffering of many of those on foot had now become very great, as they crawled along, hugging the shade of the camels with bowed shoulders and tottering steps—some mutely and uncomplainingly, while others were praying loudly and grinding their teeth with thirst. Here and there a man might be seen barefoot, or with only the rags of a pair of worn-out shoes hanging on to his bruised and bleeding feet. The large varicose veins on some of the swollen legs stood out most threateningly. With a few instances of individual suffering I will pass quickly over the horrors of this march of death.

With us was a good-looking little Bombay woman and her three children, the whole of whose story I afterwards heard. Her husband had been a small trader in Bombay, and two years before he had left his wife in charge of his business, and set out on a pilgrimage to Meccah; and experiencing little difficulty in accomplishing it, his zeal had carried him on to Medinah, but he suffered so much in health from the hardships of the journey that, finding himself out of funds, he had been afraid to venture on the return, and had written to his wife telling her that he meant to remain in Medinah for the rest of his days. On receiving this letter the plucky little woman had sold off everything she possessed, and set out to join her husband. When I first noticed her we were three days out from Meccah, and she was tramping bravely along, with the baby at her breast, and dragging two little children of four and five years old—a boy and a girl—by her side. The way that little woman bore up through the whole journey was marvellous, and her care of the three children was such that she succeeded in bringing them alive to Medinah. She would not have starved if only for the food which I procured for her; and after a time, when her case got to be known among the wealthier pilgrims, she became rather a favourite, and one of the children was often given a lift for a few hours on a camel. She was the only pilgrim in the caravan for whom I felt any compassion. She, at all events, had a reasonable motive for her undertaking.

Some of the scenes were very sickening. One old man, whose right leg was very much swollen with elephantiasis, kept up until within about six hours of the end of our present stage, when he showed the inevitable signs of being near the end. Most of the men, as they became nearly exhausted, would stagger on ahead to the leading camel and lie down until the last camel came up to them. As sure as they began to do this it would not be long before they would give in. The old fellow I watched kept it up for a couple of hours, and then lay down for good. The last Bedawin who passed his prostrate form gave him a rouse-up prod with the butt of his spear, and a jeering recommendation to move on; but the only reply from the parched lips was a hoarse delirious prayer, and another was left behind in the desert.

All the bodies we came upon were decapitated; showing that it was quite true that the Bedawi who follow in the wake of a pilgrim caravan cut off the heads and hands of all stragglers they fall in with, both dying and dead. By midnight on the last day of this march I do not believe there was a drop of water in the whole caravan; every drop that I knew of was either evaporated or had been drunk, and we still had thirteen hours before us, most of the time under a burning sun. I had often been longer without water under similar circumstances, but then I was strong and as full of life as a man could be. What the tortures of those who had to walk would be, I could not bear to think. I dreaded the revelations of the next day's light. When it came, however, it was some relief to see that most of the people who had managed to keep up until the night before, had been able to hang on through this night also; and one felt a hope that, now the wells were so near, most of them would surely hold out for a few hours longer. What terrible tempers we were all in, both pilgrims and Bedawi! Even the camels were more irascible than usual, and did the most extraordinary things with their long necks, to prevent our mounting or dismounting them. Several quarrels took place between the pilgrims and Bedawi, and in one scuffle that occurred a pilgrim was wounded by a sword-cut. Also four more camels were abandoned. During the whole of the last march we had used no water for our ablutions before prayer, but had gone through the motions of them with sand instead, as the Koran allows persons situated as we were to do so.

CHAPTER IV.

HALT AT RABIGH.

After a number of false reports that Rabigh was in sight, spread by the pilgrims, who were deceived by the mirage, the Bedawi, about two hours before noon, pointed out a grove of date-palms which had appeared to spring up suddenly out of the plain a couple of miles ahead of us.

But though it looked so close when first seen, it took us two hours to reach the Turkish fort of Rabigh, a mile inland from the port, where two or three small dhows could be seen riding at anchor, and close past which, best of all, ran a broad stream of the sweetest water we had yet tasted in the Hejaz. To reach our camping-ground we had to cross this stream, and there was a regular stampede when the water first came in sight. Even the worn camels started off into a feeble shambling trot, and could not be restrained from quenching their thirst at once. Crowds of pilgrims and Bedawi spread up and down the edge of the stream, or dabbled in it, bathing their hot inflamed feet long after the body of the caravan had moved on the two or three hundred yards farther to the camping-ground. This was a grassy open space under the walls of the Turkish fort or castle. The fort was a square building of a hundred yards on each side, the battlemented walls, thirty feet high, rising straight up from the level plain, without a ditch or other defence. But each corner of the building was flanked by a tower, mounting on its top two twelve-pounder ship's carronades, utterly useless from rust and age. There was a large gateway in the centre of the wall facing the sea. The Bedawin town numbers some two hundred huts, where fresh fish and mutton and vegetables could be procured, and the country round for a mile or two on every side was thickly studded with groves of date-palms. After the tents had been pitched and a good supply of water and provisions brought in, we soon had a plentiful hot supper ready. As we had eaten nothing but cold boiled rice, stale chupatties, and dry dates for the last three days, the fresh fish and vegetables we were able to procure here were very welcome, and soon put us all into a comfortable good-humour. Shaykh the Bo'sen, who had reached Rabigh twenty-four hours before us on his fast camel, gave us a little news. He said that a Turkish cavalry patrol, encamped a day's march ahead of us, had had two horses stolen, and he and the other Bedawi were in great consternation, not knowing what form of reprisals to expect from the Turks. He also told us that it had been ascertained that we had lost, out of our whole caravan, fifty-two pilgrims and nine camels, taking great credit to himself for having brought our own party through with only the loss of a single camel. The Turkish soldiers annoyed me here a good deal, for my fair complexion was now rather conspicuous among the Hindis. Two or three times Turkish soldiers addressed me while walking in the bazaar. One old officer strolling about our camp, and seeing me sitting near a fire, asked me if I was a Malay, and to save further explanation, I told him I was, and he was satisfied.

Our old incubus found us another camel here, and gave it the same name as his lost one. Our new Mabarak turned out a first-rate animal, and carried us well until we returned to Meccah. "Over a better piece of camel-flesh a man never crossed a leg." Towards evening, as the sea appeared to be quite close, a few of us went off to take a bathe; but after walking for half-an-hour, and on account of the mirage seeming to bring the water no nearer, we were afraid to venture farther from camp for fear of Bedawi, and so returned without our swim. In the evening the Amér took out the guns and shot a pair of pigeons, great numbers of which were flying about the country.

Under the Turkish guns we were considered quite safe from robbers, so that our rest need not be disturbed on their account, and as we were all extremely tired we slept well. For my part, it was the first night's sleep I had had since leaving Meccah, notwithstanding the packs of dogs that prowled howling and yelping round the camp. Early next morning we all rose quite freshened up and in the best of spirits. The dogs we found had done us more damage than we had suffered from the Bedawi hitherto. They had got hold of a bag of dried deer-meat in the night, and consumed nearly all of it before they were discovered. The Amér, four others, and myself went out to try and make up for this loss by shooting some of the pigeons, and it was said also we might come upon a gazelle, at a spot about a mile up the stream. As I had a double gun and a dozen cartridges in the breast of my tunic I had no fear of Bedawi, and ran off a short distance to some long grass that looked a likely place, and had just turned the corner of some reeds out of sight of my companions, when I rose a brace of quail; nothing could equal the astonishment of two Bedawi, who had followed me, when they saw me take the birds right and left. They looked upon it as the act of a madman to fire at a bird on the wing, and when they saw my birds come down, they went off and told of the feat all over the village. The Amér and the rest of our people seldom ventured to try a shot at anything in motion if they could stalk close up to it on the ground, and afterwards I thought it better to imitate them, as I had no wish to get my name up. We were shooting for the pot, and we made a good bag out of the flocks of pigeons, sometimes dropping six or seven at a volley. Before breakfast we had bagged sixteen-and-a-half pairs of pigeons, a brace of partridges, and my quails.

After that we had the rest of the day before us to do as we liked, for we were not to start until night. Some of the party took opium and went to sleep, while I went for a walk in the village. I found my fame had gone before me, and I heard the Bedawi telling one another of the wonderful shot I had been seen to make that morning. What with the blow I was said to have struck with the "empty hand" and my flying shots, I felt I was bringing myself into far too great prominence. But from my return to camp that afternoon the tide turned, and my luck set steadily against me for some time. Feeling actively idle and having nothing to do, I took it into my head to have a change of diet and do a little cooking on my own account. First I thought I would have a pigeon-pie with potatoes in it; but the cook said the potatoes had cost a piastre each, and were especially for the Amér's Englishisttoo* and muttinicutillets,† and that he would not let me have any of them *to spoil.* So I went to the Amér and asked him if he would like me to prepare him a dish that was a great favourite among sailors, very simple and nice, and as easy to make in the desert as on board-ship.

He at once told the chief cook to give me every facility for making it. As I date the beginning of my troubles from that pudding, I think the reader should know what it was like. Among our stores we had

* Irish stew, and very bad Irish stew.

† Mutton cutlets, also very bad.

flour and treacle, and the idea I had was to make a rolly-poly—nothing could be easier, one would suppose. But then the chief cook, who considered himself one of the greatest artists in his line to be found in India, and who believed the dish did not exist which he could not prepare (even down to such a foreign kickshaw as "cake"), very much resented my interference, and insisted on making the pudding himself under my directions. But I found him so intractable that, after a few preliminary instructions, I gave him up, and thought no more about him or the pudding, but went and employed myself more usefully in getting our dismantled shugduf in order for our new camel. As soon as it was ready I lay down in it and began smoking heavily, a plan I always found to banish my cravings for un-come-at-able food. I saw the supper carried into the tent, and was just thinking of taking my place at the cloth, when a cry of alarm from the tent brought me to the spot at the double-quick. Dismay was on every face, and the chief cook, standing in speechless agony, pointed first to me, as I entered, and then to the pudding on the dish in the middle of the cloth. He had tried his hand at my pudding after all, and what had been the result? With oriental ingenuity, he had contrived to impart an air of absolute ferocity to an otherwise comparatively docile and harmless—so far as I have heard—rolly-poly, as it lay curled up on the dish ready for a spring. It was not bigger than a wild cat, but in looks it exactly resembled a mad rhinoceros. All looked to me to rescue them, and I promptly seized a large iron spoon and dealt the pudding a stunning blow in the midriff; but the weapon glanced off its polished hide. With a second well-aimed blow I broke its back and finally disabled it. Every countenance expressed the joyous relief that was felt. The wound in the pudding disclosed, among other irregularities, that the cook had omitted such trifles as the treacle and suet. Still, I thought it might be eaten; so, putting a good face on the matter, I reflected a flap of its integument with a scimitar, and, by means of some gun-cotton detonating cartridges, succeeded without much difficulty in detaching portions of the interior substance. *Nunc oblavi ad gravum.* The pudding was a failure, and I got the whole blame of wasting four pounds of flour, an article we were running short of. However, it was not a very serious matter, and we made a meal out of the other good things on the cloth.

Our halt had now come to an end, and we must prepare for putting off into the desert again at sunset. Most of the begging pilgrims had been able to secure a rich supply of broken victuals, and with plenty of water at hand and the use of the fires of such as were able to buy firewood, they had not fared badly during our last halt, and now set out cheerfully, knowing that the worst of our journey was over. I had become so used to the motion of the camel that I dropped off to sleep for short intervals two or three times during the night. The moon was now growing old, and we had bright moonlight for the greater part of the night, revealing the numerous skeletons of camels

F 2

by the wayside in a very ghastly manner, but altogether much improving our condition. The camels, which had hitherto moved in one long line, were split up into shorter strings, and travelled now two or three, and sometimes four, lines abreast in the parallel beaten paths over an undulating stony plain. We had taken up a good supply of torches at Rabigh, and great numbers of these were kept burning all night. It was easy to procure a light for your hookah by calling the nearest torchbearer. Of water we had more than enough to last us, so that we need not stint ourselves; besides having some to spare for any beggars who might seem to want it badly towards the end of the march; and we again began to perform ablutions before praying.

At daylight we sighted another caravan on the distant horizon, approaching us. The two caravans came nearer and nearer, and at last passed one another, just as ships would at sea, within hailing distance. We spoke them, and they proved to be the returning Malays from Medinah. This might have been known from its orderly condition. There was not a single pedestrian attached to the caravan except the Bedawi camel-drivers.

At noon we camped. This time we pitched our camp in a pleasant little green valley, near a spring and running brook, from which the distant hills were just visible to the north-east. The inhabitants of the village in this valley were said to be the worst robbers to be met with along the whole road, so we took precautions accordingly. As we were to remain in this valley until morning, sentry duties had to be allotted for the night. I was told that my turn would come on at midnight and last until morning prayer at daylight. The day had not been painfully hot, a nice light breeze from the sea having set in shortly after daybreak, falling away at sunset, and the night promised not to be as cold as usual.

Everything went smoothly and regularly, and I was beginning to think that desert travelling need not be so bad after all.

After sunset the shoutings and volleys of musketry

kept up to scare marauders did not keep me awake long. When I was called to take my post at midnight, I found I had been enjoying a most comfortable sleep, and was rather disgusted at having to muffle up and go out and walk about with the cold barrel of a rifle in my hands. I considered it the greatest humbug. I knew there was not a man in camp who had the slightest intention of shooting anything when he fired his piece, or who would for a moment have resisted an armed Bedawin if he had walked into the camp and walked out with a load of plunder in the open daylight. The man I had to relieve was the third warrior, one of the most sensible men in the camp. He not only hurried me out quickly, but when he gave me the rifle it was not loaded. I asked him if he had any cartridges. He said: "Why do you want to waste ammunition; are there not fools enough doing that all round you?"

But I was in a bad humour, and had made up my mind that if I had any cause to fire the rifle I would hit the object, Bedawin or not. So I took a couple of rounds out with me, and loaded as soon as I got to my post. I walked up and down on my beat for a few turns, and took a drink of cold water to get myself thoroughly awake, and then sat down by my fire and occupied myself by throwing little bits of dry wood into it and making blazes. I must have been keeping some sort of a look-out—probably from an old habit of watchfulness acquired on night-watches at sea—for, during one of the brighter flashes of flame from my fire, I fancied I saw a dark object creeping along the ground about twenty yards off. I jumped to attention and watched its movements closely. There could be no mistake about it, a low black object was moving rapidly from bush to bush, and coming a little nearer to my post at every change of place. "Whatever you are you're up to no good," I thought, "so here goes;" and the next time it showed in the open I tried a snap-shot. The object stopped dead, and the low whine it gave told me I had shot a dog. In the commotion that followed the report of my rifle, nobody tried to find out who had fired the first shot. I said nothing about my little exploit at the time, and the dog remained until daylight, when it was found; and I was greatly blamed for my rashness, especially when I told the Amér I was sorry it was not a Bedawin.

CHAPTER V.

WOUNDED.

We were to have "Englishishtoo" for breakfast. Now, of all our *cuisinerie*, this was the only dish for which I had the slightest relish, and whenever we had it I used to so manage that I came in for a good share. I was obliged to do this in an underhand way, as it would never have done for me to show an open preference for such a notoriously European dish. Nobody in the party liked it, and, although the cook put about three times the proper proportion of pepper into it, everyone but the Amér declared that it had "neither taste nor smell." The Amér only pretended to like it because the dish had been a fashionable novelty when he left India, and he did not wish to appear behind the times, even in the desert, where, moreover, potatoes had the recommendation of being extremely expensive. This time I took myself out of the way when the meal appeared, and did not return until it had been over for some time. I then went to the cook and asked him what he had to eat, and he told me there was nothing but "Englishishtoo" left. This was what I had expected, for I knew that nobody took more of it than they could help—just a mouthful or so out of compliment to the Amér's supposed taste for it. I pretended to be dissatisfied, but told him to give me a good plateful, as I was very hungry; and I asked him if he could not scrape up some rice besides. This he did for me; and I took my two plates off behind a pile of boxes, and sat down on the sand to enjoy a most extensive blow-out.

Not far from me an old Bedawin was just finishing a most revolting surgical operation on a camel. I did not mind that. I could stand a great deal in those days. I only congratulated myself on the success of my little scheme, and put my first potato eagerly into my mouth with that sensation of real pleasure only to be experienced by an Irishman who had not tasted the national tuber twice for the last six months. At this crisis I saw the Bedawin just mentioned walking quickly towards me, wiping his filthy hands on his offensive matted head of hair. The astonishing circumstance of a Bedawin *cleaning* his hands should have warned me; but no! before I could draw the plate away or do anything to prevent him, this "proud son of the desert" had dived his loathsome paw slap into the middle of my *bonne bouche.* I could stand a great deal in those days, but I could not stand that. He was so overcome by the way I pressed the remainder of the mess, plate and all, on him that he had to sit down. In fact, from the hasty manner in which he dashed the scalding stew from his face and chest, I gathered that he felt rather pained, and was relieved to notice that he was unarmed, and not at all sorry to see him rush away swearing vehemently. I was more than disappointed; but after relieving my mind a little after the manner of the Bedawin, I was fain to sit down and appease my hunger the best way I could on the remaining rice. I then employed myself for a short time cleaning the two plates. All the plates carried in the desert are made either of tin or copper, and however much water may be at hand you never think of washing them. They are always cleaned with sand, which serves the purpose almost better than water; for you can rub them with handfuls of dry clean sand until they glisten, and not a grain of the sand will stick to them. I cleaned the two plates to my satisfaction, and laid them on the sand to admire them shining in the sun for a moment, and then stooped to pick them up, when—I knew what had happened—some narrow steel instrument had been driven into the back of my right thigh and, striking hard against the bone, had glanced off and passed out at the front. I felt that it had not been thrown, for it had received two distinct impulses forward; and as I felt that it was withdrawn, being sure of a second thrust, I staggered forward, and, facing round, regained my left leg standing. I saw the man who had just shared my pot-luck running away backwards and looking at me, flourishing his spear and laughing loudly in an unmistakable that's-got-you-my-boy tone of voice.

I have experienced greater pain from a slighter wound, but I never felt anything like the sudden depression* of spirits that the sight of the stream of blood flowing down my leg brought on. I dropped instantly on the sand, and stretching myself out I pressed my right hand over the wound at the back, and tried to stop the blood. I then called out to the third warrior (my camel-mate—about the most reliable man in the camp) to bring me the rifle and a cartridge, as I wanted to show him something.

He heard me, and replied: "What do you want? To shoot another dog?"

"No. In the name of God, come; I believe I'm killed."

* The depression was actual cardiac syncope or collapse, from sudden and profuse loss of blood.

This brought him at once.

"Oh Allah!" he exclaimed, when he saw the blood.

I asked him to lend me the rifle, and then set the sight at two hundred yards and handed it back to him, pointing out the Bedawin still flourishing his spear triumphantly at about that distance off. He took the rifle and tried a shot. I think he meant it; the bullet must have gone very near, for the fellow ducked as if he had been hit, and then bolted off and disappeared among a grove of date-palms. The thing had taken place in an out-of-the-way corner, behind a pile of boxes, and no one had seen it done; but now a crowd collected from all quarters, making the greatest fuss round me. I asked some of them to carry me near to my shugduf, and half-a-dozen laid hold of me and deposited me there in no time. I then asked for my bundle, and, with the assistance of the third warrior, tore up some of my cotton clothes into bandages. And now I found that the spear had not passed out at the front as I thought; but there was a round dark red blotch on the upper part of my thigh, that showed that the point of the spear had come nearly through.

Though the wound in the back of the thigh would just admit the little finger, and everybody's plan was tried, and all sorts of advice taken, we found it impossible to stanch the bleeding. Large pads of lint were scraped up and tied tightly over the wound with bandages; still in a few minutes the blood would begin to ooze out and fall in quickly succeeding drops on the sand. Two hours after I received the wound all my cotton clothes—seven pieces, each about the size of a white shirt—had been torn up, and were saturated with blood until they looked like a mass of raw flesh.

One by one the crowd that had been standing near me went about their business, with looks that said plainly: "No more can be done for him."

I felt myself getting very weak. It was maddening to think that I might die in that place, all through not being able to stop such an absurd little leak. I got into quite a rage thinking about it. I swore at the third warrior, and told him if he could do nothing for me to go away with the rest of them. I then tried my strength, and found I could not rise up into a sitting posture without feeling faint and dizzy. I then lay down quietly, and the third warrior came and put his bundle under my head, and sat down near me holding my right hand in his. He was the only one now staying by me, and I derived a certain amount of comfort from even his company; besides, he was able to give me the water, of which I was drinking a good deal, and brush off the swarms of flies that gathered over me as I lay.

After a time, as I lay on the sand, the blood still oozing slowly through the thick layers of bandages and lint, I took to contemplating the possibility of my dying, but only in a vague sort of way. I do not think, in the bottom of my heart, I believed that I should die; but, at the same time, it looked seriously like it. My companion at my side was giving me his ideas of the heaven to which I was straightway going—"a little bit invented and a little bit inferred." I think I must have had a good deal of hope left somewhere, for I was able to turn my head away and smile when he gave me a graphic delighted account of one of the angelic operations I was to undergo before attaining to a glorious beatitude: it sounded so very like instructions for cleaning a fish. I foresaw that if I went on getting weaker at the rate I was, I should not be able to double my fist soon. Then I saw the preparations for starting the caravan going on round me, and a horrid notion that I might be left in the desert alive came over me, and I felt almost the same sensation as when I first saw the blood streaming down my leg. I thought then that I had better try and do something to let my fate be known at home, if I should not get out of this scrape. The British Consul knew that I was in the country, and I had given him the address of my friends in England. I asked the third warrior to give me a piece of paper and pencil he would find in my bundle. He gave them to me, and I, with some difficulty, wrote on the paper:

"First munsel * beyond Rabigh.

"SIR,

"The bearer of this will give further information. No blame whatever to anyone.

"J. F. K."

"To H. B. M. Consul, Jeddah."

I rolled this note up and put it between my teeth, and then asked the third warrior if he would promise me to give it to the British Consul after I was dead; but if I recovered, to give it back to me when I asked for it.

"Why do you want to send a letter to that nassara?"† he said.

I told him then that I might easily tell a lie that would satisfy him; but that, as I was probably dying, I would prefer him not to ask me, but just do as I requested, without more talk. He

* Stage. † Christian.

promised he would do it, in such a way that I thought I could trust him; so I gave him the note instead of swallowing it, as I had intended to if he had made any difficulties. I was a good deal more exhausted after that; but, without having any definite hope, I felt much easier in my mind. I thought my hands looked just like a washer-woman's, and noticed two or three vultures wheeling round high up in the air above me. I became aware of people standing over me and looking at me, but I did not care to see who they were; and after that I must have died—

For dying I could die no more.

But I no more remember losing consciousness than you, reader, remember the precise moment at which you went to sleep last night.

* * * * *

The first sense that returned to me was taste, a pleasant, sweet, cool taste. I felt something being put into my mouth which I swallowed; and in time

I remembered what had happened, and began to wonder where I was, but was not sufficiently interested to open my eyes to look. I knew that my burning thirst was being quenched by some-one putting little bits of water-melon into my mouth, which was very pleasant, so I went on swallowing them as fast as I could get them down. Gradually I felt the motion of a camel under me, and opened my eyes. I was lying on my back in the shugduf, and my old friend, the third warrior, was sitting on the opposite side, cutting up a water-melon into little squares and reaching over and feeding me with them. I tried to speak, but found myself very weak; however, I did just manage to ask where I was. He told me we were about to halt, and that it was fourteen hours since I had spoken. It was coming to life from the dead. I was sure I was saved. I never felt so happy before, nor probably ever shall again. I went on eating the delicious water-melon for perhaps half an hour, and then the camel was made to kneel down, and the shugduf lifted carefully off his back with me in it. I was then left alone for some time.

I suppose I went to sleep, for the next thing I remember was the Amér and a few other people standing round me, and the third warrior removing the blanket that was covering my body and legs. I shall never forget that sight of myself—smirched and smeared from head to foot with blood which had dried black and brown, and I looked as thin as a cholera corpse.

"Wash me," I said, and as they were lifting me out of the shugduf I fainted. I remember little for the next day or two except eating water-melon. I must have slept the greater part of the time. No mother or wife could have nursed me with greater care than did the third warrior, and I soon began to get stronger. It was on the second day after coming to that I asked the third warrior to rub a piece of meat with salt and roast it in the hot ashes, which he did, and I ate about half a pound of lean mutton. After that I soon began to get better, and developed an appetite like a hyena, and was able to talk away to my camel-mate as we rode along or lay in our shugduf during the halts. If there had been any blood left in my body, the tale he had to tell me must have frozen it. It appeared that when I went off, everybody in the camp thought I was dead. As the caravan was on the point of starting, and there was no time for ceremony, it was proposed that they should just scrape a hole in the sand, put me in and cover me up. This plan the third warrior stoutly opposed, saying he did not think I was dead, and if I was, it would only be Mohammedanlike to carry me on to the next stage and "bury me decent." As he was the only one of the party who held these opinions, the majority would certainly have put me under the sand in a few minutes if it had not been for Shaykh the Bo'sen. With the Bedawi I had always assumed an air of careless recklessness, never "putting in my spoke" when they were squabbling with my companions, and had always allowed myself to be directed by them when working at loading or unloading the camels. This behaviour of mine, without my knowing it, made me a great favourite with them. So that when Shaykh the Bo'sen saw how badly I was wounded, he had jumped up on his camel and sped off to a neighbouring village where lived a hakim,* with a great name and practice, leaving orders before going that the starting of the caravan should be delayed until his return. He returned, with the hakim mounted behind him, just as some of my friends had begun to dig my grave. When the leech saw me he pronounced me alive, examined my wound, and quickly applied a Bedawin styptic, and declared that with quiet, great care, and water-melon diet, he had every hope of my ultimate recovery.

What would the reader suppose this desert doctor's fee was? *A guinea!*† The Amér gave it to him grumbling, I heard, and then gave the third warrior leave to take charge of me and put me on our camel.

On the third day after the wound the bandages began to get itchy and irritating, so that at our next halt I had myself lifted out of the shugduf and took off the bandages.

* M.D. † The English guinea is a common coin in the Hejaz.

Considering the heat of the weather and the many other unfavourable circumstances, the wound was progressing most favourably, and after a good wash it looked extremely healthy and clean. I took out of it a plug of raw cotton, that smelt strongly of common turpentine. I believe that that was the styptic which the hakim had applied, and it could have been procured in Meccah quite easily. It has, I believe, the advantage of being strongly antiseptic. So that my Bedawin hakim, undoubtedly original, appeared to be a sort of desert "Lister." From that time forward the treatment I employed for my wound was a daily wash in lukewarm water and the application of a greased bandage. It improved so rapidly, and I so speedily regained strength, that the day on which we reached Medinah, six days after receiving my wound, I was able, with the assistance of two of my companions, to walk into the town.

For the greater part of the night before we came to Medinah we had been ascending stony rugged paths, on which several worn-out camels had come to grief. We had seen the loom of the lights from the town in the sky for some time before the day broke. In the glowing imaginations of my companions it had been deemed the heavenly light said to direct the pilgrims' steps, from three days' distance, towards Medinah. Just as the sun rose we had surmounted an ascent, from which we saw spread out, five hundred feet below us, a level plain several miles in extent, and in the middle of this plain, reposing against the black rocky ridge of a mount, suddenly burst on our view the city of "Medinah the Honoured." The hill, or small mountain, rises abruptly from the plain, and the outlines of the city are egg-shaped, with the distant side of its small end against the hill, under "the shadow of a great rock in a weary land."

CHAPTER VI.

MEDINAH.

MEDINAH, when first sighted, may fairly be ranked with Constantinople from the Sea of Marmora, or anyone of the loveliest of the beautiful cities of the world. As seen from the distant birdseye point of view to which it first presents itself to the pilgrim's delighted gaze, its tall, snow-white, uninterrupted walls and numerous gilded minarets, with the morning sun gleaming over them, and the broad green belt of cultivated ground encircling it—as seen, I say, at such a time, by the way-worn pilgrim from Meccah, it is a fresh bright jewel, bounded by a vast grim barrenness of desert, an opal and pearl mosaic set in a brilliant border of shining green enamel. What a moment it was to many of us! The one aspiration of many of their lives was now accomplished. There, beneath them, reposing in the bosom of the plain, lay their goal, "Medinah the Honoured," the tomb of the Prophet, by whose side they could now lay down their weary bones to rest for ever; nor cared they how soon, in their certainty of eternal bliss.

To others of us what a glad sight it was too, after days and nights of perpetual forward, forward, yet scarcely seeming to make any advance over the drear dry miles of rocky arid desolation, to see before us the end of our apparently interminable journey at last—Medinah, which should have been named the fortunate. Walled habitations, green fields, running water, every blessing the Eastern mind could desire, were there. When first Medinah came in view the whole caravan burst into the most extravagant expressions of praise and thanksgiving to God for their deliverance from their recent perils, and for their safe arrival at their destination. Even the poor camels lifted their long drooping necks, and strained their utmost to increase their pace into a feeble staggering attempt at a "run in" at the finish.

And now most assuredly the gait of our camels kept time to that "needless Alexandrine" from Pope's "Essay on Criticism," that

> Like a wounded snake drags its slow length along.

There! it's been drummed into my ears ever since I left Meccah. I've heroically abstained, but it would out, and I must say I feel better.

Dismounting from my camel to walk into Medinah, as others did, was of course out of the question for me.

After descending to the valley, we passed over half-a-mile of sand, which gradually merged into a grassy plain; and over this the road led for about two miles up to the gate of the city, where we arrived about an hour from the time when we had first seen it. We halted close outside the gate, on an open space surrounded by Bedawi huts, and unloaded the camels, but did not form any regular camp. Crowds of Arabs came out of the city to offer lodgings and sell eatables to the pilgrims, and altogether the scene became one of almost as great animation as on the day we left Wady Fatima.

The Amér and most of our party went at once into the town to find a suitable house for us, and another for the women. The third warrior stayed with me, and assisted me out of the shugduf. I lay down on my blankets on the ground while he packed up our bundles. I told him that I had decided to make an attempt at walking into the town with his assistance, and I took the opportunity of asking him to give me back the little bit of paper I had given him, with my message to the Consul at Jeddah written on it. He soon produced it from the folds of his cumberbund, and I was in the act of tearing it up, when I changed my mind, and have preserved it ever since. Very vividly it recalls the scenes among which it was written.

The little Hindi woman and her children came to me to give me a farewell. She looked "in pitiful case;" but she was so happy at having reached the end of her journey, and at her prospects of soon meeting her husband, that she did not seem to be aware of the sore state of her feet and her swollen legs. I borrowed a rupee from the third warrior and gave it to her, and he gave her half a rupee himself. I afterwards heard that she found her husband keeping a small tea-stall, and doing very well. He must have made a good deal out of our custom while we were in Medinah, for our people went to his stall regularly.

I had no opportunity of seeing my little dark heroine again; but her bright brave face, during the whole of her terrible tramp, will always dwell in my memory. I never expect to meet with a better instance of the devotion of a wife and mother, though she was only one of those women of the East who are "kept in such degradation and ignorance" (?).

About noon—the house having been settled upon—we began to move into it; and I should have begun to dress myself, but my under-clothing had all been torn up for bandages, or was defiled with blood; in which state it was unclean, and could not be worn. Certainly, I thought, I left Meccah with "nothing but rags to my back," but I shall be returning "without a rag to my back." I borrowed a cumberbund from one of my companions, and, enveloping myself in my huge camel-hair cloak, I went in through the gate, leaning on two of my companions. After half-an-hour's walking through the streets, with an occasional rest, we reached the house. The streets through which we had come were all, fortunately for me, perfectly level. They were clean, and kept in very good order indeed for an Eastern town. There is a general air of prosperity about the place and its inhabitants that gives a very favourable impression to a new arrival: even the dogs look less mangy and hungry than in other Mohammedan towns.

The rooms we had taken were on the ground-floor of a large house, near the centre of the city, the door opening into a garden of about a quarter of an acre of date-palms. In the middle of this garden was a fine large well, full to the very brim with delicious cool water, looking dark and deep, and so fresh, with the green weeds floating on it, that it made one long for just one plunge.

I was extremely weak, and beginning to suffer a great deal of pain, so that I was compelled to go at once into the house. The room we had taken was a splendid hall—nothing less. Across the middle of the hall passed a broad paved passage; two feet below the level of the floor on each side of it, and in the middle of this lower portion of the room, was a circular stone basin of water, twelve feet in diameter, and self-supplying. Directly over this basin was an opening, between the rooms of the upper storeys, that led up to a large open skylight in the roof of the house. For light and coolness no arrangement could have been better. The raised portions of the room were matted over with a good grass mat, and the walls were cleanly whitewashed. The whole chamber looked much too wholesome and bright for us after what we had been accustomed to in Meccah.

In a corner of the room I lay down on my blanket, and the third warrior, who had seen me in, then left me to go and indulge in a big ablution, and attend to his religious duties in the Haram, as all the others of our party were now doing. As fast as they came back from the Haram, they all set to work washing again. How I envied them as I heard them sousing their skins, parched and cracked, over and over again with large vessels of water! The Amér spent all the day, when he was not at his prayers, having alternate hot and cold water baths. The splashing and laughing round the well in the garden was kept up until late on in the night. My wound was very troublesome, and I feared that my exertion of the morning had thrown it back. It was so painful that I was obliged to take a little opium that night before I could go to sleep. When I dressed my wound next morning it did not look bad, and I was able, with the help of the third warrior, to go out into the garden and have a good bathe, which had a most beneficial effect.

We were to remain ten days in Medinah, and that

would allow us fifty prayers in the Haram. But I thought it quite probable that I might have to leave Medinah without performing a prayer in the Haram at all. I might, after all my hardships, and after having actually been in Medinah, fail in attaining the object of my journey. No! I was determined I would see the tomb. For the first week I lay fretting and fuming on the floor. But after a week, at the times of prayer, when all my companions were away in the Haram, I would stand up and try to walk a little with a stick, and after a couple of days of this I felt confident that I should be able to go through the rites and ceremonies of a first visit to the Haram, as they are not very tedious. On the ninth day I determined to make the effort.

A good many visitors came in daily to pay their respects to the Amér, and we had daily calls from a number of date merchants with samples of their fruit. One of these told me that there were fifty varieties of date cultivated in Medinah. The shelibi is the finest, and is very much valued all over the East. It is said that it cannot be brought to perfection anywhere except at Medinah. It is a very large and delicious date. The Amér purchased nearly half a ton of picked fruit of this sort. The next best date is a small one, no larger than a medium-sized gooseberry. It has no stone in it, or only a rudimentary stone like a little bit of straw, which cannot be noticed in eating the fruit.

Than Medinah, I suppose that a more flourishing little city is not to be found anywhere in the East. It has a population of about twenty thousand inhabitants, probably two-thirds Arab, the rest being Turks and a small proportion of foreign residents from most other Mohammedan countries. The houses are built of the same materials as in Meccah, but are nowhere to be seen in the same dilapidated and neglected condition. I should think that the masonry and plaster is more easily kept in repair on account of the abundance of water in the district, which must induce a more uniform temperature than exists in Meccah. Under the ample fructifying solar heat, the well-watered suburbs of Medinah produce an endless variety of vegetables and fruits. A list of a day's supplies from the market would comprise perhaps all the following articles: Onions, garlic, carrots, beetroot, radishes, beans, cucumbers, and very fine grapes. In short, almost everything that can be thought of will grow about Medinah, together with such cereals as maize, wheat, and barley.

One of our daily visitors was the chief eunuch of the Haram, a very old infirm negro, who used to sit for hours telling us stories and traditions of the tomb. One of his stories, though well known in the East, may not be so well known to my readers. It relates to the only time the grave of Mohammed has been entered by a living mortal since the Prophet was buried there.

"One day"—these two words are a literal translation of the words with which the eunuch began his story, for the rest, I only remember the substance of the narrative, so must give it in my own words. "One day," a great many years ago, the attendants of the Haram noticed a most noisome smell emanating from, in or about, the Prophet's Tomb. Many days were spent in the most assiduous searching round the outside; but nothing could be found from which the smell could be thought to originate. At last a few of the moolahs* began reluctantly to admit the possibility of an impurity existing inside (though all had been unanimous in denying this at first), for the smell had undoubtedly been traced to a small aperture in the wall of the tomb. Conjecture ran rampant, and the controversy among the lights of the faith reached an appalling height. Still, all the learning of all the greatest minds of the day could not explain away that smell; it not only remained, but it was ever getting worse. One unorthodox Persian suggested the heretical thought that the Prophet himself had gone bad. He was put to such tortures that he craved to be torn to pieces with red-hot pincers as a happy release.

This wholly unexpected view, hinted at by the Persian, had the effect of uniting the wise men, though they themselves were prepared to believe the smell nothing less than the "odour of sanctity" itself, if it came to that. It would not do for

* D.D.'s.

such an opinion as the Persian's to get about and pass unrefuted. They saw the urgency of the case, and felt what terrible things unkind people might say. In a great council of moolahs, assembled from all parts of the earth, to consider this matter of the smell, a decision was come to and acted upon as follows:

The goodest good little boy that could be found, active enough to get through the hole in the wall of the sepulchre, was put into training; that is to say, was put through a course of ablutions and fastings for his extra purification, and then sent into the tomb. The boy came out again in a very short time with a dead pigeon, the cause of the smell, in his left hand, and he was found to have been struck deaf and dumb and blind. Many years passed, and the boy became an old man, and was just at the point of death, when his senses suddenly returned in time to allow him to relate these facts and expire: When he had entered the tomb he had found it brilliantly lighted, and seen sitting in the middle the Prophet with the Koran on his knees, and an angel on each side of him reading to him. The angel on the right of the Prophet rose up as he entered and introduced himself as Gabriel, and taking hold of his left hand closed it over the dead pigeon, and showed him out so politely that he never suspected the dreadful calamity that had befallen him until he found darkness on the outside and he had tried to speak.

CHAPTER VII.

THE HARAM.

At noon on the day before we left Medinah I set out to visit the Haram. I found that, though my leg was very stiff, I was quite able to walk slowly along to the nearest gate, not more than three hundred yards from our house. The level of the interior of the building is exactly the same as that of the street outside. Entering by the north-east gate there are no steps, but you walk straight in over a paved entrance, and find yourself under domed colonnades, enclosing an open gravelled square, eighty yards by fifty. Near the middle of this square there is a small railed-in patch of green, with a few palms and creepers growing on it, and spread over the square were flocks of blue-rock pigeons, feeding quite tamely among the feet of the passing worshippers. The colonnades are about thirty feet high and forty feet wide, and are roofed with three rows of small domes. This domed ceiling is supported by three rows of round pillars, and the pavement is composed of large smooth flagstones. The western arcade is set apart for the women to pray in, and is shut in from the square by a close wooden lattice-work. Walking round the eastern side of the building, you find it extends for another forty yards beyond the square, and that that part of it is completely roofed in. This roof is supported on from one hundred and sixty to one hundred and seventy round pillars, each about eighteen inches in diameter. The ceiling is divided into twelve rows of thirteen blue painted domes, and the floor is laid with marble flags, the greater part of it being richly carpeted. Near the centre of this covered-in portion of the building are two stone pulpits, plain hexagonal stone pedestals, with steps leading up to them. About twenty-five feet of the north end of the building is railed off from the rest, and placed all about are numerous gilt candlesticks and glass chandeliers.

Most of the stone work in the interior of the building is painted a light stone colour, and over many parts chapters from the Koran in gold and black letters may be seen. The whole place has a tawdry "dirty-flash" appearance, very different from the grand simplicity of the Haram at Meccah.

Being shy "of those who choose the chief seats in the synagogue," I took a seat as far from the pulpit as I could get without going into the sun, and sat down to wait for the noonday service. I had now time to observe the congregation as they assembled: more than half were Hindis, the rest being natives, with a few Turks and Persians. With the exception of a few Hindis and negroes, they all looked much more respectable and clean than a similar congregation would in Meccah. I do not believe they are a bit more honest for all that. We suffered several losses from theft while in Medinah. The Amér had the silver clasps cut off the back of his sword-belt, while he was praying in the Haram. The Medinah Arab has generally a darker complexion than his Meccah brother, his mien is much more sedate too, and his manner towards foreigners very dignified.

While I was sitting waiting for the imam to begin the service, an old Turkish officer came and sat down next to me, and seeing a new face that looked like a countryman's, he tried to get into a conversation with me. I might have found him troublesome if the sermon preceding the prayer had not soon begun. As it was, I shut him up with a rebuke for not attending to the words of the preacher, though we were too far off to hear what he said. The prayers over, I remained sitting counting my beads until the crush had subsided. Alone in that nest of fanatics, wounded and helpless, I felt anything but at home; I felt, I thought, like a dove in a hencoop, as I remembered the appearance of a poor little bedraggled pigeon that had been blown off to our vessel at sea, and so harboured by us. Properly, on my first visit to the Haram I should have had someone with me who knew the routine of the place, and could recite the proper prayers for me to follow him. I had coached myself pretty well, but now that it came to the point I rather hesitated, and wished that I had kept with one of my companions who knew me. Just at that moment the landlord of the house we were staying in passed me, and I called him to me and asked him to lend me his arm and be my guide. Now our landlord had been guilty of certain petty larcenies: he had several times come into our room at prayer-time, when everyone was away, and pocketed a few handfuls of dates and other little eatables, and I had connived at this by pretending to be asleep; but on one occasion I let him know that I saw him at it, and tipped him a wink that I would say nothing. So that when I asked him to do me a little favour he could not well refuse; and I was glad I got him, for he was a well-known man, rather a swell Arab.

The tomb is near the south-east corner of the building, and is a rectangular erection, twenty-five feet by twenty of plain square-cut sandstone blocks, and on the roof of the building immediately over the tomb is a large pear-shaped dome. It is quite unornamented, except on the south side, which has a front of open fretwork in brass, in which are three round holes, on a level with the eye, equidistant from one another, and large enough to admit the arm to the shoulder. Against the hole, supposed to be opposite the grave of the Prophet, I placed my eye, and, when I had become accustomed to the darkness, I saw, about four feet off, a stone wall with five red screens hung on it, of a size that would suggest their covering small doorways—that was all there was to be seen. These screens are said to bear the names of the people whose graves they are over, in the following order, beginning at the left: Mahommed, Abubekr, Omar —the first three Caliphs—Fatima, Mohammed's daughter-in-law, and the fifth is for Isa-bin-Maryam,* after his next appearance on earth.

Imitating others, I thrust my arm as far into one of the holes as I could force it, and waved it about a moment or two inside, that it might absorb by contact the more of the hallowed excellence therein, then withdrew it and retired. After a few

* Jesus Christ.

more prayers I was glad to return home, very fagged and rather disappointed, and lay down again.

I had just beheld a sight, after seeing which hundreds of men have plucked out their eyes, so that they might never be used to look upon anything less worthy. The practice of some fanatics has been to take a red-hot brick, and, holding it close to their faces, gaze on it till they roasted their eyes out. I felt tired and disappointed, that was all.

The noonday prayer on the next day made up the fifty prayers said in Medinah. On this day the Begum and the Amér expended large sums of money in largess. The whole of the household was "tipped." I received five rupees from the Begum and five rupees from the Amér. The caravan assembled at the gate of the city, but only the women mounted there. The donkey was allowed to come to the door of the house for me, and I rode it out through the walls and joined the caravan, which started about two hours before sunset, and was followed by a crowd of between two and three hundred beggars, for the first three miles of the road. The Amér, riding his horse, as he went along threw handfuls of small silver coins among the crowd. I gave the greater part of the money I had received that day to poor people who had come to Medinah in our company, but who were not returning with us. When we reached a turn of the road that would take us out of sight of Medinah, the caravan was halted for the pilgrims to mount. I alighted from my donkey, and, before mounting my camel, I had one last look at Medinah.

The city does not look to be more than one-third the size of Meccah, though its suburbs extend for a mile or two beyond the walls on every side but that next the hill. The walls are built of solid masonry, closely cemented in irregular layers, and are loopholed for musketry. They are a little over forty feet high, but have no ditch. Disposed at different short intervals all round them are a number of semicircular towers, about fifty feet high, projecting sufficiently beyond the plane of the wall to give a flanking fire. At the north-west verge of the city is a Turkish fort, or castle, on a rock, commanding with its guns both the inside and outside of the walls, on which the Turkish flag is displayed — differing in that particular from the Turkish forts in Meccah. Of all the venerable sanctuaries of Mohammedanism Medinah ranks second (Jerusalem being the third); and one prayer said here equals one thousand said elsewhere, except in Meccah.

CHAPTER VIII.

BEGIN THE RETURN JOURNEY—A GREAT STORM.

I WAS not sorry to be saying good-bye to it, beautiful city as it is, and desperate journey as I was entering upon. When my turn came for the mounting-ladder—for I was obliged to use that now—I found little difficulty in getting into our shugduf, where I found the third warrior had fixed everything as handy as a pocket in a shirt. When comfortably stretched out, with my old partner opposite and a large water-melon between us, I began to think that after all, and with a little experience, desert travelling might be made quite enjoyable.

To the pilgrim's homeward feet
E'en the desert's path is sweet.

Moreover, I had become accustomed to the motion of the camel, so much so as even to think it agreeable. All night we see-sawed along without any accident or alarms, passing the time between snatches of sleep in talking, smoking, and eating water-melon. At daybreak we reached the end of our first stage. It was the best site for a camp we had come to yet. The hills around were low, and clothed with dark-green verdure, and the valleys between were fresh green meadows, dotted over with grazing camels and flocks of sheep. A troop of Turkish cavalry was camped on the plain, and the troopers were at the time exercising their horses, scouring at random over the sward in every direction at racing speed. A few carried long light reeds, and were practising throwing the Bedawin spear, at which they were very expert, especially in defending themselves.

The riding was good. We passed close by one fellow who was attacked by three others, and was defending himself all round with perfect success. He relied principally on dodging and evading the darts by the rapid evolutions of his marvellously-trained horse. Twice I made sure he was hit, but he had reserved one reed for guarding himself, and just as the shaft reached him, he would interpose his own across it with a skill and rapidity amounting almost to sleight-of-hand, and with a sharp rasping click the dangerous dart would spring perpendicularly up, and fly twenty-five or thirty feet clear over his head, and fall wavering on the ground beyond him in a ridiculously harmless way. It was no child's play, for the darts were well meant, and if they hit they would have given a very severe bruise, light as they were.

We wound on past this exhilarating sight of sportive braves and pitched our tent within a hundred yards of a large well, under the shadow of a bluff hill covered with underwood. I felt the cheerful lightheartedness of a convalescent; my system seemed permeated with the delicious glow of returning health. As for eating a heavy breakfast and going to sleep in the tent with the rest, I'd twenty times rather have had to furl a flying-jib in a snow squall.

When they had all stowed away in the darkened tent, steaming and broiling under the hot canvas, I took one of the guns and a few cartridges and strolled out for a little walk, to pick up a few pigeons, or perhaps something better. The soldiers camped so near made the place safe from any large band of wandering marauders, and, with the gun in hand, I would not at all have objected to dropping upon a couple of murderously-inclined gentlemen. In my mind I had turned the tables on them. Since they only regarded me as legitimate sport, I would as soon bag a brace of Bedawi as a brace of partridges. I was not strong enough to go far away from the camp, but I sauntered about, or lay down on the cool grass under the shade of the rocks, waiting for any chance shot that might "happen along." I soon knocked over a few pigeons, and shot a hawk that *would have it.* He wheeled about over my head, attracted by the dead birds at my side, for more than an hour, and so, after covering him twenty times, I pulled the trigger. A bird of that kind can make itself quite annoying.

It was now the heat of the day, the camp was sleeping to a man. The well was deserted, so, close up under the cold shade of its low wall, I lay down with my birds and gun, to sleep or smoke away the rest of the afternoon, well out of range of the insect pests and noxious exhalations of our dirty camp. Not far from the well there was a solitary Bedawin hut, and I had just smoked enough to make me feel thirsty, when I saw come out of it two young girls with earthenware water-vessels under their arms. They were not veiled, and as they came towards me I could not help looking with more than common admiration at their lithe slender figures and graceful movements. When they came nearer I saw that they had handsome intelligent features, and were about sixteen and seventeen years of age, and evidently sisters. I must have been staring at them, for they both came up to me laughing, and said "Fortune, Shaykh." (Among the Bedawi even the gentler sex will not wish you *peace.*) "Upon you be peace," said I, for I was a devout pilgrim. As they were drawing their water it occurred to me to help them; but that would not have been at all etiquette, so I sat and watched them at work. Their only dress was a dark-blue prettily embroidered "cutty-sark," rather fascinating and very unembarrassed. All at once I thought, what a perfect "Rebekah at the Well" either of those girls would make in a picture, and the fancy took me to rehearse the scene with them. When she had filled her pitcher I said: "Let me, I pray thee, drink a little water of thy pitcher." And she said: "Drink, Shaykh," and when she had done giving me drink, she said: "Bakshish!" Too true! They both said "Bakshish," laughing wickedly at the solemn stranger's respectful manner. "Oh, hang it!" I thought, "Rebekah at the Well! Why, you wouldn't be fit to put behind a public refreshment-bar." I dropped my polite dignity; I may even admit I became rude. I sprinkled both the young ladies with the few drops remaining in the cup, and said: "Yes, there is your bakshish." Down went their pitchers, and into it they went, like pigs into porridge, with both hands baling out the contents of a large camel-trough over me, screaming and laughing like two young mad things. I emptied the contents of their own pitchers over them, and thoroughly drenched them; but I was nowhere, and got fearfully worsted. If it had not been for my wound I should have made a big splash, as it was I was obliged to ask them to stop "romping," because I was wounded. They would not believe me at first, but when they saw that I could not run away from them, but had to sit down, they stopped their fun and asked about the wound, and soon grew quite sympathetic and interested. When they had refilled their vessels, I gave them the birds I had shot, and they went away with a merry laughing "Fortune to you, Shaykh." After they had gone I lay down in the sun on a sandy place to dry, and spent the rest of the day wiping the gun and smoking, until the evening meal.

About sunset we were again under way, and found ourselves passing over the old barrenness of rock and sand. Our caravan numbered three hundred and twenty camels, and only about the same number of men walking—showing what a small percentage of the Hindis return from Medinah. Most of those walking were men who had been a few years in Medinah. I did not see among them a single one who had walked to Medinah with us. We had the same Bedawi conductors and the same camels as we had brought with us from Meccah; and it was really wonderful to see the way the camels had improved in their ten days' rest at Medinah.

The night passed without anything happening worth recording; but when the sun rose it looked very red and threatening, and the sky to the north-west was obscured by a dense yellow bank of cloud. Already the breeze was fresh, and came down the hills and out of the gullies in strong gusts. The Bedawi were hastening forward the caravan in a way I had never seen them before. They were talking to one another in an excited manner, and looking every now and again in a half-frightened way at the cloud-bank in the north-west. However, I did not need such indications to tell me that we were in for "some sort" of weather. I expected a rain storm. I would not have been surprised at a sand storm; but that I was about to witness a phenomenon that I could call by no other name than a gold storm, I expected about as much as I expect some day to be showered upon by the oft-talked-of cats and dogs.

During our journey we had often passed through districts very rich in mica; which, in certain lights, shines like burnished gold. In some places the sand was so largely composed of flakes of mica, and minute particles of this mineral, that a handful of it picked up and held in the sun close to the eye looked to be almost entirely gold-dust. Small pieces of the granite rocks about would sometimes look like nuggets of pure gold; and strewn all over the ground you could see millions of sparkling points, and here and there great shining stars of gold. I have often gone up to one of these last, which, until you become wary enough, are difficult to find; for when you shift your point of view, and change your light, they present themselves, as they really are, dull-gray paper-like translucent flakes of mica. It was one of these districts especially rich in mica that we were now passing through, and the fresh breeze was already spangling the wool of the camels with tiny, almost imponderable, flakes of this gold-coloured mineral.

The wind increased steadily, and the Bedawi exerted themselves more and more to push forward the caravan. But when I found that at the soonest we could not reach the end of the march under four hours I felt we were in for it, whatever it was. It proved to be what an old sailor would call a "buster." The view soon became obscured by a yellow haze of sand, and the sun came down close over our heads in the form of a glaring dull-red ball, in that way so familiar to a Londoner during the fogs. The wind yelled over the high rugged rocks, swept them clean, and pounced down on us in the valleys, with its burden of dust and sand, rattling a shower against us that sounded on the outside of the shugduf like hail. The poor pedestrians must have suffered tortures from the sand blowing against their bare legs and faces, for it pricked like needles, as I found by holding my hand out of the shugduf. They sheltered themselves as much as they could by getting on the lee-side of the camels and covering up their faces. The Bedawi did not seem to mind it so much. Their dress can be so arranged as to cover all but the lower parts of their legs, and their calves and shins seemed to be hardened to it. The air soon became so thickly laden with detritus that you could not see more than four or five camels ahead. The fine dust searched into the shugduf, and lodged in every wrinkle and fold in little ridges all over our clothes. The camels, the shugdufs, the men walking, the few green shrubs by the way, all became of the same light-yellow hue, spangled with gold. Though the wind was blowing with great violence the heat was intense. Perspiration was checked all over your body, still a constant desire for draughts of water was induced. Our skins became hot and feverish, and tingled painfully, and our lips dry and cracked. But by far the most interesting part of the storm to me was the shower of gold, which continued throughout the whole of the blow. At times the air was as thick with flying sparks of mica as it is with flakes during a fall of fine snow: a more beautiful phenomenon it could scarcely be possible to imagine. I collected a quantity of the dust from my clothes and preserved it in a match-box, and even in the gaslight it shows sparkles of gold throughout the whole mass.

About an hour before we got in, the wind had increased to such force that the heavily-laden camels could scarcely stand up against it, and were often blown out of the track to the left, the wind being on our right and rather with us. It appeared to me that we must be blown off their backs every moment. During one of the stronger gusts a shugduf not far behind us was overbalanced by the wind and came to the ground. Shortly after that we passed one of the advance camels, which had broken down. It was lying on the sand, and already a drift was forming round it. Through the storm we at last reached the end of our march, having left five camels on the road, two of which came up afterwards, but one of the lost ones belonged to our party. It was also said two men were missing, and a woman whose shugduf had overbalanced was brought in with a broken arm. It was, of course, impossible to pitch the tents in such a wind, so that there was nothing for it but to keep in the shelter of the shugdufs. After unloading the camels, and exposing ourselves to the pelting sand in doing so until we could bear it no longer, we covered ourselves up, to wait until the storm was past. After about a couple of hours, the wind still blowing as hard as ever, Shaykh the Bo'sen came and asked the Amér if he would care to come to the village and take shelter in one of the huts, when he could get something cooked. He said he would, and asked for volunteers to go with him. Both my companion and I offered to go.

When I had shaken the thick layer of dust off my blanket I threw it off me and got out of the shugduf. The caravan presented a very curious spectacle: under the lee of every camel and box, the forms of men were seen lying, covered with a thick layer of fine dust. As the drift had formed against the camels they had kept on raising themselves above it. All of us who were going to the village collected under the shelter of some boxes, and then, guided by the Shaykh, we set out.

Though we had a fair wind with us the pelting sand pricked one's ankles dreadfully, and we were obliged to move cautiously for fear of losing the road, which, however, suited me, as I could not have run anyhow. At this time I noticed another feature of the storm. Clouds of locusts were being whisked away before the gale, and being dashed to the ground by hundreds. Many of them appeared to be dead when they fell, and most of them would rather be trod on than venture on the wing again. The village was about three hundred yards from the caravan, and the first sign of it we saw was a row of half-a-dozen huts that had been levelled with the ground, by the force of the wind and the weight of the sand that had accumulated against them. The next time we passed the spot, the only indication of their existence was to be seen in a low ridge of sand, three or four feet higher than the surrounding level. After we had passed the fallen huts we came to another row of huts, sheltered by a high rock from the wind. Into the nearest of these we rushed, and found it filled with Bedawi belonging to the village and to our caravan. There were about twenty armed men in the greatest agitation, and the seniors among them were talking in harsh and excited voices. It was anything but a reassuring sight even to me, though I felt that the mishaps of the storm would account for their manner. The Amér, who was a little potentate at home, looked terrified; I believe he would have made a bolt for it, only the storm was about as bad to face as the Bedawi. Our conductor on first entering had entered into some hot discussion of the moment, which had taken his attention altogether from us. But after a few minutes he called one of his sons to him, a tall handsome young fellow, and gave him some directions about us. The young man then beckoned us to follow him, and we dodged out of that hut and into another a few yards off. Here we found two old women, who supplied us with pipes and coffee, and we squatted down on the matted floor and began to look nervously at one another. After a few cups of strong black coffee and a few pulls at the pungent green Bedawi tobacco our tongues began to wag.

It was easy to see the Amér had a great scare on him, and two others, the first warrior and Dirvani, were equally frightened. They distrusted the Bedawi, saying that they had been brought away from the caravan for some purpose of foul play. The others who had come with us were the old conspirator and the second and third warriors. They proved to be men; they scouted the idea of danger from the Bedawi, and said that our arms were so superior that we could hold the hut against a hundred of them; they also had the sense to see that the real danger was with the caravan, believing that if the storm lasted long at its present fury many must die from exposure.

About two hours after we entered the hut, Shaykh the Bo'sen came to us and said that he had again visited the caravan, and found everything safe as yet; and he also told us he believed the storm was over; though to me it appeared to have only reached the climax of its fury, and might take hours to die out. But he proved to be right. It had now grown so dark that we thought night had set in; but, as the Shaykh left us, it began to gradually brighten up, and shortly after the wind fell suddenly away; and we had an hour before sunset of as fine an evening as could be wished for.

When we returned to the caravan it was already unearthed, and was shaking itself free of sand. We never properly got clear of that sand till the south-west monsoon washed and blew it out of us in India. Our casualties were—two men killed (and buried at the same time); and the poor woman whose arm had been broken died that night; one camel had been suffocated, probably from being too far gone to take care of itself as the others had done.

We soon had the tents pitched and supper cooked. But sand and grit were in everything, causing the greatest discomfort. We shook and dusted our clothes and washed ourselves all over;

but shake and dust as we might, we only seemed to get dirtier. The fine dust had penetrated right through and through the very substance of the fabric of all the woollen and cotton material in the camp. A more dust-stained miserable lot of way-farers never lay down together than we were when we turned in for the night. Next morning we rose, after a sleepless night, and commenced dusting and washing again. The well was so situated that it had been protected from the sand-drifts and had not been filled up; but in other parts of the valley the sand had been piled up against the rocks in sloping banks a hundred feet high, and every little projection above the level of the valley had become a mound of sand. In one place where there had been a clump of acacia-trees fifteen or twenty feet high, only a few of their upper branches projected from the top of a sand-hill.

We were to have stayed at this place only four hours, but the Bedawi now told us that we would have to wait the whole of that day to rest and recover the camels. The sky overhead was light-blue, and cloudless, as usual, and the sun shone down on us white, bright, and powerful, as if he were trying to deny having been blurred into a hideous blood-red ball by the storm of yesterday.

CHAPTER IX.

INCIDENTS BY THE WAY.

We spent the day washing and dusting, clearing away wreck, and repairing damages; and by evening had put things about shipshape. Before taking down the tents they were emptied and beaten all over with sticks, until the clouds of dust that came out of the canvas darkened the interior. Still, when taken down and rolled up, they seemed to be almost twice their original weight. The loss of the camel which we had sustained on the previous day entailed some changes in our travelling arrangements; so that I found myself with the old conspirator for my camel-mate. He was a great talker, and entertained me all the night with his political and theological theories. The news of the recent British occupation of Quitta had just reached us in the Hejaz, and my companion's view of "General Gladstone's" (?) action in the matter were, to say the least, unique. Once I narrowly escaped incurring the good gentleman's odium theologicum by injudiciously mentioning that I had heard that Isa-el-Islaam * had once performed the miracle of turning water into wine. The old gentleman was so indignant that he would scarcely hear me out. I rued the expression of the notorious heresy almost before I had said it. He, however, put it down to ignorance and disadvantages of early training, and at once set himself to right my ideas with a will. He argued hotly and at great length, showing a familiarity with the subject I did not expect to find in a man whom one would suppose could have little sound knowledge of Christianity. He maintained that Jesus Christ, being a true believer, could not have drunk wine Himself, and that to perform such a miracle as turning water into wine was utterly incompatible with His mission of peace,

* Jesus Christ.

when, as all know, there can be no greater incitive to quarrel than wine.

He declared that the account of that miracle—which had really been the converting of wine into water—was misrepresented by Christians, in order to reconcile their belief and their practice. He then went on to cite quite a startling array of what he considered the fallacies of our New Testament; affirming that the records of the sayings and doings of Jesus Christ had been curtailed and supplemented just as it suited the notions of the infidel compilers of our version. Many of his more subtle arguments were so specious that I will abstain from giving them, lest I might appear somewhat biased myself.

Mohammedans, though believing in the immaculate conception, deny the deity of Christ; believing Him to have been only an inspired mortal. They deny His crucifixion, believing that another victim suffered in His stead—a case of mistaken identity miraculously brought about.

After exhausting for a time the subject of religion, I led the old fellow up to a little bit of historical tradition, so generally believed among Mohammedans that it must have some foundation in fact. But I found him as vague on the subject as others I had heard speak of it. It is, that the English nation once nearly became Mohammedans. Once an English king wished to embrace the faith, and sent ambassadors to—some say Stamboul, some Cairo, and others Meccah—for that purpose; but that the project fell through on account of the death of the king. I have often wondered if any clue to the tradition could be found in our history—say in some of the intrigues about the time of King John, or during any one of the crusades.

In this way and in such conversations the old fellow and I passed many an hour on the camel, and became fast friends, for I was the best listener he had in the whole caravan. For the next four days we plodded on over the rocks and sand; once we travelled sixteen hours and halted for two, and then went on for twenty-five. All the time we underwent the same trifling disasters and the same alarms as heretofore on the road. On account of the loss of a camel, my camel-mate was frequently changed, so that I had a variety of company.

One morning a youthful Bedawin, perched high up on a rock, let drive a couple of bullets at us. It seemed great fun to him, although it did not do us any harm.

I was getting quite able to walk with the camels, and would sometimes dismount and let one of my companions take my place for an hour or two. I used to carry a gun, and drop an occasional quail or partridge out of the long grass by the side of the road. At night we used to light up our way by setting fire to the dry shrubbery as we passed along, at times converting the dark rugged dells into creepy fiery infernos.

We reached Rabigh without anything particularly interesting occurring to me, though the journey was sufficiently eventful to many of my companions. We lost two of our party, servants of the Amér; one of them died during a halt, and I believe poisoned himself with an overdose of opium; the other died on his camel from a remittent fever to which he was subject. In crossing the coast plain, after leaving the rocky region, we lost five of the people accompanying us on foot, and one camel dropped out of the caravan. After a day and a night in Rabigh, and a "square meal" of fresh fish, which I roasted myself at night, I felt quite recovered. My wound had ceased to suppurate, and had formed a firm scab, so that rags were no longer needed for it.

The fish of the Rabigh waters were curious uncouth monsters. Some of them were so ugly that it would require a man to be situated as I was before he could bring himself to eat them even curried. The great heads and tails of most of them were out of all proportion to the size of their bodies, and their artificial red, green, and blue colours looked unnatural. Some of the baskets of fish I saw in the bazaar were "miraculous draughts" in the way of hues and tints; a boiled-lobster-red being the most predominant colour. For myself I bought a small shark, as being the safest and most inviting fish in the market. We were to go from this place by a slightly different route to the one we had come by, skirting along the sea for the first two days, and not being longer than twenty-four hours from water to water. Three days such as we had experienced at this stage of our outward journey would have been very trying to me in my then state of health. On leaving Rabigh the Amér and some of the more reverential of our party invested themselves in the two bath-towels which constitute the "ihram," or garb of the pilgrim to Meccah. Having once assumed it, it must not be changed until certain rites have been gone through in Meccah. It is a very scant and uncomfortable dress, and a bare head is an essential of it. Many of the pilgrims did not get into it until the day before we reached Meccah, and I, having the excuse of my wound, was one of the last to do so.

While in the ihram you must divest yourself of all frivolity or worldliness, and figure only as a pious self-denying pilgrim. My friend the old conspirator went to great lengths in this way; I had given him credit for more sense. He suddenly took it into his head, in a fit of piety, that it was sinful to smoke tobacco, and went about among us preaching his false doctrine so zealously that he brought the Amér and a dozen others over to his way of thinking. He held that the prohibition of intoxicating liquors in the Koran involved tobacco, and it was not particularly specified because it was unknown to the Prophet. He said it had been introduced by Christian emissaries of the devil from a "new world" for the purpose of trapping the faithful. He also proved that tobacco was very injurious to the health; giving many instances of disease and death brought on by its use, which had come under his observation. Some of his cases in point almost equalled Mark Twain's joke about the two drops on the end of a dog's tail followed by convulsions and death. This anti-tobacco and general abstemious craze went to such lengths with some of them that they actually gave up opium.

The coast along which we rode was a perfectly level wilderness; the surface of the ground over some large tracts was as hard and smooth as asphalt. We passed several small salt lakes or back-waters, and at one of them I dismounted and took a bathe. It was a great mistake, for the water was so salt that as it dried on me it left visible crystals, and made my skin disagreeable and sticky, until I washed in fresh water on the next day. The mirage was constant; nothing you saw, if a short distance off, appeared as, or where, it really was. A Bedawin riding past us at full speed, carrying a long spear, was in sight for more than an hour and a half. He took all kinds of fantastic shapes, and, as regards the distance, he was off at any moment; the best range-finder ever invented could not have localised him. At one time he was split up into three, with a space of something that looked like a surface of shimmering water between each part—the legs of the camel dancing along over the plain without any body attached to them, and high over them the body of the camel and rider flying through the air, and above them again the tuft of feathers surmounting his spear, looking like a bird in the air. We were constantly being deluded by visions of trees not far off, but we never came to them.

During the heat of the day sand-pillars flitted about the plain by dozens, some of them appearing to be agitated by a very powerful wind. I never came near enough to one to go into it, though I longed to investigate one of them closely. I am satisfied that those of ordinary dimensions are perfectly harmless; but the Bedawi have a superstitious dread of them, calling them devils, and blessing themselves whenever one approaches them. What added greatly to the dreariness of this horrid waste was the total absence of animal life; not a fish-jump ruffled the surface of the glassy lakes; not even the proverbial and familiar pelican of the wilderness was to be seen by the side of them; no wheeling vultures overhead; even the swarms of flies properly belonging to the caravan deserted. I almost fancied that our "inside passengers" were reduced to a policy of "masterly inactivity" for a time. (I had come to this, that when you asked a man to do anything, he usually told you to wait till he'd done scratching himself.) The carcasses of camels which we passed had the flesh dried on to the bones as hard as wood. I shall never forget one corpse, that of a man—nationality quite indistinguishable. The body had first distended to about three times its original bulk and then dried in that form. I turned it over as it lay on the sand, and it was so light I could have lifted it with one hand. It made a creaking and drumming noise as I moved it, very like the sound of shaking a rolled-up hide of sole-leather.

During the day the heat was such that I am certain the thermometer would seldom have fallen below a hundred degrees Fahrenheit; but the nights were relatively very cold, and worn out by the trying days we all slept soundly through the nights. I arrived at two conclusions with reference to that region. First, that the refraction of light by the air was so remarkable that artillery would be rendered practically ineffective. Secondly, that I would never go a Sabbath-day's journey into it again until I could do it on a bicycle, and have relays of caravans sent on loaded with iced lemon-squashes.

Before we left the plain we lost two more camels

and four of the pedestrians. One of the camels unfortunately belonged to our party, and one of the donkeys gave out. The poor jaded brute could keep up with the caravan by itself, but could not be ridden. This brought the turns at riding and walking round more quickly among us. I was walking on the morning that we reached the first isolated hill on the border of the plain; the road wound close past the south side of it. It was not more than three hundred yards round its base, so I ventured to take the gun, push on ahead, and pass it on the opposite side to the caravan-road. As there was usually a good deal of vegetation on the north side of these rocks, they were pretty sure finds of small game. I had just lost sight of the caravan, and stepped quickly out from behind a large boulder, which I had kept before me in coming up to the spot where I expected to rise the birds, when I saw before me on the ground the body of a man quite recently killed. It was that of a Maghribi, who had probably been separated from his caravan, preceding ours four days.

This hardy native of the North African desert must have supported life, after losing his way, until the night before, when he had been encountered by Bedawi and slain. The corpse was chiefly interesting to me as illustrating the frightful nature of the wound which the terrible jambiyah (Bedawi knife) will inflict. There was a gunshot in the head, and the body was much mutilated with sword-cuts; but the jambiyah wound would have been judged by any one not acquainted with the weapon to have been made with a broad axe. The thorax and abdomen were laid open from just below where the left collar-bone joins the breastbone down to the left groin, and all the viscera interposed were severed as with a razor. While inspecting this interesting object I kept my eye on the rocks, and changed my shot-charges for ball. I have no doubt the perpetrators of the deed were on the hill, but I rejoined the caravan safely.

CHAPTER X.

THE DEATH OF THE AMÉR'S UNCLE.

OFTEN, when narrating what now follows, it has been doubted that a man could go to sleep while riding on a donkey. Accustomed as I was to sleeping on the camel, I have often had the greatest difficulty in keeping my eyes open at night, both on horse and donkeyback. On the night of which I am now writing I found myself, shortly after sunset, riding on our good donkey; the donkey I have before spoken of as a great puller. His pace was so much greater than that of the camels, that he required a constant heavy drag on his mouth. I was extremely sleepy, and the night was just pleasantly cool. I muffled myself up warmly, and, after trying all sorts of dodges on my donkey, I finally thought I had eased him down to about the right speed by drawing his head into his chest and fastening the reins to the saddle. Two or three times I dozed off, and woke with a start to find him going along at about the right pace. At last I became more confident, and laying my head down on the high pommel of my Arab saddle, I dropped off sound asleep.

I slept for a long time, and then, "oh what an awakening!" I was in the midst of a vast yellow plain, with the dark cloudlike hills visible round the horizon, but not a sign or vestige of my companions anywhere. I was a "castaway" in the desert. For all the evidence to the contrary, I might have been the only inhabitant in the world. I must say I felt rather queer for the first minute or so, but I soon pulled myself together. There was a little moon, and the white donkey I rode stood out very conspicuously in its light. I did not want to be picked up sooner than I could help by any bands of prowling Bedawi, so I took a stone and laid it on the end of the donkey's bridle, and went off a hundred yards or so and sat down to review the position, over a pipe. I knew that, if I was in the road at all, all the chances were that I was in advance of the caravan. Besides, I could not have got so far to the rear as to lose sight of my companions without having been snapped up by the Bedawi, who are always on the look-out for stragglers in that direction, and who would look upon it as flying in the face of Providence to let such a godsend as a solitary well-dressed man and a good donkey slip through their hands. I sat smoking for about half-an-hour, during which I worked out the caravan's course and distance since I had been with it—partly by dead-reckoning and partly by stellar observation. I remembered that it was to have halted at midnight, and then determined that it was about that time now. I also fancied I recognised a hill on the horizon as one we had passed about sunset. I decided that I would ride for that hill at the best speed I could, ascend it, and look out for the fires of the camp. If I could not see them I would then wait till daylight, and allow the donkey to graze and rest near the hill; then, finding the camel-track, hasten forward after the caravan, trusting to nerve and my sword-bayonet if I should fall in with Bedawi.

I had little fear but that I should overtake the caravan, and considered it by no means the worst scrape I had ever been in. My course once decided on, I remounted and set off, as I judged, exactly retracing my steps. I proved to be right, for I had not been ten minutes in the saddle when I saw the caravan, about a quarter of a mile off, coming up a gentle slope in the plain.

When I rejoined them I looked as unconcerned as I could; but the Bedawi had missed me, and laughed in a very warning manner as I appeared among them. Some of them made remarks to the effect that I had been very lucky, but had better be more careful. There was no need to tell me that; I took care never to mount that donkey at night again. Next day I offered to ride the donkey all day through the hottest of the sun rather than at night. Everyone was willing, most of them preferring the shade of the shugduf during the day. The donkey seemed to know it was getting to the end of its journey, and pulled harder than ever, and I was very glad when, about an hour after sunset, I was relieved by the Amér's uncle. He was a decrepit old man. I don't think his actual years were over forty, but he was utterly broken down and prematurely aged, by long-continued indulgence in opium. When I changed places with him I warned him, whatever he did, not to go to sleep, and told him the trick the donkey had played me on the night before. His manner showed me at once that he had been taking an extra allowance of his darling drug. I felt very much afraid on his account. Before mounting the camel I walked some distance by his side, trying to impress on him the necessity of keeping wide awake, but he only kept on answering: "Good, good!" and I could see he was half asleep before I left him. I took the precaution of taking the lame donkey from the man who was leading it, and tying it on behind the other, to act as a sort of drag, hoping to retard the pace of the first donkey a little. My anxiety about him did not prevent my falling into a sound sleep in the place just vacated by the doomed man—for I had a presentiment that he was doomed—as soon as I lay down in the shugduf. I had slept for about two hours when the stopping of the camel awoke me, and I became aware that some excitement was going forward at the advanced part of the caravan. The news soon reached us: the Amér's uncle had been found by the side of the road badly wounded and insensible, with a large stone rolled on him. They took him up and put him on a camel, and at the next halt he was brought into the tent and his wounds dressed.

I saw him before he was bound up; he had a number of bad bruises and abrasions over his head and back, and one very severe cut from the right elbow down the back of the arm to the wrist. Consciousness returned to him, and he was able to give an account of what had happened. Of course, he went to sleep on the donkey as soon as I left him, and the next thing he knew he was woke up with a thump on the back from a stone. The caravan was nowhere to be seen, but all round him in the partial darkness he saw human figures flitting about among the rocks, and, as he described it, "raining stones on him." This is one of the Bedawin modes of attack when without firearms, or when they do not wish to use them. Their idea is to draw your fire on to their quickly-moving bodies, which you are expected to miss, and then, if some lucky stone has not done it, to close in and finish you. In this case these elaborate tactics were quite uncalled for. The poor old fellow, though he had two loaded pistols in his belt, never thought of using them. He sat quietly on the donkey praying under the shower of missiles; he had not even a worm-turning-point, for he sat and prayed to the last. As I heard him tell it I almost wished I'd been in his place. The Bedawi, finding that their stone-throwing was not producing the desired results, and concluding most likely that their victim was unarmed, began to draw closer, and one of the daring robbers, with intrepidity that must have gained him a lasting fame among his tribe, came up behind the old fellow and hit him a whack on the back with a long stick, and then ran away. Others, seeing that no resistance was offered, came up and repeated the whacks—they appear to me to have been trying if he was alive—and then a fellow came near enough to give him the cut on the arm, and another hit him on the head and knocked him senseless. Probably the caravan came up at this crisis, before they had time to strip and despatch him; so they rolled a big stone on him to keep him quiet until the caravan passed, and then hurried off out of sight with the donkeys. It would have been perhaps as well if the old fellow had been left to their mercy, for he lingered on for two days in the greatest suffering, and on the day before we reached Meccah he died.

At the first halt after losing the donkeys, Shaykh the Bo'sen offered to recover them for two pounds. (The ruffian! though he did save my life.) This the Amér agreed to give him. About twenty of our Bedawi then went off fully armed, with their matchlocks loaded and burning fuses. They returned in a couple of hours with the donkeys. I have no doubt but that some of our conductors were the very men who had stolen them. They gave us the most graphic descriptions of the hard-fought battle in which they had recovered them, and showed a good deal of blood; but the only wounds were to be found on the hind-quarters of our good donkey. That animal was so badly gashed that it was rendered useless for the rest of the journey. As we came nearer to Meccah it was curious to note how the brusque authoritative manner of our Bedawi conductors changed. Having in view the early settling-day and possible bakshish, they became almost civil to us. In proportion as the Bedawi became subdued, the spirits of the pilgrims rose and their confidence increased; it was significant of this that, on the last day before we reached Meccah, a Bedawi was wounded by a pilgrim in a scrimmage with swords, and no retaliation was attempted by the others. The Amér was in great tribulation over the death of his uncle, which happened at our last halt; but he smothered his sorrow in opium, and concluded that it was a very blessed and desirable end to be killed on the pilgrimage.

The old fellow had been conscious just before he died, and had made a last request that, as we were only a few hours distant from Meccah, he should be taken to the Holy City to be buried. When the breath left him we rolled him up in calico, intending to put him on a camel, but at the last moment the Bedawi demurred to carrying the body at all, and then only consented on condition that they were given a most extravagant payment for the use of an animal for that purpose alone. To this the Amér would not agree; so we hastily buried the old fellow where we were. I thought, as we placed a few bushes and stones over the shallow grave, how very easily that might have been my fate once. I came in for the reversion of the old fellow's ihram, which was a very good thick one. We had not enough of the rough bath-towels, which form the most comfortable and fashionable pilgrim's garb, to go round the whole party, so that I had had to use a couple of strips of thin white calico; but now I came in for the uncle's swell and comfortable dress.

On the afternoon of the thirteenth day after leaving Medinah, and thirty-six days after we had set out from it, we returned to Wady Fatima. We made no halt there, but all who were able dismounted and walked the rest of the way into Meccah, by the side of the caravan. Just as we dismounted it was the time of afternoon prayer, and I went to fill a small pot of water from the skins on the water-camel for my ablution. In doing this I received a kick from the camel. It was in this way: In drawing off the water you walk along by the side of the animal, untie the neck of the skin you are taking the water from, holding the pot under until full; then closing the mouth of the skin with one hand, you put the pot on your head or under your arm, and have both hands to retie the mouth of the skin. The camels were going rather unsteadily, and I was a long time fumbling about doing this, when all at once the brute stopped dead, lifted up its nearest hind-leg, as if it was going to scratch the top of its back, and then lashed out, hitting me on the lower part of my chest. I was lifted off the ground and came down on my face on the hard stony ground. The agony was awful; I felt as if my whole inside was torn up; I turned on my back, closed my eyes, and asked the people about not to touch me. I lay for two or three minutes, suffering tortures, before I could rise; when I did get up, my companions near me remarked how sick I looked. I saw that there was blood on my ihram, my hands and knees were very much torn by my fall, and there was a bit of a "gravel rash" on my right cheek. After being kicked by a camel, it strikes one as quite puzzling how such an apparently soft-cushioned pad as a camel's foot can strike so hard, and yet I do not think that even an iron-shod hoof can do more execution. The camel's kick is a study. As it stands demurely chewing the cud, and gazing abstractedly at some totally different far-away object, up goes a hind-leg, drawn close in to the body, with the foot pointing out; a short pause, and out it flies with an action like the piston and connecting-rod of a steam-engine, showing a judgment of distance and direction that would lead you to suppose the leg gifted with perceptions of its own, independent of the animal's proper senses. I have seen a heavy man fired several yards into a dense crowd by the kick of a camel, and picked up insensible.

My accident happened very unfortunately; for the blood defiled and broke my ihram, rendering a reinvestment and purification necessary. This entailed half-an-hour's ablution and prayer. We had now no water left, the skin at which I had been having run itself dry before anyone could take my place and tie it up. The only thing to be done was to push forward ahead of the caravan, to a small tank said to exist by the roadside, and take my old calico ihram with me and put it on again. Some of my companions, who had been a little jealous about my coming in for the dead uncle's ihram, said very ill-natured things about dead men's clothes bringing no luck; but of course I could only laugh good-temperedly, at the same time feeling the force of their remarks none the less. I managed reinvestment and ablution all right.

CHAPTER XI.

PASS THROUGH MECCAH TO JEDDAH.

Towards evening we began to get among the outlying habitations of Meccah. Great crowds assembled to see the Hindi caravan from Medinah come in. Old women came up to us and asked if we were from the tomb of the Prophet of God, and on being told that we were, devoutly kissed the hem of our ihrams. After Medinah, how dirty and unwholesome the narrow steep streets of Meccah appeared! and yet I can assure the reader that the feeling with which I entered Meccah was one of relief, and a sense of security amounting almost to the homeward-bound feeling with which one arrives in port after a long voyage in an unseaworthy ship.

As we passed through the streets the caravan

broke up, and the different parties separated from it and went to the parts of the town where they intended to stay. We went into the very centre of the city, to the house in which we had formerly lived. Almost at the door there lay a dead camel-foal, partially devoured by the dogs, and the air was redolent of it, bringing the fact that we were at last back in Meccah most forcibly home to us. When the door of our large room was unlocked and opened, for the first time since we had left the house, what an atmosphere there was in it! The dust lay on the boxes and bundles that had been left behind so thick that it could be scraped up in handfuls, just as one gathers up a thin layer of snow. The camels lay down in the street outside, and while they were being unloaded a party was detailed to clean the room, then the Amér and his principal companions went to their devotions. Myself and my old camel-mate received orders to watch all the property, as it was taken off the camels and laid in a great pile outside the door, until the room was made habitable, when it could be removed inside. It was very late that night when we finished our devotions and packed ourselves into the close stifling room, head and tail, like sardines in a box—quite as oily, and, it occurred to me at the time, almost as brainless.

The Amér had been so pleased with the horse he had taken with him to Medinah that he determined to buy two more in Meccah to take to India, and the next day he spent in choosing them. About a dozen were brought to the house when it became known that he was buying. They were chiefly owned by officers of the Turkish garrison, and were all good animals. He bought two young bay entires for one hundred dollars each, getting the saddles and bridles thrown in after a great deal of bargaining.

The town was not nearly so crowded as it had been when we left it, still a great number of pilgrims remained in it, and hundreds came on each day of our stay, begging for a return passage with the Amér. Four days were spent in Meccah, during which the Amér laid out a great deal of money in precious stones and bars of gold, procured in the country. The Bedawi who had conducted us hitherto were retained to take us to Jeddah, and on the afternoon of the fourth day after our arrival, the camels were brought to the door, and in a few hours everything was in readiness for our final leave-taking.

It had been settled that I should take charge of one of the horses and ride to Jeddah on it. The horse that I was to ride was a very young thing, and was expected to be rather restive and require some management; but after I had been on him a few minutes I found that a kinder horse you could not have. He would not walk any closer to the camels than he could help, but once give him his place and he would keep it until you changed it, no matter what it might be, and he was guided by the lightest pressure of the reins against his neck. My feelings, as we left Meccah behind us, were such as cannot easily be defined; they were something like the happiness one feels on falling in an unexpected stroke of fortune; and yet I could scarcely realise that in less than two days I should be in the company of Christians and Englishmen. It seemed as if I had not seen a countryman for years and years, whereas it had only been a few months. But what a complete separation from the world and my kind it had been! I began to wonder what I should say to the first Englishman I met, and how it would sound to hear English talked as the common language again. I spent most of the night as we rode along talking to myself in English, and practising saying "Good-morning;" for my own language on my own tongue had really come to have an unfamiliar sound to me. About an hour after daylight we came to a halt at Haddah, and half the distance between Meccah and Jeddah was accomplished.

All day we stayed there, and I felt impatient during a halt for the first time since I had been travelling with camels. I should have liked to have jumped on a horse and spurred off at full speed; but it would not have done. I could not sleep or eat, and the sun appeared as if it would never go down. I passed part of the day basking in a stream of running water that flowed near the camp, and was driven out of that by a little

Bedawin child. I think the episode is worth recording, as showing how early the principles of murder and robbery are instilled into the native youth, if indeed it is not an hereditary instinct. When I went into the water I had taken off my clothes and hidden them under some stones, in case some pilfering Bedawi might creep up and steal them when I was not looking. I must have lain some two hours, with the delicious cool stream rippling over me, when I saw a small almost naked child behind some stones coming stealthily in my direction. I saw the little vermin meant some mischief, and got a big stone ready for him, at the same time letting him know that I could see him. I expected he would run away, but not a bit of it; he came boldly up to me and shouted the Bedawi "Stand and deliver!" (Haat fleus!*), holding out his little hand, flourishing a large knife, and looking as fierce as may be. The boy was not more than fourteen years old, and I confess I admired the boldness of his little enterprise.

* Give money!

But here was a predicament for me! You can never tell how far the madness of a youthful adventurer like this may carry him; he looked to me as if he had the most perfect confidence in his ability to go through with it. I did not want to hurt the boy, or I might have squashed him there and then with a big stone. Catching hold of him would have been altogether too risky. I was naked, and he had a sharp knife with which he might have given me a nasty cut, lay hold of him as I might. It requires a good deal of nerve to handle a rat even, when you are certain of a bite. I tried to represent to him how preposterous his demand was, when he could see I was perfectly naked. But he only repeated his "Haat fleus!" in a more threatening way, and flourished his knife nervously close to my abdomen. He knew my clothes were somewhere about, and my manner only encouraged him, and made him think that he had got hold of a poor unresisting pilgrim that he could "get away with." For a moment I thought of running and leaving my clothes, until I could come back with a big stick and get them. I really thought once that the boy would try and give me a taste of his knife. In the meantime I conceived the following plan: I led him to my clothes, pulled them out from under the stones, and made them up into a neat hard bundle, as though I intended to give them to him; but instead of that, I let him feel what my prowess would be in a bolster fight, and knocked him sprawling with a swinging thump from my bundle, and then bolted off and was out of range before he could even gather himself up and return it with a stone. But I heard him scream his infantile defiance after me until I came within sight of the camp. I then stopped and put on my clothes. I told the story to my companions, and it gave rise to a good deal of mirth; but they all agreed that you could expect nothing else from "the sons of devils who called themselves true believers, but never prayed."

At sunset we set out for our last march in the desert, and after an uneventful night we sighted the sea, the white walls of Jeddah, and half-a-dozen English steamers riding at anchor in the port.

Shortly after we entered the gates of the town I saw a Frenchman I had known before, but he did not recognise me in my native costume, though he looked very hard at me, as if there was something about me he could not quite make out. I should very much like to have spoken to him, if it was only to hear his voice; but I did not wish to undeceive my companions as yet, out of consideration for their feelings, so I went on with them to a lodging-house close down near the water's edge. Here we were to put up until a passage could be engaged for us in a suitable ship.

I promise you I did not stay to breakfast on currie and rice that morning. As soon as I could wash and change my tunic and turban, I hurried out and spent one rupee of the two and a half that I possessed on a mutton cutlet, with white bread and coffee, in a French restaurant not far off. Over a smoke and glass of cognac in this place I had a conversation with two or three Frenchmen. I told them where I had come from, and my circumstances, and they offered to provide me with

European clothes, which I was glad to accept; though I did not put them on at once.

The next thing I did was to go to the British Consulate, to remind them of my former visit. I do not think they ever expected to see me there again. They most likely thought they had seen the last of me when I left them to go to Meccah. The Consul was away in a gun-vessel at the time, but the gentleman acting for him kindly offered to do his best to get me a passage to Bombay; when I told him I would rather work as a sailor than be compelled to remain as I was. He also gave me all the latest news to read; which was very welcome.

I remained away from my old companions all the day. After talking to a countryman I almost dreaded going back to my fellow-pilgrims; and positively hated the title of Haji, by which we now ostentatiously addressed one another, and which I had been through so much to obtain. Their habits and ways, that had been my own for months, suddenly took the most degraded and disgusting form in my eyes. I was without funds, so that I could not well leave them at the moment. I walked about the streets until the night began to get cold, when I was constrained to return to the house and litter down in the old style in the crowded rooms. How beastly it did seem, under the reaction that had come over my feelings!

At daybreak I rose and left the house again. I walked about near the beach, looking at the ships, and regarding them in the light of so many homes; as indeed they would have been to me could I have got on board them. I meant, when the shops opened, to make a good breakfast out of my remaining rupee and a few coppers.

In walking through a rather crowded bazaar towards the restaurant, I came upon a little crowd assembled round a Hindi woman and a young boy, who was doing some very feeble street tumbling. Probably she was the widow of some pilgrim, trying to make a little money to carry her home to her friends. I thought I would give them a copper, and put my hand into my pouch, where I had seven coppers and one rupee. Although all the coins were about the same size, I did not think it likely that I should come upon the rupee. I just pitched out the first that came into my fingers, without looking at it. Of course it was the rupee. Neither the admiration of the crowd nor the looks of gratitude from the woman and boy repaid me for the disappointment.

You may judge what sort of a humour I was in when I returned home without my breakfast. I told the Amér there and then that I was going to leave him, and enlist in the Sultan's army. At first he laughed at me, and pretended he thought I was joking; then he tried reproaches and abuse, and finally entreaties; reminding me that he was going to give me five hundred rupees a month, and a troop in one of the cavalry regiments he supported for Government of his own native state. I then told him if he would give me the money to pay for my own passage I would remain with him. I explained that I wanted the money because, being a sailor, I could get a passage for myself cheaper than a landsman. The real reason was that I knew that, though the passage-money was now thirty rupees, it would be down to ten before the ship would get her full complement of passengers; so that I would clear twenty rupees by the transaction. Such are the shifts to which private research is occasionally put. The Amér would not have let me leave him at that time for a good deal, so he gave me the thirty rupees I asked him for.

That day he engaged a passage for the whole of his suite, in a large two-thousand-ton English steamer, that was advertised to sail on the next day. I spent the whole of the day away from my companions, chiefly down at the boat-landing, talking to the crews of the ships' boats. I met a man who only three years before had been A.B. in a large London sailing-ship in which I was second mate. Though we had been a year and four months in the same ship, and he had been in my watch the whole time, he did not recognise me. I talked to him for two hours in broken English, without his having a glimmering of whom he was talking to; showing how my unshaven chin and eastern costume had metamorphosed me. When I did declare myself, and change my voice, the man was still inclined to be incredulous, but, to his astonishment, I proved my identity. On the same day I looked up some of the English captains of the steamers, and asked them to let me work my passage with them; but they told me they had heard of me at the Consulate, and had decided not to give me a passage, for fear of offending the pilgrims they intended to carry. I called at the Consulate, and was told that no captain would give me a passage unless I travelled as a Mohammedan.

It was no use "kicking against the 'bricks'"—as I once heard it put—so I must content myself to remain as I was, and travel with the Amér to Bombay.

The sailing of the ship in which he had taken passage was put off from day to day, for five days; and, as I had foreseen, the price of the passage gradually went down, until, on the morning of the day on which she actually did sail, it went down to ten rupees. Then I got hold of an old Hindi beggar, and sent him into the office to take out a ticket in my name, and gave him a rupee for his pains.

CHAPTER XII.

ON BOARD SHIP.

The whole of our party went off to the steamer in three large lighters, and we had little difficulty in embarking ourselves and our property. The three horses followed in a fourth lighter. When it came alongside, though there was a little jump of a sea on, the horses were quiet and did not appear in the least frightened. I was standing on deck, in the gangway, to watch them come in, and I remember thinking that it was very foolish to blind them with such enormous cloths as they had folded round and round and over and over, and tied securely on their heads. But most idiotic of all, their legs were tied together, and then about a fathom of line leading from their leg-lashings to the gunwale of the lighter was there made fast. There were two horses in the midship compartment of the boat, and the one on the side nearest the steamer was soon slung, steam turned on, and up he rose; but as he was lifted off his feet he lunged out and gave his companion a nasty kick. The other poor horse rose in a startled rear as the boat rolled. No one was at his head; there was nothing whatever to keep him inboard; over the gunwale he went, and hung at the side of the lighter, with his hoofs just level with the surface of the water. Here was a position!—one horse drowning instantly; another hanging outside the ship, thirty feet above the lighter, and lashing out its legs so wildly that it looked momentarily as if it would struggle out of the slings and fall; while the third, in the forward compartment of the lighter, was doing its best to follow its companion overboard.

The Arabs and negroes in the lighter capered about aimlessly, swearing and shouting; but attempting nothing to save the two horses. The ship's deck was so crowded with excited and exclaiming pilgrims that the ship's people who were taking in the horses were lost to one another, and their work had come to a standstill.

It was easy to see what ought to have been done. The horse hanging at the derrick should have been landed at once, and then an effort made to hook the other on and heave it out of the water, before it was too far gone. The confusion of unintelligible and contradictory orders, the crowding of loudly-crying and praying pilgrims, made individual action of any kind useless.

It appeared probable that all three of the beautiful animals would be lost. The miserable impotency one feels at such a crisis! Without the authority or power to direct others, and uncertain and hesitating about the best course to pursue oneself, twenty ideas flash across my mind in the twentieth of a minute, but none of them will meet the emergency. I turned away from the scene, and tried to calmly take in the whole case. There stood the Amér and the principal members of his suite on the bridge, wailing and wringing their hands in unison, and executing contortions sympathetic to every flounder of the drowning horse. For him the only hope now lay in cutting his legs clear, and giving him a chance to save himself. There was no immediate way down to the boat, and I had no knife about me; I could only ease my feelings by yelling at the people near it to cut the horse's legs clear. It was some relief to see that the third horse had become steady, and was standing safely in the boat. Just then a tremendous plunge of the animal in the water broke the ropes holding its fore legs; but that did not mend matters, for it now hung in a way that would have made it more difficult to get at him with a sling.

The ship's people now came to their senses, and swung the suspended animal in-board, and landed him, frightened and trembling, on the deck, where the crowd soon gave a wide berth to his lively heels. I now took a knife from a sailor, and jumped on the chain-runner as soon as it was unhooked from the horse, and in an instant was lowered into the lighter. To knock down a couple of niggers who were in the way, and cut the drowning horse adrift, was the work of three seconds; but it was too late. I question if it would have done much good at any time. Twice his head came to the surface, but it was so enveloped in wet cloths that it might as well have been at the bottom. The ropes round his legs got more entangled, and would have hampered him so that, even if he had had the sense and strength left to make a swim for it, he could not have struck out properly. Three times I was on the point of jumping in the water to endeavour to free the animal; three times I put my hands together for a dive; but the horse, as it sank down in the clear transparent blue, gave such terrific struggles as to put me off each time. I stood and watched it. His powerful young life was hard to quench; from first to last it must have been between three and four minutes in the agonies of its extreme distress before it ceased to strive and its energies collapsed. Then the dead body rose to the surface, and was towed alongside by the ship's boat to be hove on deck.

Poor fellow! It was he who had brought me away from detested Meccah. A short acquaintance with some animals serves to foster a very strong attachment. As he lay on the deck his wet skin looked more beautiful and glossy than ever, and his head as lovely; but the eye was glazed. I am not ashamed to say I felt strongly affected, and could not return to the part of the deck where he lay until I knew he had been delivered over to the sharks.

Now that I was cooler I was glad I had not jumped in after the horse, for I well knew that a drowning horse instinctively gets on the top of every solid object it encounters in the water. I have heard two or three instances of men being drowned in that way while swimming horses.

The third horse was taken in without any mishap. I saw it out of the lighter myself, taking care that there should be no more of the melancholy mismanagement that had already been so disastrous.

In the scenes above described I had thrown off

all semblance of a Mohammedan, and talked in the most undisguised English, making copious use of very emphatic nautical expressions; so much so that the ship's people knew I was an Englishman, notwithstanding my costume and close-clipped hair. The officer who had been superintending the taking in of the horses came to me, thinking I was the owner. I soon put him right, told him who I was, and explained to him all the circumstances. We then went together to the Amér, as he wanted to know if the owner of the horse considered the ship in any way to blame for its loss. The Amér had regained his composure, and resigned himself to circumstances like a true fatalist, as he was. When I interpreted the officer's question to him, he merely replied: "God gave, and God has taken away." He then praised me for my efforts to save his horse, and noticing that I had lost my tarbouche, it having fallen overboard as I went down into the lighter, he ordered me to be given a very handsome one of his own. I then went forward and made myself known to the sailors, and they at once gave me the run of their forecastle and the run of my teeth. I then deposited my bundle in an empty bunk, and took up my quarters there for the rest of the passage.

The Amér and about fifty other wealthy pilgrims were first-class passengers, who lived in the cabin and were allowed on the poop. I had taken a third-class ticket, which only allowed me the use of the main and lower decks, so that the Amér, of necessity, could see but little of me during the time we were on board. I hoped—though I did not care much—that he would not find out where I lived. Besides the first-class passengers, the ship was carrying one thousand three hundred third class. When I state that these were all huddled together, men, women, and children, indiscriminately, and were so put to it for space that there literally was not room for all to lie down at the same time, it will be understood why, to many of the pilgrims, the sea voyage has greater terrors than the land journey. During our passage of twenty-one days to Bombay, not a day passed without its death; and on one fine morning three corpses were dragged up from the foul lower-deck, out of the midst of a reeking throng of penned-up human beings.

During the whole passage I was never once asked for by the Amér. A couple of days before the ship reached Bombay I dressed myself in the clothes of an English sailor, and walked about among the pilgrims. The change in my appearance was so great that I believe I might have spoken to any of my old companions without their knowing me.

On the morning of the day on which we arrived in Bombay I shaved and put on my European rig, and afterwards stood on the deck and heard my pilgrim friends asking one another about me, and wondering what part of the ship I was in. There were many more places in the ship than they knew of, and I kept myself out of the way of all my Mohammedan acquaintances, until I saw an opportunity of bundling my kit into a boat and slipping on shore alone. I then entered my name on the books of the Sailors' Home, and nobody would have suspected that the young English sailor who ate as much cold pork for his supper that night as any other three men at the table, had been the zealous Mohammedan devotee of a few weeks before.

A few days afterwards I met the Amér in the street. Either he did not know me, or he thought me an undesirable acquaintance and cut me. If the latter, I can only hope that the reader who has accompanied me through this pilgrimage will not have formed the same opinion, and intend to do likewise should we ever be thrown together.

CHAPTER XIII.

THE HEJAZ.

I CANNOT pretend to add anything to our geographical or natural knowledge of the country known as the Hejaz. Indeed, it would only be presumption in me to attempt to supplement, with my necessarily crude conclusions and opinions, work which has already been so thoroughly done by my exact predecessor, Captain R. F. Burton. But as many intelligent and otherwise well-informed Englishmen have not been ashamed to confess to me that they had no precise idea of the whereabouts on the earth's surface of Meccah, and as only the other day I observed that a writer in "The Thunderer" itself spoke of "Hejaz" as though it were a town or city, I may venture to offer some short description of the country and people.

The country is bounded on the north by the Land of Midian, subject to the Pasha of Egypt, and extends down the coast of the Red Sea to about the twentieth parallel of latitude. To the eastward it comprised territory reaching from the coast to the great central plateau of the Nedj, the home of the Arab horse, and subject to Wahabi rule.

The Hejaz is subject to the Sultan of Turkey, and every considerable town is garrisoned by his troops, and the roads are kept open by patrols of Turkish cavalry. Although the Turks maintain their authority with a strong hand, in a harsh semi-barbarous manner, they but inefficiently protect travellers through the country, and would be powerless, until largely reinforced, to resist any general rising of the natives, especially if armed with modern and serviceable weapons. I do not think that such a revolt is at all improbable, but rather I should say imminent; for the detestation of Turkish rule is shared alike by both town and desert Arabs; and should these so far overcome their antagonism to one another, as to unite against the common enemy, Turkish tenure would not be long in the land. Moreover, in such an event the pilgrims would join the natives with a zeal even greater than their own.

The two chief cities, Meccah in the south and Medinah in the north, are distant from one another, by the shortest road, about three hundred and sixty miles, and this distance is accomplished on swift camels in six days. The next chief inland town is Taif, distant seventy-five miles east-south-east from Meccah, at a considerable elevation above that city, and situated on the southern rise of the highest mountains in the Hejaz, the Gazuan range, on the tops of which snow remains throughout the year. The two chief ports are Yembu and Jeddah. Yembu is the port of Medinah, and possesses a considerable import trade for the supply of its chief town. Also many pilgrims to both the great sanctuaries disembark there. Here the Sultan's authority is supposed to begin to the northward.

Jeddah is the port of Meccah, and is situated on the coast exactly west of its chief town. It possesses a commodious and safe harbour, though somewhat dangerous of approach, and a trade so considerable that lines of English steamers call regularly, and during the pilgrim season fleets of seven or eight large vessels are often seen riding there at one time. Numbers of European merchants and agents reside in Jeddah. Natives of every country under the sun may be seen in its crowded bazaars, and the products of the same may be bought in its shops and stalls. Excepting in two particulars it bears a strong family likeness to every other town in the Hejaz, especially to Meccah; and these are, that the place is not interdicted to intoxicating drinks or Christians; but these abominations to the true believer are strictly confined to the very circumscribed space enclosed within its walls. The town covers an area of probably two miles in circumference, and the whole of this space is thickly built over, except along the water's edge, where large open spaces are left, and where exist a few squares connected with the most ruinous fortifications.

It is outside the walls of Jeddah that Mohammedans locate the Tomb of Eve. I did not visit it; but from the descriptions of my companions who did, it cannot be much changed since Burton's day. He describes it in these words:

"I now proceed to the last of my visitations.

"Outside the walls of Jeddah lies no less a personage than Sittna Hawwa, the mother of mankind.

"The boy Mohammed and I, mounting asses one evening, issued through the Meccan gate, and turned towards the north-east, over a sandy plain. After half-an-hour's ride, amongst dirty huts and tattered coffee-hovels, we reached the *enceinte*, and found the door closed. Presently a man came running with might from the town; he was followed by two others; and it struck me at the time that they applied the key with peculiar *empressement*, and made inordinately low congees, as we entered the enclosure of whitewashed walls.

"The Mother is supposed to lie, like a Moslemah, fronting the Kaabah, with her feet northwards, her head southwards, and her right cheek propped by her right hand. Whitewashed and conspicuous to the voyager and traveller from afar, is a diminutive dome, with an opening to the west; it is furnished as such places usually are in El-Hejaz. Under it, and in the centre, is a square stone, planted upright, and fancifully carved, to represent the omphalic region of the human frame. This, as well as the dome, is called El-Surrah, or, the navel. The cicerone directed me to kiss this manner of hieroglyph, which I did, thinking the while that, under the circumstances, the salutation was quite uncalled-for.

"Having prayed here and at the head, where a few young trees grew, we walked along the side of the two parallel dwarf walls which define the outlines of the body: they are about six paces apart, and, between them, upon Eve's neck, are two tombs, occupied, I was told, by Usman Pasha and his son, who repaired the Mother's sepulchre.

"I could not help remarking to the boy

Mohammed that, if our first parent measured a hundred and twenty paces from head to waist, and eighty from waist to heel, she must have presented much the appearance of a duck. To this the youth replied flippantly, that he thanked his stars the Mother was under ground, otherwise that men would lose their senses with fright."

* * * * *

"The idol of Jeddah, in the days of Arab litholatry, was called *Sakhrah Tawilah,* the Long Stone. May not this stone of Eve be the Moslemised revival of the old idolatry?"

But for the Turkish authority in the Hejaz, Christians would not be tolerated by the natives even in Jeddah, and their residence on the holy soil is a standing grievance to the Meccans. Daily they may be heard to groan out "Christians in Jeddah—battal! (bad)." I have no hesitation in saying, though I may risk the charge of offering an immature opinion, that should any political or fanatical ferment arise in the Hejaz, one of the first results will be the massacre of all the Europeans in Jeddah. As a Nazzara (Christian) in the Hejaz, I should feel safer in Meccah itself than in Jeddah, at this moment. Found by the authorities, in Meccah, I might perhaps—as was the case with an Englishman who attempted the pilgrimage in 1876—be mercifully and ignominiously expelled as an idiot; but should an outbreak occur in Jeddah I would expect no quarter.

I know that a man-o'-war is usually within easy reach of the port; but Englishmen have a habit of closing their eyes to the strongest evidences of this description of danger; and our consuls are murdered every year, and our subjects assassinated for want of timely precautions.

How easily the fanatic who assassinated the late Shereef of Meccah,* little more than two years after I had seen him at Arafat, while in the act of shaking hands with H.B.M.'s Consul, at Jeddah, might have turned his knife against the "Sahib!"

I do not believe that the Consulate at Jeddah, with all its advantages of proximity to the scenes,

* March 14th, 1880.

and apparently trustworthy emissaries, obtains one word of true information as to the situation of affairs in the interior.

Now and again there reaches us a short tantalising paragraph in one of the daily papers, seemingly penned by someone from a vague rumour, and making meagre allusion to a great and important political movement in a country which is perhaps the most influential of the Mohammedan Powers. In these days of universal intercommunication and rapid and certain spread of the most trifling news-matter, to and from the most out-of-the-way corners of the globe, what could better show how isolated and cut off from Christian supervision are the doings in the Hejaz. Who can know what alarming projects or conspiracies may not at this moment be on foot in Meccah, that centre and hotbed of Mohammedan intrigue? For my part I regard the Christians in Jeddah as sitting on the safety-valve of the Hejaz, and sooner or later an explosion inevitable.

It is not the Bedawins so much as the settled

Arabs who are to be feared. The nomads of the wilderness must have some powerful motive or influence to unite them. Nothing short of a great leader, with a new faith, licensing universal plunder, would do it. So split up into tribes and clans are they, that no ordinary cause would serve to induce a long-sustained concerted action on their part. Their arms too, which nothing would persuade them to exchange for superior weapons, are worthless. No crescentade which might be organised by them, no matter how widespread or of what dimensions, would be formidable to any but the first few unprepared victims.

The Bedawi in stature and form resemble the Bengali, but are wiry, tough, and probably weigh ten stone, where a Bengali of the same inches would weigh nine. Their costume has already been described, with many of their customs. Profes-sedly they are Mohammedans of the Shafei class, but they make no outward show of that religion; such rites as I have seen them perform in the Haram at Meccah more resembled pagan or idolatrous worship. They devoutly kiss the black stone, and run seven times round the Kaaba. During prayer their attitudes and prostrations are extremely grotesque, not in the least resembling those of any recognised Mohammedan sect. While on the road in the desert I have never seen them occupied in any act of devotion whatever.

From what I have hitherto said about the Bedawi, his character will, I suspect, have impressed the reader unfavourably; but there really is much in the desert man to admire: his hospitality, and genuineness as a scoundrel, and above all, his untiring energy and hardihood—qualities in which he differs so much from all other Easterns. He makes no excuse for his acts of violence and depredation, nor claims any religious motive or sanction for them.

He openly declares himself an outcast and brigand, at enmity with everything approaching civilisation. His points of honour with his clansmen are numerous and extremely nice, and the murder of a relation is inherited, as a blood-feud, from father to son, until it is revenged. The knowledge of this makes them chary of killing an enemy outright; besides which, as in all savage states of society where man has little but his life to lose, he does not, as is generally supposed, undervalue it. The Bedawi, though undoubtedly a brave man, is also a very discreet one. He considers everything fair in war, and will never, except under a very strong incitive, expose himself to unnecessary danger. Though swords flash out at a word, the wounds given are always trifling, the cuts being directed at the limbs, and few Bedawi are to be met whose legs and arms have not a number of long black cicatrices to show. On receiving a wound gun-powder is immediately applied to it and rubbed in: this blackens the scar and makes it conspicuous for life.

The three national arms of the Arab are the gun, spear, and sword.

The guns are usually matchlocks, with a short butt, not more than a foot long, and a stock extending throughout the whole length of the barrel. In the most admired weapons the barrels exceed five feet in length, the metal in them is very heavy, and at the muzzle and breech it is as much as half an inch thick, in cases where the barrel is reinforced by rings. On account of the great length of barrel and thickness of the metal admitting the use of a heavy charge of powder, with but slight vibration, the guns are adapted for throwing a spherical bullet to a great range with precision; but the sights are of an exceedingly primitive description, so that a Bedawin with a gun he is accustomed to, takes about a minute and a half to get on to a fixed object. I have been told that they make some very fine shooting when they do fire; but though I have several times seen reputed good shots trying their hands at short ranges, I have seen nothing but the worst of bad practice from them. Pistols are also carried by the Shaykhs; these are in nearly all cases flint and steel; many are of European manufacture. I inspected one very handsome pair of English silver-mounted duelling pistols, from the belt of a Shaykh, with their one-time owner's name on a silver plate let into the hilts, "R. Williams, 1808." If they could have told their own history, I undertake to say that they would have had some strange tales to tell of the vicissitudes and adventures which landed them eventually where they were.

The spears in common use are of two kinds. The long one, exceeding twelve feet, is used when mounted. Its shaft is made of the male bamboo from India, and is decorated with one or two tufts of ostrich-feathers under the head. The shorter one is used by footmen, and is by far the best-judged and most serviceable weapon I met with among the Bedawi. It never exceeds eight feet in length, and I have seen them only half that length. It is composed of three parts, of equal length. The extremities are iron, and the centre a round shaft of hardwood, the thickness of a man's thumb; the blade is four-sided, and flattened rather in one direction, and at its broadest part is not more than half an inch, and gradually tapers a couple of feet to a fine point. The iron of the butt-end is the same length as the blade, about a third the entire spear, but is round and not so finely pointed or gradually tapered, it being only used for sticking in the sand to stand the spear. In use, this weapon is retained in the hand, and might be very fairly opposed to the bayonet, but I have seen it launched with great accuracy and penetrating power up to a distance of thirty yards. The swords seldom exceed two feet in length, are much curved, sharp on both edges, and finely pointed. They are always worn across the body, in front of the girdle, with the hilts to the left. Some of the wealthier Shaykhs carry the well-known Persian sword. During the whole of my stay in the Hejaz I did not see the faces of twenty women. In the three remarkable instances in which I met with good-looking ones I have recorded all the circumstances. Though there may be a few very sweet faces among the young girls, they soon come to maturity, and age early. Only haggard old crones, of an ugliness truly repulsive, present themselves to the stranger in the camps.

The exports of the Hejaz are few, and I believe the following short list will comprise all:

Kohl, or powdered antimony, used for making up the eyes by darkening the rims. This properly belongs to the toilet of the women, but it is often used with good effect on the eyes of some dissipated old opium-eater, or to heighten the gleam in the optics of a young dandy. Henna, the crimson dye used by women to make their nails pink, and sometimes by Hindi women to colour the whole of both their hands and feet a deep red. This custom also is not strictly confined to the women. Hides, dates, zemzem water, balsam of Meccah—a universal specific—gold, precious stones, talismans, charms—and I know of no other products sent out of the country.

CHAPTER XIV.

PILGRIMS IN ENGLISH SHIPS.

The sea-portion of the journey is regarded by the Hindi pilgrims as entailing greater hardships than any other portion of the whole pilgrimage. Apart from the ordinary sickness and inconvenience experienced by landsmen on a sea-voyage, they are crowded together by hundreds on the filthy wet decks of small steamers, and do not receive as much care or attention as cattle would under similar circumstances. Water and firing is supposed to be served out to them, but in all else they bring their own supplies. So crowded are they sometimes that I have seen weaker pilgrims and women, prostrated by sea-sickness, go for three days without water, on account of the greediness of the stronger, and carelessness of those whose duty it was to see to its proper distribution.

I regret to say that there are men among my brother-sailors in the East who treat the natives, over whom they may be "dressed in a little brief authority," with a brutality and harshness such as they would never have the boldness to show towards the meekest of their own countrymen. I have seen a mate of a ship kick in the mouth a woman who was kissing his feet, all because she had lost her ticket, valued at ten rupees. My blood boiled as I heard the coward cursing the cowering wretch, in a voice that sounded like a railway-train crossing a bridge. When such is the conduct of the officers, of course the sailors follow their example, and every ignorant stoker who is master of a few broken sentences of that barbarous jargon, half-Portuguese half-Hindostani, spoken by native sailors in English ships, exercises what he fondly imagines a native curse, on every helpless passenger who gets in the way of his very superior self and intelligence.

I have sat in a room and heard Englishmen telling, with boisterous mirth, how a sea came and washed twelve Hajis overboard, and swept the property of nearly all the rest from the deck; and how, all their supplies being gone, the captain, after keeping them on nothing until they began to end their misery by jumping overboard, generously gave them a few buckets of beans from the cargo.

These things do happen yearly under the English flag, and I think some of our slave-trade suppressing resources might be turned to investigating outrages on humanity nearer home with advantage.

I do not mean to say that barbarities are practised as a rule on the pilgrims in English ships, but ill-treatment and overcrowding are so common as to call for increased official supervision. Also, there is often much mismanagement on the part of charterers and agents of the pilgrim-ships, causing great suffering to the native passengers, for which the ship's people are in no way to blame. One instance I will quote which came under my knowledge. This instance will not bring me under the censure of anyone, as I believe no one was to blame, and it reflects nothing but credit on all my countrymen concerned.

It happened on board the very ship in which I took passage from Jeddah to Bombay on the immediately-preceding voyage. She had been placed in the pilgrim service only, and carried no cargo. After landing her native passengers from Bombay at Jeddah, a few days before the coming off of the great pilgrimage to Arafat, she was put on the berth to make an intermediate trip to Suez before returning to Bombay. This was to put in the time she would otherwise have been waiting at Jeddah, until she could secure her full complement of passengers to India.

The pilgrims who embarked at Jeddah for Suez numbered about a hundred—not enough to pay for coals, one would have thought; and these were all Arabs from different parts of North Africa—the most objectionable class of pilgrims that could be got together in numbers.

The lower classes of them are the dirtiest people I know—excepting, perhaps, a few tribes in the Arctic; they are bold and daring to a degree, and possess an average physique equal, if not superior, to any Europeans. Men of the most splendid muscular development are common among them. On the way up to Suez smallpox broke out among the ship's crew, and she was not allowed to land her pilgrims at the termination of the passage. After lying four days in the roads, and burying four of her sailors, on a distant sand-spit on the opposite side of the bay to the town, the Egyptian authorities ordered her down to Tor, a small anchorage on the Sinaitic shores of the Gulf of Suez, to lay out forty days' quarantine. While at Suez the ship had not been allowed to maintain any communication with the shore, but on going away they were allowed to *leave one sick man behind them*, who, we heard afterwards, died in Suez of the smallpox. No other deaths occurred on board the ship, and the epidemic left the ship as suddenly as it had appeared.

The pilgrims, on arriving at their new destination, and understanding what was to be their fate, were of course highly enraged; but as all their arms had been taken from them on coming on board, and they were so few, numbering little more than double the ship's company, it was not feared but that they would be managed without difficulty.

At first things went on smoothly enough, but in a few days the pilgrims found that, husband their stores as they might, they would soon be exhausted. They had only supplied themselves with food for the passage up, and no provisions could be procured at the place they were now in; no inhabitants were seen during the whole time the ship was there, and the country presented nothing but bare, hot, naked rocks and mountains. They were offered a daily ration of ship-bread per man; but this Christian food they said they must rather die than accept. As they became more and more pressed by hunger, their behaviour became more noisy, and at length quite mutinous. Knowing that the ship's people could not understand them, old men would stand up and harangue the crowd, evidently counselling some strong measures. At night they would sit about in excited groups, discussing their position volubly and threateningly.

After a time, driven by starvation, they seemed to have agreed that if they could obtain Christian food by stealth or violence they might eat it, but would as yet accept no gift. At first they would watch the cook, and the moment his back was turned purloin any little scraps lying about; they would watch the sailors lay down their pipes, and steal them. Then they grew bolder, and one stalwart Moor, finding a boy smoking alone, took the pipe out of his mouth by force. They took every opportunity to insult the men and officers of the ship, and the practice of snatching men's pipes from their mouths became quite common; but for the captain's express orders to bear with them as much as possible, things must have come to a climax sooner. However, arms were made ready early, and preparations set on foot to meet any serious movement on the part of the Arabs.

One day a crowd rushed into the galley, just as the cabin dinner was being dished up to send aft, and turning out the cook, devoured everything. Now they simply took all the eatables that came in their way. The sailors' rations were stolen from them as they carried them along the decks, the galley rifled at each meal, and, to make a long story short, they had charge of the ship.

This could not be put up with longer, and they must be shown that they had gone too far. The captain's arrangements for offence and defence were made. From the poop to the midship bridge there ran a gangway bridge, which could be raised and lowered. On this midship bridge two armed sentries were posted, with orders to allow no Arabs on to it. There were two other ways on to the poop from the main-deck; these were inside the poop, behind two stout doors on each side the deck, which could be closed. Placed inside these doors were the two ship's guns, loaded to the muzzle with links of chopped-up chain. The position of these guns was such that the doors might be thrown open for a moment, the deck swept fore-and-aft on both sides with the terrible discharge, and instantly after, the doors closed before the guns. On the poop were placed all the arms and ammunition: twelve rifles, six revolvers, six bayonets, and a miscellaneous assortment of sharpened files, belaying-pins, knives, and—hardest lines of all for the Arabs—a selection of the most useful of their own weapons. But the greatest reliance was placed on the hot-water hose, from which a stream of boiling water could be discharged half the length of the ship. Still the captain hesitated to show his strength, and every endeavour was made to induce the Arabs to eat Christian biscuit peaceably; but they would not, and soon brought things to a head. A young lad was coming to the cabin with a dish of hot currie, when two Arabs waylaid him, and as they attempted to seize the dish, he threw the contents over them. They caught hold of the boy and were very severely ill-treating him, when the captain and a number of the crew came and rescued him. More Arabs gathered round and more sailors. A row was imminent. The captain was struck; that was enough. He went up on to the bridge and blew three short blasts upon the steam-whistle. It was the signal for all hands to assemble on and inside the poop, at posts which had already been allotted to them.

As soon as the captain and two sentries reached the poop from the midship bridge, the fore-and-aft gangway was triced up. In a quarter of a minute every white man in the ship was in his place. The Arabs were almost as quick, and ready to battle. They rushed aft in a body; but there was no way on to the poop for them, unless they scaled the front in face of the crew. At first they contented themselves with gesticulating and howling defiance, and then one splendid young fellow stepped to the front, and, calling to the others to follow him, actually leapt at a bound from the deck and caught the poop-railing. The captain's revolver was at his breast in a moment. He looked back, saw those behind him hesitating; so, glaring in the captain's face, he tore open his shirt, and forced his naked breast on the revolver, so suddenly that the captain must have had a steady hand, or it would have gone off. Just at that moment an old quartermaster—the man who told me the story better than any of the others—reached over the captain's shoulder and knocked the brave young fellow's brains out with a blow of an iron belaying-pin.

In the meantime, where was the hot water? For the first few seconds of discharge, the water that has been in the pipes is cold. So the hose was put overboard for a minute, until the water direct from the boiler should reach its mouth. When it was found hot enough, the water was cut off and the nozzle swung in-board to be directed at the Arabs. The sailor who was doing this, either out of mischief or by accident, allowed a few drops of the boiling fluid to escape in a sparkling crescent over the crowd on the main-deck. The effect was magical.

On discovering the murderous instrument in the hands of the Christians—rather than be boiled running about—they surrendered unconditionally. Within two hours they were all landed on a small island near, supplied with sails for tents and covering, and given puncheons of bread and water, as much as they could consume. They were very glad indeed to accept it before they got away, and they lived quite peaceably among themselves, occasioning no more trouble until they were landed at Suez, where the Egyptian Government put them under an armed escort until they were clear of the country.

NOTE.

[From *The Athenæum*, July 23.]

THE MECCA PILGRIM.

Godalming, July 19, 1881.

I HAVE just returned from the United States, and observe that some doubt has been cast upon the authenticity of statements made in my book, " Six Months in Meccah," both as to my ability to perform the pilgrimage, and with regard to the story of the English lady whom I met in Meccah. I would wish to state that

I am the son of the Rev. William Keane, for many years senior canon of the Cathedral, Calcutta, perhaps one of the best speakers of native dialects in India. I have spent seven years of my life among Mohammedans, and at one time I served three years as officer on board a ship carrying a Mohammedan crew. The latter experience would be quite sufficient to give me a thorough knowledge of the Mohammedan language and customs. My pilgrimage to Meccah was no rash experiment or accident, but the outcome of a long-cherished project. I have now in my possession a private letter, addressed to me by the English lady whom I met in Meccah, which proves most conclusively that the statements made in "Six Months in Meccah"—so far at least as she is concerned—are correct.

I hope these statements will satisfy those who have read my book that I did perform the pilgrimage to Meccah.

My publishers are now about to issue the record of my journey from Meccah to Medinah, which many of the reviewers of "Six Months in Meccah" have asked for.

J. F. Keane (Hajj Mohammed Amin).

* * * * *

With reference to the "Lady Venus," who received so much incidental mention at my hands in describing my life in Meccah, I feel called upon to add the following few remarks:

"The Lady Venus" is not a fancy name, but a literal translation of "Begum Zarah," the name by which she was known in Meccah. Throughout the whole of the inquiry, instituted by the Government, to ascertain the truth of my statements concerning her, she has been extremely reticent as to her antecedents. But she has admitted that she is English, and it has been discovered with tolerable certainty who she really is.

She is now amply provided for in India, and has expressed a desire that she be left unmolested in that country, in her present retirement, and the obscurity of a native home.

Every possible inducement has been held out to her to return to Christianity; but as she remains obdurate, nothing can be done for her, and I unquestionably can give no more publicity to her case, or divulge anything further concerning her.

THE END.

CHARLES DICKENS AND EVANS, CRYSTAL PALACE PRESS.

Glossary

This glossary lists Arabic and other non-English words used by Keane. It also gives information about selected places mentioned in his text. There is some variation in Keane's spellings and modern standard Arabic transliterations are given in brackets where appropriate.

aahal (*'iqāl*): head-ring made of camel hair.
aba (*'abā, 'abā'ah*): woollen cloak.
amér (*amīr*): leader, prince, local ruler.
Arafat ('Arafāt): a plain about 12 miles (20 kilometres) south-east of Makkah, the scene of one of the essential rites of the pilgrimage, the "Standing at 'Arafāt". The pilgrims assemble here on the "Day of 'Arafāt" (09 Dhū'l-Ḥijjah), continually repeating the *ṭalbīyah* prayer (*q.v.*).
bakhshish, bakshish (*bakhshīsh*) tip, gratuity.
Bedawi, Bedawin (*badawī*, pl. *badū*): Bedouin; tribal, nomadic pastoralists.
Begum (probably from Turkish *bīgam*, a feminine formation from *beg*, a chief or lord): title used in Muslim India to denote a lady of high rank, especially a prince's widow.
Bimbashi: an Egyptian/Ottoman military rank, equivalent to Major or Lieutenant-Colonel.
Bismillah (*bismi'l-Lāh*): "In the name of God"; said by devout Muslims before performing any task or action, however simple.
Caluma (*kalimah*): literally, "word". The Muslim profession of faith or *shahādah*, the first of the Five Pillars of Islam: *Ashhadu an lā ilāha illā 'Llāh, wa ashhadu an Muḥammadun rasūlu 'Llāh*, that is, "I bear witness that there is no god but Allāh and I bear witness that Muḥammad is the Messenger of Allāh."
Darwaysh (*darwīsh*): dervish; a member of one of the Muslim orders of ascetics; a religious mendicant living a wandering life of self-denial, in search of enlightenment and living on charity.
Dirvani: steward in charge of supplies.
djin, jinni (*jinn*, a collective noun): "genies", inhabitants of the spirit world, invisible beings, either harmful or benevolent, which may interfere in the lives of mortals.

El-Sai (*al-Sa'ī*): the walking or hurrying back and forth between the hills of Ṣafā and Marwah in Makkah, in imitation of Hagar in her desperate search for water for her son, Ishmael. Formerly just outside the Ḥaram, its course, or *mas'ā*, is now included within the extended confines of the sacred enclosure. The word has the root idea of endeavour.

fakir (*faqīr*): literally poor man. Beggar, mendicant pilgrim.

Haji (*ḥājj, ḥajjī*): honorific title of a Muslim who has performed the *Ḥajj*, or Annual Pilgrimage to Makkah.

hakim (*ḥakīm*): title of a learned doctor of medicine and philosophy.

Haram (*Ḥaram*): literally, "restricted". "forbidden", "sacred". The Great Mosque in Makkah, the sacred enclosure around and including the Ka'bah, is called *Al-Masjid al-Ḥaram* ("the Sacred Mosque") but is referred to in familiar terms (as Keane refers to it) simply as the *Ḥaram*. In its proper sense, the term denotes the sacred areas enclosing each of the cities of Makkah and Madīnah, as well as the Temple Mount in Jerusalem. The two former places are often known as *Al-Ḥaramain al-Sharīfain*, or "The Two Noble Sanctuaries".

harami (*ḥarāmī*): thief.

harem (*ḥarīm*): literally, "forbidden [area]" or "inviolable [place]". The women's quarters; the private, domestic area of an Arab Muslim household, as opposed to the male, public section".

hasabat, al- (*ḥaṣbah*): the singular form means "measles". Keane uses the plural to mean pustules. He also states that the same word means "pebbles", but, although from the same root, this is a slightly different word, *ḥaṣbā'*, a collective noun.

Hegira (*al-Hijrah*): the migration of the Prophet Muḥammad and his small band of followers from Makkah to Madinah in 622 AD. The Muslim era is calculated from the beginning of the month of Muḥarram in that year.

Hejaz (al-Ḥijāz): the mountainous, western region of the Arabian Peninsula, from the Gulf of 'Aqabah in the north to some distance south of Makkah and Ṭā'if. Today it is entirely within the Kingdom of Saudi Arabia.

Hindi: a Muslim native of India, as distinguished from a Hindu.

Hindustani: the dialect of Hindi spoken by Keane, a lingua franca used by Muslims in India; also known as Urdu.

hookah (*ḥuqqah*): a water-pipe, hubble-bubble.

Iblis (*iblīs*): a name of the devil; a fallen angel.

ihram (*iḥrām*): literally "consecration". The state entered into by a

pilgrim in order to perform the Ḥajj, symbolised by the two pieces of seamless white cloth that he dons, by extension known by the same word.

Indian Mutiny: Keane refers simply to "the Mutiny", the 1857–58 uprising against British rule in India, which was triggered by the belief that cartridges were being greased with animal fat, an idea equally repugnant to both Muslims and Hindus. Starting at Meerut, the Mutiny spread throughout northern India. Delhi fell, and Cawnpore (Kanpur) and Lucknow were besieged. When the British finally regained control, some Muslim mutineers sought refuge in the holy cities of the Ḥijāz.

jambiyah (*janbīyah*): the curved dagger with decorated haft, worn usually in an ornate sheath, corresponding to the *khanjar* of southern and eastern Arabia.

janlo: Keane uses this word to mean a deep pool, but its origin is obscure.

jebel (*jabal*): hill, mountain.

jehad, jihad (*jihād*, from *jahd*, "effort"): holy war, sanctioned by religious authorities and aimed at extending Islam among non-believers. The Muslim equivalent of the Christian "crusade".

jinni (*junaih*): literally "guinea". A gold sovereign or pound.

jumo: Keane uses this word for the prescribed ablutions for prayer performed without water when none is available, for example in the desert. It is not clear what word he means. The Arabic word is *tayammum*.

Kaabah (Ka‘bah): literally "cube". The large, square stone structure in the centre of the Ḥaram at Makkah. It is covered with the *kiswah*, a black cloth embroidered in gold thread with verses from the Qur'ān, which is replaced anew every year. The Black Stone (*Al-Ḥajar al-Aswad*) is embedded in one corner of the Ka‘bah. The original building is believed by Muslims to have been erected by Ibrāhīm (Abraham), the primordial monotheist according to Muslim belief. It is towards the Ka‘bah that Muslims turn to perform the five daily prayers, wherever on the globe they may be.

Kadi, Kasi (*qāḍī*): judge of the Islamic Law (*Sharī‘ah*) appointed by a ruler or government.

kaffir (*kāfir*): unbeliever, infidel, non-Muslim.

kismat (*qismah*): fate, destiny, preordained by God.

kohl (*kuḥl*): a preparation of pulverised antimony, used to darken the edges of the eyelids in order to impart greater brightness to the eyes.

Koran (*Al-Qur'ān*): literally "the Reading" or "the Recitation". The holy scripture of Islam, believed by Muslims to have been revealed verbatim by God, through the Angel Gabriel, to the Prophet Muḥammad, in a series of revelations between AD 610 and 632.

kufiyah (*kūfīyah*): square cloth, folded and used as a head-dress, held in place by the *‘iqāl*.

kurbash: bastinado, punishment by beating of the feet.

Labbayk: literally "Here am I, at thy service". The first word of the *ṭalbīyah* prayer (*see* Talbiyat).

Maghribi: a person from the west (*gharb*, or place of the sunset), i.e. North Africa, corresponding to Libya, Tunisia, Algeria, Morocco and Mauritania.

Mameluke (*mamlūk*): literally "owned", "slave". Member of a military class, originally of Turkish slaves, ruling in Egypt from the mid-13th century to 1517 AD, when the Ottoman Turks acquired Egypt and the Ḥijāz. The Mamluks remained powerful until they were finally crushed by Muḥammad ‘Alī Pāshā, ruler of Egypt, in 1811 AD.

Meccah (Makkah al-Mukarramah): Originally called Bakkah, the holiest city of Islam, where its most sacred sanctuary, the Ḥaram (*q.v.*), is situated. It was the birthplace and early home of the Prophet Muḥammad but rejected his teaching, wherefore he migrated to Madīnah. He later returned briefly to the city with his followers and eventually it was brought into the fold of Islam.

Medinah (Al-Madīnah al-Munawwarah): literally "the Radiant City". The oasis and town, originally called Yathrib, to which the Prophet Muḥammad migrated with his followers in 622 AD as a result of persecution in Makkah. The first Muslim community was established in Madīnah and there the Prophet died in 632 AD. His tomb forms part of the Prophet's Mosque, which is built over the site of his house. It is Islam's second holiest city.

Midian: the northernmost part of the Ḥijāz, the mountainous region adjacent to the Gulf of ʻAqabah.

Mohammedans: a follower of Muḥammad, but, as Keane says, an appellation not used by the people so called by others. The correct term is the Arabic word Muslim, commonly spelt, as by Keane, Moslem.

Moolah, **Moulah** (*mawlā*; in Hindustani, *mullā*): literally master, lord, patron. In India it has come to mean a religious scholar, teacher or doctor of the Law.

moonshi (*munshi'*): used primarily in India for a writer or teacher.

Moulvi (*mawlawī*, from the same root as *mawlā*): used in India of a judge, doctor of the Law etc, and prefixed to the names of learned men.

Mount of Mercy (Jabal Raḥmah): the small rocky hill on the plain of ʻArafāt that is the focal point of the "Standing" at ʻArafāt during the Ḥajj.

muezzin (*mu'adhdhin*): the one who calls the people to prayer in the mosque.

Mufti (*mufti*): legal expert or functionary, who may be a *qāḍī* or his assistant.

Muna (Minā): the name of a valley and small town about 3 miles (5 kilometres) south-east of Makkah, which only comes to life during the Ḥajj, when pilgrims gather there to perform the rite of stoning the three *jamarāt* or pillars (Keane's "obelisks"), representing Satan.

Mussulman: archaic term for a Muslim used by early English writers, now obsolete. It is derived from the Arabic plural form of Muslim: *muslimūn*.

Muzdalifah: an area between ʻArafāt and Minā (*see* Muna), 2 miles (3 kilometres) from the latter, where pilgrims spend the night after the Day of ʻArafāt, on their way to the stoning of the pillars.

Nassara, **Nazzara** (*Naṣārā*, plural of *Naṣrānī*): Christians, possibly connected with Al-Nāṣira, that is, Nazareth.

Nawab (*nuwwāb*, plural of *nā'ib*, "representative"): an Indian

Muslim ruling prince or powerful landowner. It is unclear whether the plural form came to be used in error or honorifically.

Nedj (Najd): the upland desert steppe forming the centre of the Arabian Peninsula, bounded on the east by the Dahnā' sands, on the south by the Empty Quarter, on the north by the Great Nafûd, and on the east by the Ḥijāz mountains. Home to the House of Sa'ûd and of the Islamic reform movement of Shaykh Muḥammad bin 'Abdu'l-Wahhāb in the 18th century AD. Its western reaches, peopled by Bedouin tribes, drain towards the lower-lying eastern side, where the wadis and depressions of lower Najd have supported widespread oasis settlement since early times, for example at the Saudi capitals of Al-Dir'īyah and Al-Rīyāḍ (Riyadh). Keane's spelling probably represents his pronunciation.

ottoman: a divan, a low cushioned seat, usually without back or arms, set against a wall.

Pacha, **Pasha** (*bāshā*, from Turkish): a provincial governor or other high official in the Ottoman Empire. When used as a title, it follows the name; e.g. Ibrāhīm Pasha.

parra (in English, para): a small Turkish coin, one fortieth of a piastre.

piastre: a Turkish coin, one hundredth of a pound (*see jinni*). The word comes from Italian "piastra", a plate [of metal], and is related to the English word "plaster".

Ramazan (*Ramaḍān*): the holy month of fasting, ending in the 'Īdu'l-Fiṭr (literally Feast of the Fast-breaking), which is the second most important festival of the Muslim year, after the 'Īdu'l-Aḍḥā, which marks the end of the Pilgrimage.

ratl (*ratl*): a weight of variable amount but here probably the Egyptian weight of about a pound avoirdupois or 449.28 grams. The Syrian *ratl* was over three kilograms.

riyal (*riyāl*): a coin at various times of gold or silver and still the unit of currency in several Middle Eastern countries. The name was probably introduced by the Portuguese, who established a presence in the area in the early 16th century.

Shafei (*Shāfi'ī*): adherent of one of the four great *madhhab*s or schools of Sharī'ah law in Sunni Islam: Shāfi'ī, Ḥanbalī, Ḥanafī and Malikī.

Shaitan (*shayṭān*): Satan, devil, fiend.

Sheréf (*sharīf*): Honorific title borne by male descendants of the Prophet Muḥammad through his daughter Fāṭimah and 'Alī ibn Abī Tālib. In the Ḥijāz, the most prominent sharīf was known as the Grand Sharīf, or Sharīf of Makkah, and ruled the towns and tribes under the suzerainty of the Ottoman Sultan in Constantinople. During Keane's visit, the Sharīf was Ḥusain bin Muḥammad bin 'Abdu'l-Mu'īn, of the Dhawī 'Awn clan.

shibriyah (*shibrīyah*): a camel-borne passenger litter.

shikari (Hindustani, *shikārī*): a sportsman or hunter, a sportsman's assistant.

shugduf (*shuqdhuf*): a camel-borne passenger litter.

Talbiyat (*ṭalbīyah*): the pilgrim's prayer; the words the Qur'ān attributes to Ibrāhīm (Abraham), calling mankind to the Pilgrimage:

Labbayka 'Llāhumma labbayk
Labbayka 'Llāhumma labbayk
La sharīka laka, labbayk
Inna'l-ḥamda wa'l-ni'mata laka wa'l-mulk
La sharīka laka, labbayka 'Llahumma labbayk.

Tallukdar (from Persian *ta'alluqdār*): the holder of a *talluk* (*ta'alluq*), or hereditary estate in India, or the officer or tax-collector in charge of a sub-district.

tamarind: fruit of the tropical evergreen tree *Tamarindus indica*, used as a food (it is rich in vitamin C) and to make drinks and medicines.

tarbóuche (*ṭarbūsh*): tarboosh, fez; a flat-topped, brimless cap.

tawaf (*ṭawāf*): the circumambulation of the Ka'bah. The pilgrim makes seven counter-clockwise circuits as one of the principal rites of the Ḥajj.

wadi (*wādī*): a valley, generally dry, but which may become a roaring torrent after heavy rain.

Wady (*or* **Waddy**) **Fatima** (Wādī Fāṭimah): the large wadi whose broad watercourse provides much of the route between Jiddah and Makkah. Pilgrims leave Wādī Fāṭimah just east of Hadda to proceed towards Makkah, whilst the *wādī* itself trends north-eastwards to Jumūm.

Wahhabi (Wahhābī): an adherent of the Islamic reform movement of Shaykh Muḥammad bin 'Abdu'l-Wahhāb, which arose in

Najd in the mid-18th century. It was known to outsiders as Wahabism, and his followers as Wahabis. The movement inspired the rise of the First Sa'udi State.

Zarah: the name Keane gives to the mysterious "English" Muslim lady he met in Makkah. "Zarah" is clearly Keane's corruption of *zahrah*, meaning "flower" or "beauty", or of *zuhrah*, meaning "beauty" or "light", both common Muslim given names. The related word *Zuharah*, from the same root, refers to the Evening Star, the planet Venus. Keane translated Zarah as Venus, either out of ignorance of the distinctions in Arabic or, perhaps more likely, to add spice to his tale for his Victorian readership.

Zem Zem (Zamzam): the name of the well located about twenty metres south-east of the Ka'bah, inside the Ḥaram. The spring of Zamzam is believed to have appeared when Hagar and her son, Ishmael, had exhausted the water left by Ibrāhīm (Abraham).

zenana (Persian, *zanāna*; from *zan*, woman): the women's section of an Indian Muslim household or the women themselves, equivalent to the Arabic *ḥarīm* and the Turkish *haramlik*.

Index

This index to J. F. Keane's two books includes all names of people and places in his text, as well as a comprehensive listing of themes and topics. Particular entries relating to the author himself are listed under Mohammed Amin. The numbers (**1**) and (**2**) denote *Six Months in Meccah* and *My Journey to Medinah* respectively. Spellings follow the author's.